Chinese Technology Transfer in the 1990s

Chinese Technology Transfer in the 1990s

Current Experience, Historical Problems and International Perspectives

Edited by

Charles Feinstein

Chichele Professor of Economic History, All Souls College, Oxford, UK

Christopher Howe

Professor of Economics, School of Oriental and African Studies, University of London, UK

Edward Elgar
Cheltenham, UK • Lyme, US

Published by
Edward Elgar Publishing Limited
8 Lansdown Place
Cheltenham
Glos GL50 2HU
UK

Edward Elgar Publishing, Inc.
1 Pinnacle Hill Road
Lyme
NH 03768
US

A catalogue record for this book is available from the British Library

Library of Congress Cataloguing in Publication Data

Chinese technology transfer in the 1990's : current experience,
    historical problems, and international perspectives / edited by
    Charles Feinstein, Christopher Howe.
        Includes bibliographical references and index.
        1. Technology transfer—Economic aspects—China.   2. Technological
    innovations—Economic aspects—China.   3. Technology and state—
    China.   4. Competition, International.   I. Feinstein, C. H.
    II. Howe, Christopher.
    HC430.T4C465   1997
    338.951'06—dc21   96–39590
                                                                              CIP

ISBN 1 85898 245 6

Typeset by Manton Typesetters, 5–7 Eastfield Road, Louth, Lincolnshire LN11 7AJ, UK.
Printed and bound in Great Britain by
Biddles Ltd, Guildford and King's Lynn

Contents

List of Contributors

Paul A. David, All Souls College, University of Oxford

Ding Jingping, Foreign Affairs Bureau, Chinese Academy of Social Sciences

John Enos, Magdalen College, University of Oxford

Charles Feinstein, All Souls College, University of Oxford

Christopher Howe, School of Oriental and African Studies, University of London

Jiang Xiaojuan, Institute of Industrial Economy, Chinese Academy of Social Sciences

Tang Shiguo, National Research Centre for Science and Technology Development

Nick von Tunzelmann, Science Policy Research Institute, University of Sussex

David Wall, School of Oriental and African Studies, University of London

Xu Jiangping, Institute of Industrial Technology, State Planning Commission

Yin Xiangshuo, Fudan University, Shanghai

Zheng Youjing, Institute of Quantitative Economics and Technological Economics, Chinese Academy of Social Sciences

List of Figures

List of Tables

Preface

In 1993 a delegation of social scientists from the British Academy visited China as guests of the Chinese Academy of Social Sciences (CASS). One of the purposes of the visit was to discuss the operation of the reciprocal exchange agreement between the Academy (working jointly with the Economic and Social Research Council) and CASS. In the course of the discussions it was suggested that it would be valuable to supplement the visits of individual scholars by a joint seminar. It was agreed that the issue of technology transfer was a topic of great importance and mutual interest, and that discussion of both historical and contemporary aspects would provide a very suitable theme for such a seminar. As a member of the British delegation, Charles Feinstein undertook to carry forward the proposal and to invite the British participants.

The papers included in this volume were originally presented at the resulting seminar, which was held in Beijing in April 1995. The arrangements in China were made with great efficiency by the Institute of Industrial Economics on behalf of CASS, and the success of the meeting owes a great deal to the contribution made by Professor Ding Jingping, Deputy Director of the Institute, and by Mrs Ding Yi, Chief of the Scientific Research Division. It is also very appropriate to record the valuable support for this initiative given initially by Mrs Wu Lingmei, who was at that time Chief of the European Division of the Foreign Affairs Bureau of CASS.

We hope that this collection of papers will both make a useful contribution to better knowledge and understanding of the problems of technology transfer with which China will be dealing in the 1990s, and also convey something of the stimulating character of the seminar in Beijing.

C.H.F.
C.H.

Introduction

Christopher Howe

TECHNOLOGY TRANSFER IN TWO SYSTEMS

The efficiency of technology transfer and innovation has long been regarded as the touchstone of the quality of an economic system. In market-based societies, as Paul David shows here in Chapter 1, the character of innovations and trade secrets has called for special arrangements (patents, apprenticeship traditions, etc.) designed on the one hand to reward innovation and, on the other, to ensure its controlled diffusion. In the period before the Second World War, however, technology was at the forefront of western debates about the relative merits of capitalism and socialism.

On one side of this debate was Joseph Schumpeter, who first made the crucial link between theories of innovation and development and who later came to the view that both activities were necessarily and beneficially related to monopolistic industrial structures, at least in the short run.[1] Against this, critics of capitalism, including economists such as Paul Sweezy and Maurice Dobb and scientists such as J.D. Bernal, argued that monopoly and concentration were the main reasons for capitalism's failure to exploit the discoveries of science in the broad social interest.[2] For them, the unused patent for the ever-burning electric light bulb was a defining symbol of capitalist waste. Dobb also argued that the inability of market systems to cope with problems of excess capacity and 'technological unemployment' made technology a drag on economic progress.[3] Later, even such a relatively dispassionate analyst as Edith Penrose was concerned that the international monopolization of the combination of patents and trade 'know-how' posed a serious threat to world economic efficiency.[4]

Early apologists for socialism believed that the dilemmas posed by innovation could be resolved in socialist systems: systems where public ownership would predominate and where planners rather than profit-driven capitalists would allocate resources. The planners, it was believed, would invest in human capital, shoulder the risks inherent in innovation, take account of all linkages and positive external effects, and make investments using time horizons far longer and closer to social optimality than those of the private businessman.[5] But as Charles Feinstein shows in Chapter 3, the experience of the Soviet Union proved disappointing. For in spite of some spectacular successes (space technology, for example), major Soviet innovation was rare and industry in general was technologically backward and lacking in the incremental improvement of processes of the kind achieved by firms in market economies described by John Enos (Chapter 6) and Christopher Howe (Chapter 2).

The analysis of the Soviet problems, however, was not conclusive, even in the west, until the 1960s and 1970s – some thirty to forty years after the beginning of the Soviet experiment. To China, therefore, embarking on its own institutional revolution in the early 1950s, the Soviet model was the dominant, natural influence; and whereas the Chinese were aware from the outset of the errors of Soviet agricultural collectivization and their implications for China, they had no reason to doubt the superiority of Soviet industrial and technological systems and policies.

THE SOVIET PHASE OF TECHNOLOGY POLICY: 1953–60

The main task for China in this period was to secure efficient transfer of known, foreign techniques and to adapt and improve these in the light of Chinese characteristics, including labour abundance, raw material configurations, and existing resources in the modern and traditional sectors. Two aspects of the early programme stand out: the dominant role of the Soviet Union as the single supplier of new technologies; and the priority accorded to the defence-related industries.

Overall, what is striking about the technology transfer in this phase is how successful it was. Important new process technologies were introduced, especially in the metallurgy and chemical sectors, and new products appearing in these years included vehicles, machinery of all kinds, man-made fibres and chemical products. Moreover, improved management of existing resources and some incremental improvements led to productivity gains (including gains in total factor productivity) both in industry as a whole and in individual industrial sectors such as steel, where progress mainly took the form of the modernization and enlargement of facilities left by the Japanese.[6]

What factors explain these successes? First, we should not ignore the skills and capabilities accumulated in industry before the Anti-Japanese War. In Shanghai, in particular, machinery, shipbuilding and textiles all made important transfers of western and Japanese technologies, in part as spill-overs from foreign direct investment (FDI) in the city.[7] Second, during the First Five-Year Plan (1953–57) choices were relatively simple and government priorities clear and coherent. This coherence reflected the advantage of having one major supplier of new industrial technology since this ensured at least minimal standardization and integration.

Most interesting of all, however, was the fact that, whatever Soviet motives at the time, the underlying concept of technology transfer appears to have been a broad one –something, as Paul David (Chapter 1) argues, conspicuously lacking in western thinking about the problems of technology transfer to 'developing countries' during the 1950s. For the Soviet transfer included not only the 'hardware' of whole plant and other capital goods imports to China, but also the blueprints, technical literature, training programmes and personnel exchanges required for a full transmission of 'know-how' and tacit information. Soviet assistance also extended to the upgrading of higher education and the establishment of a Soviet-style network of research and design institutions, as well as to the practice of formulating long-range science and technology plans.

In spite of its successes, these programmes were in serious difficulty by the late 1950s. This reflected not only China's macroeconomic mismanagement and the Sino-Soviet political rift (which led directly to the abrupt withdrawal of all Soviet technicians from China), but also more narrowly technological factors as well. One of these was that the speed of technology transfer embodied in the fifteen-year perspective plan (1953–67) and the Five-Year Plans within this was over-ambitious, allowing insufficient time for full transfer and absorption of skills to take place.[8] Indeed, some of the plants planned in the mid-1950s did not come on-stream until 1969–70 – ten years behind schedule. Further, unlike the Soviet Union, China's low level of economic development required the continuation of small-scale, semi-mechanized productive and service sectors and the Sino-Soviet strategies for technology transfer and improvement did little or nothing for this important element of the economy.

Apart from these specific problems, China also began to report evidence of the systemic shortcomings common to Soviet-type systems, including lack of continuous productivity growth and innovation in existing enterprises. The key dysfunctional features of the system were reported to be the gulf between quasi-autonomous research and development (R&D) facilities and industrial enterprises; the unwillingness of managers to take risks in a system that provided rewards and punishments reflecting success in plan fulfilment and physical indicators; and the problems created by planning based on physical norms. Productivity norms governing basic processes (e.g. coal per unit of electricity, raw cotton per metre of yarn, etc.) are the essence of a physical planning system since, without them, planning is reduced to *ad hoc* bargaining between the planners and individual enterprises. Yet precisely by predetermining these relationships and rewarding plan fulfilment based on them, the rationale and incentive for *improvement* in them is lost.[9]

Thus the Soviet relationship and system provided an effective mechanism for achieving an heroic, once-for-all transfer of a limited number of technologies and in enabling the Chinese to acquire much of the codified, tacit and contextual knowledge associated with these. What they did not do was to implant a system for discovering and diffusing the incremental gains to be had from learning by using and learning by doing, or to impart to the Chinese a sense of the complex, routine, day-to-day relationships required for successful innovation and productivity growth in the long run.[10]

These comments are not simply a western-oriented, retrospective commentary on events. By 1958 Mao had himself become very critical of the industrial system; and while there was much that proved disastrous in Mao's thinking and policy in these years, he was correct in perceiving that because of its strong elements of centralization, bureaucracy and coercion, Soviet planning was destructive of a creativity that should be based on first-hand knowledge of local circumstances and on the incentives provided by local and individual empowerment. He also grasped the point that planning based on common technological norms could not work effectively in China where varying vintages of capital (with widely differing norms) were unavoidable.[11]

THE PROBLEMS OF RELATING TO THE MARKET ECONOMIES: 1960–78

When China began to rethink these problems in the mid-1960s it was faced with new issues and possibilities. In place of one major supplier, China could now shop for technology throughout western Europe and, increasingly, even in Japan, with whom tentative rapprochements were being made.

In this phase, anti-foreign politics, Maoist emphasis on decentralized, inspirational management, rejection of foreign investment and an explicit preference for self-sufficiency were all-important. The underlying philosophy for technology transfer appears to have been that while some foreign technologies remained essential for the large-scale sector, they could be acquired with minimal foreign contact and no respect for foreign intellectual property rights. Thus the technology import programme for 1964–66 consisted mainly of targeted whole-plant and other hardware imports, coupled with plans for copying and reverse engineering.[12]

Apart from the ideological and other restraints on technology transfer, a short-term attitude to it was reinforced by the prevailing trade system. For whereas in the 1950s trade plans (and contractual commitments) extended over several years, by the 1960s this had been abandoned in favour of year-to-year planning in which the composition and level of trade were, to an important extent, determined by the harvest in the previous autumn. None of this worked well. The time period for planning was too short and by comparison with the 1950s, when 'know-how', contextual and codified knowledge came packaged together, the attempt to manage with minimal, arm's-length, market-based relationships failed to take account of the realities involved.

The Cultural Revolution

The first phase of the Cultural Revolution (1965–70) brought even these tentative experiments to an end. However, the seriousness and ever-widening character of the technology gap were well understood by Zhou Enlai and Liu Shaoqi. Zhou had played a major role in the Twelve-Year Programme for Technology and Science (1956) and, in December 1964, had made his historic call for the Four Modernizations – including that of technology. Liu, on the other hand, was reportedly particularly concerned about the development of the electronics revolution then gathering pace in the west and Japan; while both must have perceived the defence significance of gaps and the need for major technology acquisitions in oil and chemicals that would enable China to increase its supply of fertilizer and take advantage of the downstream possibilities created by exceptionally high growth rates in crude oil output.[13]

There thus followed a further spurt of whole-plant imports, in part taking advantage of China's resumption of normal relations with the United Sates and Japan (1972). This phase culminated in contracts for a huge steel complex at Baoshan (Shanghai) in 1978 which, in a completely new turn of policy, was designed to be fed by imported ore supplies.[14]

The effectiveness of this phase of technology transfer (1972–78) remains controversial. On the one hand, technology transfers were hampered by continued emphasis on whole-plant imports with insufficient attention to 'know-how' and the wider transfer of management and technical skills. Transfers were also affected by the collapse of China's educational and research systems during the Cultural Revolution; by politically ambiguous foreign-trade policies; and by the general disorder of planning and co-ordination that made it difficult to keep installation schedules and plans to bring technology imports and new plant on stream at reasonable capacity levels. While much of the blame for this lies on the Chinese side, western and Japanese exporters (many desperate for orders in the post-oil-shock recessions) were also at fault for signing contracts without fully acquainting themselves with Chinese conditions and absorptive capacity.[15]

However, an alternative view of this phase (from the Japanese whole-plant exporters) emphasizes that many of the problems of the 1970s were echoes of the 1950s, another period when Chinese impatience tended to outstrip reality. The Japanese point out that by the mid-1980s most of the problematic plants were operating successfully, reflecting the eventual success of Chinese learning efforts and of the Japan–China knowledge transfer.[16]

Summary of the Pre-reform Period

Summing up the pre-reform experience, we may say that, whereas in the 1950s technology transfer between China and other planned economies was reasonably successful, the collapse of the Soviet connexion left China with unprecedented problems in relating to market economies. These were found to be insoluble without significant internal planning reform; without a revolutionary transformation in political and cultural attitudes to the outside world; and without some willingness to experiment with joint ventures and foreign investment.

It is true that some highly specific, state-led technology enterprises did succeed, even in the difficult years. One achievement was in nuclear fission, where the Soviets believed that their withdrawal from China would be fatal to Chinese ambitions.[17] China also succeeded beyond expectation in establishing the technology for China's oil extraction industry.[18] Against this, we must note some very high-priority technology transfers that failed badly. Prominent among these was the Spey engine contract with Rolls Royce. This was intended to enable China's Xian-based aircraft-manufacturing capabilities to jump from twenty to only ten years behind the contemporary technological frontier. But it proved far too ambitious a leap for the time, and revealed that China lacked the sophisticated, complementary technologies and skills (especially in metallurgy) that were needed for success.[19]

These judgements are made mainly on the evidence of case studies and Chinese self-analyses. Further evidence of the problem is to be found in estimates of long-run trends in total factor productivity and other indices. According to one uncontroversial estimate, the trends for the state-owned manufacturing sector as a whole were as shown in Table 0.1.

Table 0.1	*Total factor productivity in state-owned industry, 1952–78*
(average annual rates of growth, per cent per annum)

	1952–57	1957–65	1965–78
Series I	7.4	−1.4	0.8
Series II	9.3	0.3	1.2

Note: Series I and II represent weightings for labour and capital inputs of 0.4 and 0.6, and 0.6 and 0.4 respectively.

Source: Tidrick, (1986, p. 4).

Although the data for the First Five-Year Plan reflect some special factors, they generally confirm the overall pattern shown, made up of a successful Soviet phase, chaos during and after the Great Leap Forward, and weak technology transfer and domestic innovation during 1965–78.[20]

TECHNOLOGY TRANSFER AND INNOVATION IN THE CHINESE REFORM

The reform of the Chinese economy which began in later 1978 has been accompanied by a major effort to raise the level of research and development, and to accelerate both its application to the economy and the transfer of foreign technology to China. This is made clear in the chapters by Tang Shiguo and Jiang Xiaojuan, and has been confirmed by the State Council as recently as May 1995.[21]

In Chapter 4, Xu Jiangping identifies three phases in the technology transfer element of this programme: a rapid phase of state-led growth 1981–87; stagnation during 1988–91; and a final phase of accelerated transfer in which the driving forces have been the influx of foreign direct investment and the growing importance of enterprise-level decision-making.

Throughout the whole period, however, the government has retained a major role. It has done this by establishing the broad framework for science and technology policy and industrial innovation as well as detailed technology programmes – the latest of which extends to the year 2010. The state has also been active in raising the status of science and technology staff and in improving incentives through the establishment of new forms of intellectual property rights, prizes and the creation of a market for technology contracts. Particularly significant also has been the support for continuous, on-going technical progress to enhance the productivity and quality of output in old enterprises as distinct from earlier policies that concentrated on technology showpieces and new investments. Clearly, it is hoped that progress of this kind will be increased by the incentives generated by the general marketization of enterprises' activities but, in addition, the problem has been recognized by the provision of special funds for investment in technical renovation (Jiang Xiaojuan, Chapter 7 in this volume).

In the most recent phase, the role of foreign direct investment (and especially that by the Japanese) has been particularly striking. In Chapter 8 Tang Shiguo points out that in 1993 alone Japanese investment was almost as large as in the whole of the decade of the 1980s. While these flows are unlikely to continue to grow at such high rates, it is clear that a new era in Sino-Japanese economic relations is opening with consequences for technology transfer and enhancement on a scale of importance that matches the Soviet effort in the 1950s.

The impact of the reform era is already clear. New products and processes (particularly in the consumer goods sector) have come on stream and, in the widest possible sense, China is being drawn into contact with world industrial and scientific communities on a scale unimaginable just a few years ago. For the future, new long-term plans published in the summer of 1995 recognize the linkage between technology and economic reform policies and include the target of raising the share of science and technology expenditure in gross domestic product to 5 per cent.[22] These plans also show awareness of many existing problems, including the difficulties of ensuring that technology initiatives reach the small-scale firm, and the seriousness of the losses to China caused by the migration of many of China's younger and highest-quality research workers.[23] None the less, as the discussions in these papers and current evidence reveal, in many respects the objectives of technology reform are not being attained, and many issues remain unresolved and contingent on the outcome of the wider arguments about economic organization.[24]

One crucial, continuing debate is that on the role of government and the balance between centralization and dispersal in resources for technical renovation. In Chapter 5 Ding Jingping particularly emphasizes the need for enterprises to achieve more independence and more authority over investment and technology decisions; but this is not a unanimous view. Some are still arguing for the crucial role of government, not only in setting the frameworks, but also in deciding on individual projects, as in the past. Articles referred to by Jiang Xiaojuan in Chapter 7 point up the dilemma posed by the shortage of resources on the one hand, and the high failure rate of many renovation projects on the other.[25] Another debate, discussed in Chapter 9 by David Wall and Yin Xiangshuo, is that between foreign providers and Chinese users of imported technology as to what the appropriate level of technology for China's current state of development should be. These differences, currently still being argued out in the context of the consumer goods industries, will surely become even more intense as the question of the future of the Chinese automobile industry unfolds and the role of foreign capital and technology in this is decided.

Finally, a topic touched upon by Nick von Tunzelmann (Chapter 11) and Christopher Howe (Chapter 2) is the value to China of study of the Japanese and other international experience of technology transfer and industrial policy. This is a subject already of interest in China, and in terms of the Chinese debate our papers provide some ammunition for both sides: they show on the one hand the crucial character of government's guiding hand, yet on the other the indispensable importance of learning in the individual firm, local networks, and 'bottom-up' initiatives and decision-making.[26] Less ambiguous is the message that successful technological transfer is most likely to occur in societies where general levels of literacy and education are high. This is crucial for China, where overall illiteracy is still 20 per cent and only 2.1 per cent of the population have university-level education.[27] Thus as the world economy approaches a new millennium, China, by virtue of its enormous scale, its complex history, and its current policy conundrums, seems set to be the main theatre in which a dramatic interplay between technology and economic development will be played out.

NOTES

1. Schumpeter (1934, ch. 2; 1951).
2. Steindl (1966). A closely associated contemporary, Joan Robinson, while highly critical of capitalism in many respects, was actually neutral about the relationship between monopoly and invention (Robinson, 1933, pp. 168–9).
3. Dobb (1967, pp. 38–40).
4. Penrose (1951).
5. A positive evaluation of Soviet arrangements for technological advance by an American specialist is that by Campbell (1960, ch. 8). A theoretical case is outlined in Brus and Laski (1989, p. 11).
6. Clark (1973).
7. For the textiles case study, see Nishida (1990, ch. 3).
8. Soviet advisers subsequently reported that they had urged a rate of industrial growth well below the 14.7% per annum adopted in China's First Five-Year Plan, but were overruled by an impatient Mao. In the 1980s the Japanese were to make similar claims in relation to the Baoshan contracts (see below, p. 5). For the strategy of the Plan, see Wang (1989). Mikhail Klochko (1963, p. 34) reported on the unrealistic ambitions of Chinese science and technology plans and on the unrealistic, even 'magical' expectations that the Chinese had of the Soviet experts at this time.
9. The Soviet use of 'norms' reflected the fashion in the 1920s for industrial standardization and Taylorism and also Lenin's confidence in the 'engineering' approach to economic planning, see Jasny (1961, p. 39). Norms have to be kept up to date, but Chinese norms atrophied and became increasingly unusable between 1958 and 1978; hence the first task of the planners in the early 1980s was to begin the laborious task of bringing norms for the planned sector up to usable standards.
10. Gains from 'learning by doing' reflect the accumulation of small improvements discovered through the experience of *manufacturing* a piece of equipment. Further gains are made as *users* absorb and apply their experiences. In practice, learning by doing and using will tend to interact as users feed back their ideas to manufacturers (Rosenberg, 1982, pp. 120–40). In many contemporary high-technology industries, users and producers now work so closely at every stage from R&D and design to final use that the distinction between doing and using is disappearing. The 'unheroic' character of technical progress in an early market economy is suggested by the fact that, according to a witness to a British House of Lords Committee in 1857, the core textile process in the UK at that time consisted of 800 minor innovations, of which the carding process alone was protected by sixty patents (see Hobson, 1916, pp. 79–83). For a broad industry case study of the way in which periodic major product innovations generate continuous streams of process improvements see Stobaugh (1988, ch. 2). A company case study with evidence of the scale of the long-run productivity gains from incremental innovation is Hollander (1965).
11. The labour aspects of this are surveyed in Howe (1972).
12. An excellent account of this period is Heymann (1975). This includes a comprehensive listing of whole-plant imports and a discussion of Chinese copying and reverse-engineering experiences. Among the smaller-scale products which the Chinese worked on in the

1960s and 1970s were the Hasselblad camera and the exceptionally high-quality fuel-injection mechanisms of British truck engine manufacturers. According to British sources, had the Chinese engineers succeeded in reverse engineering the fuel-injection mechanism, the savings made by illegal copying would have been enormous. But they were unable to do so, and after wasting considerable resources and several years working on the problem, they finally had to enter into licensing agreements.

13. Chinese crude oil output increased sevenfold between 1965 and 1975 (*1993 Zhongguo gongye jingji tongji nianjian*, p. 38). A detailed account of the development of the refining and petrochemical sectors in the relevant period is Kambara *et al.* (1985, ch. 4). The technical information in this is based on frequent visits by Japanese specialists to oil fields and plants as well as on knowledge of the documentary sources.

14. Weil (1982). The project is also discussed in the context of the Sino-Japanese Long-term Trade Agreement in Howe (1990).

15. The lessons to be learned from this phase are summed up in Chen (1981) and Lin (1981).

16. Yokoi (1990).

17. Klochko (1963, pp. 185ff).

18. The development of the oil industry focused on the Daqing field, which the Soviets helped to discover but abandoned long before it was on stream. Progress of the field was closely monitored by the Japanese (who wished to buy the oil) – and who were particularly impressed by the development of enhanced recovery techniques that kept the field's output at high levels for years after maximum production levels had been reached. A recent book (Zhang *et al.*, 1986) has thrown important light on many aspects of the technological progress achieved in Daqing.

19. These comments are based on briefings from British commercial sources.

20. The special factors include a continuation of the post-war recovery and the intensification of old plant use by means of shift-work. These were both once-for-all improvements still working their way through the system in the 1950s.

21. *Resolution of the Central Party Committee and State Council on Accelerating Progress in Science and Technology* (6 May 1995).

22. Ibid.

23. See also 'Renmin Ribao bemoans outflow of good scientists' (1995). According to this, in 1994 the top five out of thirty-five postgraduates in physics at Beijing University went abroad; three of the top five in biochemistry; and a further eight from physiology and biophysics. The article also quotes an 82-year-old professor at the Beijing Medical University as saying: 'My first students are over sixty years old now but their students have mostly gone abroad. So we cannot retire now.'

24. For data on the low technological standards of industrial enterprises and on low and declining quality standards, see 'Firmly grasp economic construction and turn it in the direction of raising efficiency' (1994) and 'Develop enterprises towards [improved] quality and efficiency' (1994). The latter reported surveys that showed that only 15 per cent of Chinese industrial enterprises currently had capital equipment that met the international standards of the late 1970s and early 1980s.

25. In particular the articles by Hua and Wang. I am grateful to Professor Jiang for supplying the texts of these articles.

26. It is currently estimated that there are at least 1,000 Japanese specialists working in Chinese research institutes of various kinds (see Jackson, 1996). A good example of Chinese concern with foreign systems and technology acquisition is 'The Secrets of Technology Transfer by Japan and the Four Asian Dragons', in Zhong (1992).

27. Data reported by Zhang Weimin, Head of Population and Employment Statistics, State Statistical Bureau (1995).

REFERENCES

1993 Zhongguo gongye jingji tongji nianjian, [Chinese Industrial Statistics Year-book], (1993), Beijing: China Statistical Publishing House.

Brus, W. and Laski, K. (1989), *From Marx to the Market: Socialism in Search of an Economic System*, Oxford: Clarendon Press.

Campbell, R.W. (1960), *Soviet Economic Power: Its Organization, Growth and Challenge*, London: Stevens.

Chen Huiqin (1981), 'The trend in technology imports must be changed', *Jingji guanli* [Economic Management], 4, 22–5.

Clark, M.G. (1973), *The Development of China's Steel Industry and Soviet Technical Aid*, Ithaca, N.Y.: New York School of Industrial and Labor Relations.

'Develop enterprises towards [improved] quality and efficiency' (1994), *Renmin ribao* [The People's Daily], 20 May 1994.

Dobb, Maurice (1967), *Papers on Capitalism, Development and Planning*, London: Kegan Paul.

'Firmly grasp economic construction and turn it in the direction of raising efficiency' (1994), *Renmin ribao* [The People's Daily], 9 May.

Heymann, Hans, Jr (1975), 'Acquisition and diffusion of technology in China', in *China: A Reassessment of the Economy*, Washington, D.C.: Joint Economic Committee, 678–729.

Hobson, J.A. (1916), *The Evolution of Modern Capitalism: A Study of Machine Production*, London: George Allen & Unwin.

Hollander, S. (1965), *The Sources of Increased Efficiency: A Study of the Du Pont Rayon Plants*, Cambridge, Mass.: MIT Press.

Howe, C. (1972), 'Industrial relations and rapid industrialization: some Far Eastern cases. China', *Bulletin of the International Institute of Labour Studies*, 10, 48–84.

—— (1990), 'China, Japan and economic interdependence in the Asia Pacific Region', *China Quarterly*, 124, 662–93.

Jackson, S.F. (1996), 'Lessons from a neighbour: China's Japan-watching community', in C. Howe (ed.), *China and Japan: History, Trends, and Prospects*, Oxford: Clarendon Press, 155–78.

Jasny, Naum (1961), *Soviet Industrialization, 1928–1952*, Chicago: University of Chicago Press.

Kambara, Tatsu *et al.*, (1985), *Chugoku no sekiyu sangyo* [The Chinese Oil Industry], Tokyo: Saiwai Shobo.

Klochko, Mikhail K. (1963), *Soviet Scientist in China*, London: Hollis & Carter.

Lin Senmu (1981), 'The lessons of the 22 whole plant imports', *Jingji guanli* [Economic Management], 12–14.

Nishida, Judith Mary (1990), 'The Japanese influence on the Shanghaiese textile industry and implications for Hong Kong', University of Hong Kong, unpublished MPhil thesis.

Penrose, E.T. (1951), *The Economics of the International Patent System*, Baltimore, Md: Johns Hopkins Press.

'Renmin Ribao bemoans outflow of good scientists' (1995), Foreign Broadcasting Information Service CHI-95-09, 25 April.

Resolution of the Central Party Committee and State Council on Accelerating Progress in Science and Technology, 6 May 1995, reported in *Xinhua yuebao* [New China Monthly], June 1995, 70–5.

Robinson, J. (1933), *The Economics of Imperfect Competition*, London: Macmillan.

Rosenberg, N. (1982), *Inside the Black Box: Technology and Economics*, Cambridge: Cambridge University Press.

Schumpeter, J.A. (1934), *The Theory of Economic Development: An Inquiry into Profits, Capital, Credit, Interest and the Business Cycle*, Cambridge, Mass.: Harvard University Press.

—— (1951), *Capitalism, Socialism and Democracy*, 3rd edn, London: George Allen & Unwin.

Steindl, Josef (1966), 'Capitalism, science and technology', in C.H. Feinstein (ed.), *Socialism, Capitalism and Economic Growth*, Cambridge: Cambridge University Press, 198–205.

Stobaugh, R. (1988), *Innovation and Competition: The Global Management of Petrochemical Products*, Boston, Mass.: Harvard Business School Press.

Tridrick, Gene (1986), *Productivity Growth and Technological Change in Chinese Industry*, World Bank Staff Working Paper n. 61, Washington, DC: World Bank, 1986, p. 4.

Wang Guangwei (1989), 'The basic tasks of China's First Five Year Plan', in C. Howe and K.R. Walker, *The Foundations of the Chinese Planned Economy: A Documentary Survey, 1953–65*, London: Macmillan, 10–19.

Weil, M. (1982), 'The Baoshan steel mill: a symbol of change in China's industrial development strategy', in *China Under the Four Modernizations, Part 1*, Washington, D.C.: Joint Economic Committee, 365–93.

Yokoi, Yoichi (1990), 'Plant and technology contracts and the changing pattern of economic interdependence between China and Japan', *China Quarterly*, 124, 694–713.

Zhang Lizhong et al. (eds) (1986), *Keji jinbu yu Daqing fazhan jianshe* [Technological Progress and the Development of the Construction of Daqing [Oil Field]], Beijing: Science and Technology Materials Publishing House.

Zhong Yukun (1992), *Yinjin jishu de jueqiao* [The Tricks of the Trade in Technology Import], Beijing: Science and Technology Materials Publishing House.

1. Rethinking technology transfers: incentives, institutions and knowledge-based industrial development

Paul A. David

CONCEPTUAL BEARINGS: THE SUBJECT'S NATURE AND SCOPE

As an aspect of the study of the 'diffusion' of innovations, the economic analysis of technology transfer phenomena has been coloured by periodic shifts of the vantage point from which that larger subject area has been viewed. Some of these shifts in perspective have occurred in response to the waxing and waning of interest in the connections between technological development and international economic and political relations, while some have been coloured by rather specific policy issues having to do with scientific and technological knowledge and its exploitation for commercial (and, in some cases, military) purposes. Still others have reflected the influence of deeper reconceptualizations of the relationship of diffusion to the whole complex of processes involved in technological change.

Not surprisingly, then, 'technology transfer' has meant many different things to different economists, management practitioners and national and international policy-makers over the course of the past several decades. My purpose in this chapter is not to attempt to survey the field, but, simply and much less ambitiously, to draw attention to a number of significant regards in which a fresh look at the issues of technology transfer is called for in the light of recent theoretical work on the economics of information and the role of knowledge in economic growth.

Even in its more restrictive meanings 'technology transfer' usually has been identified with one or another aspect of the process of technology diffusion, that being the subject area broadly concerned with the dissemination of knowledge about technological practices and consequent changes in the distribution of the population of potential users across the set of feasible techniques. To be clear about the terminology before going any further, I should say that here I am using 'techniques' quite comprehensively to refer to specifications of products and methods or systems of production, which may or may not be embodied in particular artefacts, such as materials, machines or instruments. 'Technology' then is simply knowledge about techniques, to which some significant degree of reliability or dependability is attached by those possessing it.

Within the broad category of such knowledge various functional types may be distinguished:[1] *generic technology* refers to general properties of materials and principles for their transformation and combination into systems and products whose performance attributes can be described; *infratechnology* refers to sets of methods, scientific and engineering databases, models, measurement and quality standards that support and co-ordinate the investigation of fundamental physical properties of matter as well as the practical implementation of generic knowledge that gives rise to *applied product and process technologies*; the term *craft technology* is sometimes associated with forms of knowledge that enable the possessor to accomplish specified tasks in designing and producing useful artefacts, without necessarily divulging or even being conscious of the 'instruction set' that is implicit in those operations.

Improvements in the state of each of these kinds of knowledge can be termed technological 'innovations', even if that usage does permit some degree of ambiguity to persist; innovations in the state of technical (or scientific) knowledge can emerge in a particular social context as a result of the creation of truly novel techniques, hitherto unknown to any of the agents in that context, or through the discovery, acquisition and application of pre-existing knowledge by agents who previously had not possessed it. The former of these modes is usually given the label 'discoveries and inventions', whereas the latter mode of change, when viewed from the global, system perspective, is conventionally referred to as technology 'diffusion'.[2]

When we speak of technology transfer, then, it is in reference to the transmission of knowledge of one or more of the foregoing sorts, quite possibly separately but more usually in conjunction with knowledge of other kinds. The channels of transmission may involve trade and transfers of materials, of designs, blueprints, scientific papers and patents, formulae, manuals, databases, instruments and machinery, as well as the physical relocation of people possessing specialized technical information and craft skills. But it is only a shorthand form of expression to conflate 'technology transfer' with the acts of exchange involving those elements and embodiments of technology, or with the array of transactional modes through which deliberate knowledge-exchanges are effected. Licensing, subcontracting, technical co-operation agreements, joint venture arrangements, management and training contracts, turnkey project contracts, direct foreign investments, and sales of capital equipment and materials are transactional modes that figure prominently in the modern literature devoted to international technology transfers.

Yet it must be borne in mind that the existence and use of these mechanisms does not in and of itself signify how completely or effectively the pertinent knowledge-transfer is being accomplished.

Furthermore, it is one thing to transfer technological knowledge effectively, and quite a different matter to impart *technological capabilities* to individuals, organizations and still larger social aggregations that previously had lacked them. Technological capability does not inhere in the knowledge that is possessed, but in the ability to make effective use of technological knowledge to satisfy material wants. It therefore entails a command of a far wider field of economically relevant knowledge and competences that are often associated with the concepts of organizational, institutional and societal capital.[3]

In this rethinking of the evolving treatment of the subject at the hands of economists, the particular themes I wish to develop are these: (a) the growing appreciation of the complex and peculiar nature of scientific and technological knowledge as economic assets, and of the consequent problems of contracting for some forms of economically relevant information; (b) the ambiguous role played by intellectual property in technology transfers; (c) the limitations on knowledge diffusion as a dynamic driver of international convergence in technological practices and productivity levels.

Although to do this will hardly require me systematically to reconsider the whole intellectual history of the subject, it may be useful none the less to introduce and motivate my discussion of the foregoing three themes by recalling the major transformations that have taken place since the 1950s in the content of the economics literature appearing under the rubric 'technology transfer'. Almost unavoidably, given the goals of brevity and coherence, the following cursory review will suffer for being not only highly selective, but personally idiosyncratic in its account of the way the main currents of research in this area have shifted since I first entered it, as a student of economics at Harvard some forty years ago.

A BRIEF INTELLECTUAL HISTORY

During the latter part of the 1950s and the early 1960s, that is to say, in the heyday of enthusiasm in the industrially advanced countries for programmes of economic development assistance, 'technology transfer' was synonymous with the design and organization of efforts by western governments and international agencies to disseminate information and practical knowledge about techniques of production that were familiar in their economies but somehow had failed to come into widespread use among what then were referred to as the 'less-developed countries' (LDCs). Much of the expertise in this area initially was focused on finding the most effective channels through which to impart 'better knowledge', following from the presumption that the technologies in use in the west were manifestly superior. That was an orientation that many of the programme administrators and advisers recruited for this work brought from their prior experiences – in agricultural extension services and similar organizations in civilian 'mission agencies' of their own countries, dealing with health service, education and transportation in their own countries.[4]

Thus, at that time the technology transfer problem itself was thought to be primarily one of information dissemination; of locating influential members of the local, recipient community who would help overcome the predictable resistance of the other 'locals' to abandoning the familiar in favour of anything novel. The question of why it was that people in the target community somehow had failed to seek out and adopt the putatively 'best' methods, including those that were embodied in specific capital equipment (electrical pumps for water wells, gasoline tractors) and special materials (hybrid corn seeds, chemical fertilizer, insecticides and fungicides), was not one that automatically commanded careful attention in this context. In the same fashion, observed behavioural differences among members of the selected population of farms, firms or households, in their acceptance and continued use of the techniques being transferred to them, glibly were ascribed to differences in their inherent attitudes towards change *per se*, or to variations among their individual susceptibilities to the particular mode of information dissemination and persuasion which had been utilized by the transfer agents.[5]

The next discernible phase in the modern evolution of thinking in this vein saw development economists becoming concerned with planning criteria for investment projects, and therefore directing attention to the 'which?' of technology transfer activities, rather than to the question of 'how?'. The signal issues were whether or not many of the technologies which lent themselves most readily to 'turnkey' modes of transfer really constituted appropriate technologies for the recipient economies. As attractive as the transfer mode appeared to the would-be providers of integrally packaged and externally financed technical systems (steel plants, electricity power stations, chemical plants and petroleum refining facilities), doubts were occasioned by the fact that such systems, typically, had been designed and engineered for deployment in advanced industrial economy contexts. Under the prevailing macroeconomic factor endowment conditions that obtained in many poor countries, it was not a self-evidently efficient allocation of resources to promote the introduction of technologies that had proved commercially successful where capital (and foreign exchange) was comparatively cheap, where skilled technical staffing could be readily found locally to repair and maintain sophisticated continuous production systems (while unskilled labour was comparatively dear and inelastic in supply), and where transport and input supply conditions were suitable for ensuring the high throughput rates and continuous utilization necessary for spreading the large fixed costs of indivisible plant and equipment over a large volume of standardized production. Through such sceptical questioning, and doubts about the length of time before the recipient economies would be able to develop an indigenous capability to operate and further improve upon such technologies, the strands of the economics literature that drew upon Stephen Marglin's and Amartya Sen's theoretical treatments of the development planner's choice of technique problems became conjoined with the more philosophical and political themes of the 'Small is Beautiful' movement for appropriate technologies.

One consequence, surely unintended by the contributors to that literature, was the gradually growing appreciation of the importance of distinguishing between the set of 'feasible production techniques', defined by the prevailing state of technological knowledge, and the proper sub-set within it that was formed by the 'available production processes'.[6] The latter, having been selected for implementation in the setting of particular factor- and product-markets, over time would tend to build up around themselves a body of learned expertise that was not only technical but organizational and transactional, and so would appear as the more salient, more reliable candidates for deliberate 'transfer' across organizational or societal boundaries.

In the west during the 1970s, and in the US particularly, the term technology transfer lost its previous exclusively international connotations and began to be applied in reference to certain domestic public-sector technology diffusion efforts, namely the deliberate search for commercial applications of technical developments that had been generated in the pursuit of other, non-commercial missions. The promotion of 'spin-offs' from military and non-military R&D was an activity that agencies such as NASA and the Department of Defense undertook as part of their public relations strategies, in search of support for their primary missions. In committing themselves to the goal of bringing about a higher rate of such 'transfers', greater consciousness developed of the historical role taken by the US federal government in supporting the application of agricultural R&D to improving farming practices through the work of the Department of Agriculture's experimental stations, and to the role of the agricultural extension service as an information diffusion agency.[7]

At a very basic level this approach reflected the dominance of the so-called 'linear model of innovation', which placed diffusion as the end-stage of a unidirectional sequence. The latter was envisaged as proceeding from fundamental scientific discovery to applied science, to invention, and thence, via improvement and development of the invention for purposes of economic exploitation, through to the innovative act of commercial introduction by a business firm; whence, if things went properly, there followed the final stage of adoption and increasingly widespread acceptance by 'the market'. With this schema in mind, it was an easy step for non-commercial mission agencies conceptually to hive off the end-stage 'task' of securing adoption of some spin-off product, technique or management method; by neglecting the significance of the actual web of two-way information flows and feedback channels of influence that link the processes of initial adoption and of incremental adaptation to field conditions and technical design refinements through which successful innovations frequently must pass, it could be made to appear natural and sensible for such agencies to try to organize technology transfers as 'top-down' programmes, employing 'change agents' and demonstration projects.[8]

Paralleling the mission-oriented public-sector experiments with domestic technology diffusion in the advanced economies, and reflecting the fact that expansion of business into new market areas through direct foreign investment had become a major strategy of emerging multinational and transnational companies during the post-Second World War boom, the problem of technology transfer re-emerged as matter of specialized concern for intra-organizational management in the private sector. Concurrently, during the mid-1970s, worries had been voiced in some US government circles about the possibilities that, in addition to direct foreign investment, other channels of international technology transfer such as patenting and patent licensing and exports of instruments and production machinery were causing international leakages or unintended spillovers of information relating to 'high-tech' industries, and that these might find direct and indirect military applications in nations rivalling the US. In an effort to bring more empirically-based considerations to bear on these issues, studies began to be undertaken, most notably by David Teece (1976) and others inspired by Edwin Mansfield (1982), to re-examine the presuppositions on which such suspicions rested.

Their starting-point was to question the empirical foundations for the assumption in most of the information-theoretic literature that the costs of communicating information about proven technological opportunities were negligibly small. Investigations of this kind into the micro-foundations of technology transfers sought to quantify the speed with which innovations in various industrial and technical fields diffused internationally; to estimate the costs of successfully transferring information about production methods between organizations; to gauge the impact on such costs of variations in the technical capabilities of the initiating and recipient firms, and in the nature of the environment(s) in which the foreign subsidiaries of multinational firms were operating.[9] It was found in some research-intensive industries, such as plastics and semiconductors, that 'imitation lags' for the introduction of specific products (between the US and other countries) varied inversely with the follower country's relative R&D performance efforts in the industry in question. Transfers of the technology for manufacturing products by multinationals to their foreign subsidiaries tended to be the mode favoured in the case of products that had been added most recently to the transferor's product line, whereas when licences, joint ventures and other channels were used the average ages of the products involved were higher.

Teece's (1976) earlier investigations of the costs of transferring product designs to overseas subsidiaries of US multinationals (mainly in the chemicals, petroleum refining and machinery industries) showed that there were very substantial costs of transmitting and absorbing the additional know-how required to put the technology into actual operation. These averaged about 20 per cent of total project costs and were additional to the costs of transmitting knowledge that was 'embodied' in capital goods, blueprints, specifications and special materials. They included the costs of pre-engineering technological exchanges, engineering costs associated with transferring process or product designs and the associated process- or product-engineering, as well as R&D costs entailed in adapting and modifying the technology to suit local conditions. They also included the pre-start-up training costs and the outlays made during the initial 'shakedown' and 'debugging' phases of learning required for the plant to achieve its designed performance specifications. The more extensive the experience that the transferring organization previously had acquired in furnishing subsidiaries with the technology in question, and the narrower the gap between indicators of the technical capabilities of the two participating organizations, the smaller were the transfer costs in relation to the total size of the project (see Mansfield *et al.*, 1982, ch. 8).

Whereas the microeconomics and microsociology of intra-firm 'transfers of technical practice' formed a natural centre of focus in the corporate technology management literature of this period, a more macroeconomic policy perspective began to recast discussions of technology transfers during the 1980s. This was the concern, again one primarily voiced in US government circles, that the diffusion of technological information, whether as an intended or as an unintended consequence of private-sector activities, was promoting international convergence in technical capabilities. If so, it was feared that this might be contributing to accelerated erosion of the position of economic and technological advantage that the US had enjoyed earlier in the post-Second World War era. A preoccupation with the role of technological leadership in securing superior 'competitiveness' began to replace the national defence security worries of the 1970s (which had focused on possible leakages of 'defence-sensitive' technologies from the west to the east). This new 'techno-mercantilist' source of anxiety now caused civilian technology transfers to be viewed increasingly as problematic, rather than as a *desideratum* of international economic integration.[10]

These concerns undoubtedly were exacerbated by adverse trends in the US commodity trade balance, which previously had shown strong surpluses for all the R&D-intensive manufacturing industries. The role of technology gaps arising from the imperfect and delayed diffusion of technological knowledge had been noted in the international trade theory literature of the previous decade, where it was treated as a benign feature of the new pattern of international specialization that called for new and heterodox styles of modelling, especially the product-cycle models of trade and the related empirical studies of R&D intensity of trade flows that featured in the line of research initiated by Raymond Vernon (1970). In the mid-1980s, however, economists' attention shifted more to examining the role of scientific and technological information spillovers and imitation by the follower nations of production methods and products in productivity convergence and 'catch-up' on the part of some of the rapidly industrializing follower nations. Emblematic of this latter shift was William Baumol's (1986) virtually exclusive concentration on unavoidable spillovers of scientific and technological information as the putative process underlying long-run tendencies towards convergence of the levels and rates of growth of productivity and real income per capita among the industrial and industrializing economies.[11]

The subsequent emergence in the 1990s of scientific and technological 'knowledge' and knowledge-generating capabilities at the centre of the formal analytical constructs being explored by 'new growth theory' has opened the way for the subject of technology transfer to regain a key position in discussions of the dynamics of economic development, North–South trade and capital flows, and long-term tendencies toward convergence or growing inequalities in the international distribution of income and wealth.[12] The mathematical models that have been put forward to illuminate these phenomena are most certainly an important advance over their predecessors. They do explicitly recognize that the diffusion of innovations from the technologically more advanced, high-productivity regions to the rest of the world (the South, in their stylized parlance) is neither automatic nor instantaneous. Further, they acknowledge that the costs of access by producers located in the south to innovations generated elsewhere will be affected by the prevailing regime(s) of intellectual property protection, and so at least accord symbolic notice to the powerful influence that legal and other institutions have upon the transmission of scientific and technological knowledge among agents and economies, and therefore in channelling or impeding the transfer of technology.

In the genre of 'technology gap' models of trade, to choose one influential and illustrative example, the differential pace of technological progress is usually depicted as the force creating international divergences in comparative advantage and asymmetries in national patterns of foreign trade. It is supposed that additions to the stock of knowledge generated in one country will have positive externalities for firms located there, but do not diffuse rapidly across national borders, even though there eventually will be international 'spillovers' and imitation (based on reverse engineering) by producers in other countries. General equilibrium models of North–South technological development and trade, such as those constructed recently by Grossman and Helpman (1989, 1991), suggest that the transfer (imitation) of technological innovations generated in the North and their application to the production of tradeables in the initially lower-wage South must work to increase the specialization of the two regions. According to this analysis, which assumes full employment and labour malleability, commodity production in the North is forced to contract by the southern 'imitators' of the North's technological innovations, and the displaced workers of the north are absorbed in R&D activities there, which leads to increases in the global rate of technological progress. Everyone benefits thereby!

What should we take from all this when considering the role of technology transfers and the scope for technology policy measures in the developing countries? How reasonable is it to identify the economies of the latter with the stylized, technologically laggard 'South' of the currently fashionable models? How informative is the characterization of the processes of technological innovation and diffusion ('transfer') in these models and of the way those processes may be affected by policies concerned with intellectual property protection and other, infrastructural conditions?

I must say that when I read these stylized analytical exercises, the overwhelming feeling I experience is that an awful lot has been 'lost in translation'; that is to say, lost in the passage between the understanding that economists have gained about the mechanisms of interorganizational and international technology transfers, and the 'stylized facts' encapsulated in the formal terms of these ingenious and mathematically tractable models. In my view, at least, it is both unfortunate and unnecessary that much of the empirical wisdom, and many of the nuances of analysis of the workings of the institutional and organizational devices employed in technology transfer arrangements, all of which have been so patiently accumulated over the preceding decades of research and field experience, should be simplified to the point of distortion in the course of restoring the subject to its present position of prominence in the models of the 'new trade theory' and 'new growth theory'. What follows in these pages, therefore, is proffered as a modest contribution to a much needed rethinking of the analytical treatment of the subject of technological transfers.[13]

TACIT KNOWLEDGE, CODIFIED INFORMATION AND TRANSACTIONAL DIFFICULTIES

The basic conceptualization of technological knowledge in much of the growth and trade theory literature is that it is all codified information and, because it is unambiguous and cheaply transmitted, to prevent such information from 'leaking out' is difficult, except during comparatively brief intervals of time following its initial acquisition. Competitors, it is supposed, will soon learn enough of a new technique to borrow it. A related, variant view is that the essential technological knowledge is embodied in the very design of the product, and hence, with some effort and expense, it can be retrieved by 'reverse engineering'. There is certainly enough that is true in the foregoing characterizations, particularly when they are applied to the situation of inno-vating firms in the technologically and industrially advanced countries. But, because they convey only a part of the truth, the picture that emerges tends to understate the very considerable problems that may attend the inter-organizational transfer of complex, modern technologies and, *a fortiori*, the difficulties of contractual arrangements to achieve this in many of the world's developing countries.

Yes, there is codified technological knowledge, but there is also uncodified, tacit knowledge which is complementary to it. In contrast with codified knowledge, tacit knowledge refers to a fact of common perception that we all are often generally aware of certain objects without being focused on them; they are none the less important in forming the context that makes focused perception possible, understandable and productive. No less than other hu-man pursuits, scientific and technological endeavours draw crucially upon sets of human skills and techniques that have been acquired experientially and are transferred between people by demonstration, by informal personal instruction, advice, consultations, rather than being reduced to explicit and codified methods and procedures. Yet, without the latter contextual know-ledge which forms a major ingredient of 'expertise' in those fields, even quite elaborately codified sets of explicit instructions may be difficult to interpret properly. Production processes that are implemented by people trying to follow the codified instructions without access to the complementary tacit understanding of experts often fail to deliver immediately outputs of the expected quality, and others continue for long periods to produce below the rates anticipated.

Some of this tacit knowledge consists of the details and material specifica-tions that have been omitted from the 'blueprints' intentionally, or simply because they are so 'standard' in the country where the design originated that specifying them is regarded as unnecessary. Others may reside in the exper-tise accumulated by production engineers or of the plant operators at the sites where the technology was first implemented. The more complex the process, or the product design, the greater the dimensionality of the tacit knowledge problem. For example, as Edward Steinmueller (1989) has pointed out, the knowledge involved in effective production of advanced information technology products entails far more than the transfer of a set of blueprints. Differences in the availability of individual components, subtle effects resulting from seemingly minor adaptations in design to accommodate local least-cost methods of manufacture, the necessity of achieving interoperability with other information technology systems that are not 'standard', all may frustrate attempts to implement a patented process or product design. This is especially so if that attempt is made in a foreign industrial setting, without access to the tacit knowledge of agents who have experience getting the technology to work in its original setting.

We may say that the greater is the technological distance between firms, in terms of the degree of overlap or disjointedness in the domains of their production experiences, the more serious is the problem posed by tacit knowledge. Tacitness itself implies that the agents will not have a conscious, focused perception of what it is they know (and that others may not know) which is critical for successful operations. The smaller the set of analogous experiences, the more difficult it is likely to be for one firm to elicit from the other the list of subjects about which it should be seeking further information. This last is an aspect of the generic difficulty of arm's-length contracting purely for information: because knowledge is infinitely expansible so that mere possession of it does not preclude its possession by others, to describe completely the 'commodity' that is to be exchanged for valuable consideration, in this case, would be tantamount to delivering the goods themselves. In addition, the greater is the asymmetry in the distribution of knowledge between the contracting parties, the more severe become the principal–agent problems that add to the costs of contracting and monitoring contract compliance.

Of course, common training of skilled personnel and easy mobility of such personnel will help greatly in overcoming some of these problems, and hence they tend to raise the likelihood of rapid, successful implementation when codified technologies are 'transferred' from one unit within a multinational corporation to an overseas subsidiary. Co-operative industry-sponsored programmes and public investments in establishing infratechnologies that are standardized across national borders would, for the same reasons, tend to lower the costs of negotiating arm's-length contractual arrangements for licensing technologies developed abroad by making it easier to describe what the techniques and products in question are supposed to do. Such measures would also reduce the need to contract for the provision of the complementary tacit information.

It thus seems unwarranted simply to assume that technology will automatically 'leak out' to developing countries, in much the same way, albeit with somewhat longer lags, that knowledge about innovations tends to become ubiquitously diffused among competing firms in the technologically advanced region of its origin. A corollary of this proposition, however, is that the successful transplanting of advanced technologies may have important externalities in building up stocks of tacit knowledge in the receiving country, and these will make it cheaper and less risky to transfer other analogous or technically related innovations. The development of technological competences in a particular field, especially one such as information technology that has pervasive applications across a range of industries and sectors, will also make it more feasible for potential borrowers to monitor the advance of the knowledge frontier, and so to identify the most competent innovating firms from whom they might seek to acquire access to the newest relevant techniques. Acquisition of competencies of these sorts can be viewed as forming a particularly critical technological capability and may well be termed 'learning to borrow'. But rather than seeing this as a priority item only for countries that are technologically laggard, it has been argued that the emerging paradigm of 'innovation through recombination' (which is currently exemplified in high-technology fields such as biotechnology and computer software design) will make 'borrowing capability' a strategic core competence for firms operating on the technological frontier itself, regardless of where they may be physically situated (see, for example, David and Foray, 1995).

The self-reinforcing, positive feedback mechanisms to which the foregoing observations have pointed imply that there may be marked divergences in the rate of imitation or 'technology absorbing capacity' across industries, and even across broad sectors of developing economies. These have remained largely unrecognized in the 'technology gap' literature, however, because the latter has focused attention upon positive feedback mechanisms that operate to generate divergences in rates of innovation in the industrially advanced countries. Exploring the properties of open economy models that incorporate positive feedback affecting the rate of technology borrowing or 'imitation' alone, or which combine them with positive feedback in the rate of innovation, undoubtedly would uncover much richer dynamics. It also is likely to suggest policy implications rather different from those that have emerged to date.

INTELLECTUAL PROPERTY PROTECTION AND TECHNOLOGY TRANSFER

One of the longest-standing traditions in the economic analysis of intellectual property issues is the antithesis that is discerned between the incentives provided for invention and innovation by the award of patent and copyright protection, on the one hand, and the discouragement of widespread utilization of new knowledge that results from the exercise of those monopoly privileges. Producers of innovations, it is therefore supposed, should be favourably disposed towards strong protection for intellectual property rights, whereas technology 'users', and especially those seeking to deploy the latest advances in technical process and product design, should oppose such regimes. Many of the well-known recent 'trade gap' models serve to reinforce this view. They start from the premise that under conditions of free trade the production structures and immediate economic interests of the developing countries (i.e. 'the South') would be promoted by freely 'borrowing' whatever new technologies they were able to reverse-engineer or simply copy; whereas the interests of 'the North' are seen in these models as being bound up almost exclusively with the generation of new processes and products.

This further entrenches an already deeply-rooted notion: namely, that there is an unavoidable commercial conflict between the technology-borrowing developing economies and the technology-generating developed world, centring on issues of protection for intellectual property. In the 1960s and early 1970s, the United Nations Conference on Trade and Development (UNCTAD) articulated the charges of many developing countries that the international intellectual property system was biased against them, in that it gave monopoly rights to foreign holders of patents and copyrights at the expense of consumers in their countries (see Mody, 1990; UNCTAD, 1991). The explicit justification offered for not subscribing to international patent and copyright conventions was essentially a distributional or equity argument: poor countries at their 'stage of development' ought not be asked to pay for knowledge that would ultimately be part of the universal heritage of mankind.[14] In the event, India, Brazil and Argentina, among other countries, passed laws restricting the scope of intellectual property protection.

Although the international system of protection was somewhat strengthened during the 1970s by the expansion in the number of signatories to the Paris Convention for patents and the Berne Conventions for copyright protection, during the 1980s the US, supported by other industrially advanced countries began to press for a much greater strengthening of the machinery to enforce compliance on the part of the signatories, as well as seeking to induce the 'hold-outs' to join. Increasingly, trade sanctions have been threatened in bilateral trade negotiations, if not actually invoked by the US in pursuit of that goal. The recent difficulties that have arisen between China and the US over the latter's implementation of so-called 'anti-piracy' laws pertaining to copyright and trade-marked products may be seen to be merely the latest round in this longer process.

This is an arena of much contention, one into which I must try to enter with utmost caution and delicacy, and that only for the purpose of pointing out that the foregoing portrayal of the 'North–South' conflict is overly simplistic. Crudely stereotypical conceptualizations of some of the subtle issues concerning the role of intellectual property in technology transfers cannot help resolve the real conflicts that do exist, and it obscures some respects in which the general interests of the developed and developing economies may be more closely aligned than is often supposed. It is upon the latter, more hopeful possibilities that I wish to focus on the present occasion.

One of the general arguments that has been made for 'harmonizing' the international treatment of intellectual property by strengthening the protection accorded to patents, copyrights and trade-marks in developing countries is that the latter would benefit from greater direct foreign investment by multinational firms (see, for example, Sherwood, 1990). It is claimed that, where the regime of protection for intellectual property is non-existent or weak, direct foreign investment is discouraged and that when investment does occur, it is more likely to be confined to wholly owned subsidiaries or to the transfer of older technologies. I have two reasons, however, for putting these contentions to one side. First, many factors influence direct foreign investment decisions, and there is little systematic empirical evidence to support or contradict the assertion that the insecurity of intellectual property exerts powerful adverse effects among these, except possibly in the cases of the chemical and pharmaceutical industries, and in choices about the location of overseas R&D facilities (see Mansfield, 1993, ch. 5). Second, direct foreign investment by multinationals in wholly owned subsidiaries is treated by the governments of some developing countries as politically problematic, and is judged by others as likely to be at best a rather ineffective channel for transferring technological knowledge to indigenous industries, especially not in ways that enhance the host country's technological capabilities. Therefore, it seems more important to consider how the efficacy of other modes of transfer, such as joint ventures and arm's-length licensing agreements, is affected by the nature of the prevailing intellectual property regime.

It might also be remarked that the technology gap trade models (reviewed earlier) do not envisage the rate at which innovations are imitated by producers in 'the South' as being governed by capital inflows from the North; in so far as they consider licensing as a channel through which technological knowledge flows to the South, the effect of weak or non-existent intellectual property protection is supposed to be to increase the rate of knowledge flow by lowering the costs of imitation. Here, again, there is a dearth of convincing empirical evidence. What there is, however, seems more fully consistent with the contrary and rather plausible view that the licensing of technology to non-subsidiaries in developing countries becomes a comparatively more important transfer mode when the recipient's patent system more closely resembles that of the licensor.[15] Consistency of treatment, rather than 'strength' of protection, may well be what matters most in intellectual property matters.

In setting out the logic of the case for viewing intellectual property protection as an institutional mechanism that can be used to facilitate rather than impede the absorption of foreign technologies, it may be enlightening to begin with some historical perspective on the institution of patents. Far from having been designed as a device for stimulating inventive activity, which is the way in which they are seen today, patents originally were granted to promote the 'borrowing' of technology![16] The English term 'letters patent' is a literal translation of the Latin *litterae patentes*, which refers simply to open letters. These were the official documents by which certain privileges, rights, ranks or titles were conferred and publicly announced; hence they carried the seal of the sovereign grantor on the inside, rather than being closed by a seal on the exterior. Patents began as instruments used by noble or republican governments in later medieval and early Renaissance Europe primarily to induce the transfer and disclosure of foreign technologies. In the fourteenth century, when England was an industrially and technologically backward realm in comparison with many provinces of continental Europe, such grants were found to be effective in gaining access to foreign technologies through the immigration of skilled foreign craftsmen.[17] It was desired that the foreign master craftsmen should not simply transfer their production activities to England, but by so doing should introduce English apprentices to the 'mysterie' of their respective arts. However, because maintaining control over the activities of these newly skilled workers would be difficult if not impossible once they had risen to journeyman status, a cohort of potential domestic competitors would thereby be created. Obviously, it was from this that any forward-looking foreign master wished to be protected by the grant of a monopoly.

It has become conventional in popular accounts of the development of intellectual property protection in the west to assign great significance to the Venetian Senate's passage on 19 March 1474 of the first general patent law. Most modern authorities, however, view this statute merely as codifying prior practice rather than enunciating any 'novel' principle. The law required the registration of any 'new and ingenious' device not made hitherto within the Venetian domain, and prohibited all private parties save the inventor from making it for a period of ten years, on pain of penalties for violation of the code. Yet it appears that between 1474 and 1490 very few patents were issued under the Venetian code; this despite the fact that the period right through to the middle of the sixteenth century saw the continued granting of many patent *privileggi* that conferred exclusive production rights for terms varying between five and eighty years, as well as monopolistic trade privileges. Despite the rising interest in invention, and the spread on the continent of Europe of the use of patent grants to encourage the development of new industrial practices as an instrument of mercantilist policy in France during the mid-sixteenth century, in England the first clear provision for 'patents of invention' – as distinct from the technology transfer franchises sometimes referred to as 'import patents' – did not emerge before the seventeenth century.[18]

Many of the basic features of the patent as we know it today are better suited to its initial purposes and pre-eighteenth century historical contexts than to the subsequent use to which the contrivance has been put. The disclosure provisions of modern patent systems, for example, were an essential and natural aspect of the effort to induce foreign artisans to reveal a 'mystery' and train domestic craftsmen in such pursuits. Making the conduct of the trade or craft (and the consequent training of apprentices and journeymen) a readily monitored condition for enjoying the privilege conveyed by the patent was a quite straightforward arrangement. Indeed, the transmission of knowledge that in large part belonged to the tacit repertoire of the master craftsman (and which, even where it might be codified in instructions, say, for the reproduction of particular textile weaves, most likely would have been held as a guild secret) was the whole object of the exercise. Protecting the instructors from the competition of their students, by giving them a monopoly of the trade, directly addressed the incipient 'spillover' problem: there was no way in which those they trained were likely to benefit, except by setting up in competition as soon as they learned the 'mysterie' of the trade.[19]

Two aspects of the brief institutional history just related seem especially apposite to my argument that even in present-day conditions the international transfer of production technologies, and the creation of associated technological capabilities among the receiving firms and industries, can be facilitated by protecting intellectual property rights. First, the story draws attention to the general proposition that in granting a monopoly privilege one provides a corrective, albeit of the 'second-best' variety, to the problem of underinvestment in the international transfer of industrial know-how that is caused when transferors recognize that others will benefit from the resulting 'learning externalities'. Second, my historical digression linked the use of patent rights with the transfer of technological knowledge of a form that was largely tacit, involving artisanal practices that typically were kept secret and uncodified, and, in the conditions of the times, often were unamenable to usefully complete codification.

To expand briefly on the first of these observations: there are many circumstances in which faster technological advance, and consequent welfare improvements, might be secured by employing a monopoly as the means of 'internalizing' the benefits that would result, not only from worker training effects, but more generally from the incremental modification and adaptation of a new technology to the new and different circumstances of an economy that was structurally dissimilar to the one in which the basic innovation had originally been developed. When private production of a durable good is subject to learning-by-doing that generates process improvements and managerial and worker skills that cannot be protected as trade secrets, there is reason to suppose an industry composed of competitive suppliers will perform suboptimally from a social welfare standpoint.[20] If the industry in question was supplying a new technology embodied in a machine, or some other producer good whose adoption (and the attendant producer surpluses therefrom) depended upon progressive reduction of its supply price, the dynamics of the diffusion and incremental improvement of the new technology would be affected adversely by the externalities of the learning process. Not being able to capture the benefits of future cost reductions that are a by-product of gaining more production experience currently, the rate at which competitive firms would travel down their learning curves, and at which the price of the industry's product would fall, would be suboptimally slow. By correcting the externality, the grant of a monopoly franchise for production of the new good could lead to a second-best welfare optimum *even when there was no prospect of future inventions being induced by the promise of patent rights.*[21]

The difficulties that the complementary role of tacit knowledge creates in successfully transferring incompletely codified technological knowledge from advanced to developing countries suggest that involving firms from the former countries via co-operative ventures and technology support and training contracts will be in the interests of firms in the latter countries. (And one should consider, too, that there will be the positive externalities in the form of 'learning to borrow', as already has been noted.) While information asymmetries and monitoring difficulties make it virtually impossible to write efficient contracts specifying the transfer of tacit knowledge, it is possible to design contracts for the successful implementation of technologies by bundling the provision of assistance together with the licensing of the use of codified information such as patents and copyrights, as Ashish Arora's (1991) analysis of the mechanism design problem has shown. This simplifies the monitoring of contract compliance as well, and avoids the limitations on the involvement of indigenous technical personnel that have proved to be a drawback of turnkey projects.

But if protection for such property is weak in the borrowing country, the originating firm is unlikely to enter such contracts. The implication of this is clear: the would-be borrowers of technology have an interest in a regime of stronger protection for intellectual property established by statutory measures and judicially enforced not only through legal apparatus permitting the prosecution of infringement suits, but by the protection of trade secrecy rights. Inasmuch as trade secrecy laws protect the right to enter into contractual relationships of confidentiality, they should be seen in this context less as an alternative to patent and copyright protection for innovators, and more as a measure of additional security for licensors who would be damaged by the 'leakage' of valuable knowledge that would not otherwise be disclosed to third parties. Trade secrecy rights are in this sense complementary to those elements of the system that permit effective transmission of tacit knowledge by bundling training and other services together in formal licensing contracts.

The thrust of the foregoing is distinct from, but not at odds with, the contention of Chin and Grossman (1990) that both technology-generating and technology-borrowing regions stand to gain from an international regime that provides strong protection of intellectual property, because the prospect of licensing patents to the 'South' would stimulate a faster rate of innovation in the 'North'. While it is a useful step towards revision of the simplistic 'ineluctable conflict' view of North–South divisions over intellectual property rights protection, Chin and Grossman (1990) have simply re-emphasized the potential externalities of lending encouragement to innovation in the North. Instead, by focusing on the conditions for successful transfer of codified and tacit information regarding innovations that *have already been made* in the north, the foregoing analysis suggests that the South would gain even when there was no incremental innovation-inducement effect of extending intellectual property protection into its own markets.

TECHNOLOGY TRANSFERS, TECHNOLOGICAL CONGRUENCE AND CONVERGENCE

This discussion should close on a broader, qualifying theme. Even if attention has been centred up to this point on problems of relying upon market incentives to transfer technological knowledge, and on the role played by the treatment of intellectual property in structuring and facilitating such transactions, it must be kept in mind that the latter is but one element of the larger property rights regime. Property rights, in turn, form only a single side of the complex, multifaceted social and institutional infrastructure shaping a society's ability to access and absorb the economically relevant knowledge in the world around it.

In a recent paper Moses Abramovitz and I (1996) sought to organize under two broad headings the conditions that govern the abilities of countries to achieve relatively rapid rates of productivity growth: those that govern the potential of different countries to raise their productivity levels, and those that influence their abilities to realize that potential. The productivity convergence hypothesis tells us that one proximate determinant of countries' relative growth *potential* is the size of the productivity differentials that separate them from the leader, because these reflect the gap between their average technological practice and the technological frontier. Manifestly, however, the record of growth does not conform consistently to the predictions of the unconditional convergence hypothesis. The implicit assumption underlying the unconditional formulation of the convergence hypothesis, namely that countries are 'otherwise similar', in reality is not fulfilled. There are often persistent conditions that have restricted countries' past growth and which continue to limit their abilities to make the technological and organizational leaps that the convergence hypothesis envisages.

The potential of laggard countries to raise their productivity rapidly by closing the technology gap can, in turn, be grouped into two categories. The first consists of the limitations of what Abramovitz has termed 'technological congruence'. Such limitations arise because the frontiers of technology do not advance evenly in all dimensions; that is, with equiproportional impact on the productivities of labour, capital and natural resource endowments, and with equal effect on the demands for the several factors of production and on the effectiveness of different scales of output. They advance, rather, in an unbalanced, biased fashion, reflecting the direct influence of past science and technology on the evolution of practical knowledge and the complex adaptation of that evolution to factor availabilities, as well as to the scale of markets, consumer demands and technical capabilities of those relatively advanced countries operating at or near the frontiers of technology.

Thus, as the 'appropriate technology' movement was correct in recognizing, it can easily occur that the resource availabilities, factor supplies, technical capabilities, market scales and consumer demands in laggard countries may not conform well to those required by the technologies and organizational arrangements that have emerged in the leading country or countries. Although technological choices do adapt to changes in the economic environment, there are strong forces making for persistence in the effects of past choices and for 'path-dependence' in the evolution of technological and organizational systems. These may render it extremely difficult, if not prohibitively costly, for firms, industries and economies to switch quickly from an already established regime with its associated trajectory of technical development in order to exploit a quite distinct technological regime that had emerged elsewhere under a different constellation of economic and social conditions.[22] The laggards, therefore, face varying degrees of difficulty in adopting and adapting the current technical practices of those who hold the productivity lead.

The second class of constraints on the potential productivity of countries concerns a more vaguely defined set of matters that has been labelled 'social capability', a term coined by Kazushi Ohkawa and Henry Rosovsky (1972). It covers countries' levels of general education and technical competence; the commercial, industrial and financial institutions that bear on their abilities to finance and operate modern, large-scale business; and the political and social characteristics that influence the risks, the incentives and the personal rewards of economic activity, including those rewards in social esteem that go beyond money and wealth.

Over time there is a two-way interaction between the evolution of a nation's social capabilities and the articulation of societal conditions required for mastery of production technologies at or close to the prevailing 'best practice' frontier. In the short run, a country's ability to exploit the opportunities afforded by currently prevailing best-practice techniques will remain limited by its current social capabilities. Over the longer term, however, social capabilities do tend to undergo transformations that render them complementary to the more salient among the emerging technological trajectories. Levels of general and technical education are raised. Curricula and training facilities change. New concepts of business management, including methods of managing personnel and organizing work, supplant traditional approaches. Corporate and financial institutions are established and people learn their modes of action. Legal codes and even the very concepts of property can be modified. Moreover, experience gained in the practical implementation of a production technique enhances the technical and managerial competencies that serve it, and thus supports further advances along the same path. Such mutually reinforcing interactions impart 'positive feedback' to the dynamics of technological evolution. They may for a time solidify a leader's position or, in the case of followers, serve to counter the tendency for their relative growth rates to decline as catch-up proceeds.

On the other hand, the adjustments and adaptations of existing cultural attitudes, social norms, organizational forms and institutional rules and procedures is neither necessarily automatic nor smooth. Lack of plasticity in such social structures may retard and even block an otherwise technologically progressive economy's passage to the full exploitation of a particular emergent technology. New technologies may give rise to novel forms of productive assets and business activities that find themselves trammelled by features of an inherited jurisprudential and regulatory system that had never contemplated even the possibility of their existence. The problems emerging today in the sphere of intellectual property protection for innovations arising in the fields of biotechnology and computer software amply illustrate difficulties of this kind. For laggards, the constraints imposed by entrenched social structures or the absence of specific pieces of institutional infrastructure may long circumscribe the opportunities for any sustained catch-up movement.

To summarize the general thrust of the qualifications for the present discussion that emerge from my work with Moses Abramovitz: countries' *effective* potential for rapid productivity growth by catch-up are not determined solely by the gaps in levels of technology, capital intensity and efficient allocation that separate them from the productivity leaders. They are restricted also by their access to primary materials and more generally because their market scales, relative factor supplies and income-constrained patterns of demand make their technical capabilities and their product structures incongruent in some degree with those that characterize countries that operate at or near the technological frontiers. And they are limited, finally, by those institutional characteristics that restrict their abilities to finance, organize and operate the kinds of enterprises that are required to exploit the technologies on the frontiers of science and engineering. A continuing critical re-examination and adjustment of their institutions affecting the treatment of intellectual property is therefore only one among a rather large number of important items to keep on the agenda of reform for developing and developed countries alike.

NOTES

1. For further discussion of some of the distinctions that follow, see David and Foray (1995, esp. pp. 19ff).
2. Much confusion over terminology in this area can be avoided by being explicit as to whether the frame of reference is macroeconomic or globally systemic (so that true novelty is the *sine qua non* of 'innovations'), or whether it is microeconomic (the individual, household or firm, which may be held to be 'innovating' in regard to its own routines, even when imitating the methods already in use elsewhere).
3. See Westphal *et al* (1984), wherein 'technological capability' is defined as 'the ability to make effective use of technological knowledge...[and] the proficiency of its use in production, investment, and innovation'.
4. This orientation is well-reflected in the material surveyed by Rogers (1962).
5. At a later point attention shifted to considering the social network structure of the target community as a determinant of communication speed and the effectiveness of technology transfer programmes (see Rogers and Kincaid, 1981). But this pioneering work remained largely unnoticed in the economics literature devoted to modelling diffusion until very recently, when some of the same insights have been arrived at via other routes in studies of the diffusion of competitive network technologies. On the latter see, for example, David and Foray (1994).
6. For an early development based on this distinction, see Salter (1960). The corollary proposition, that techniques implemented and improved upon under one regime of factor-price conditions would not necessarily be found to be economically dominant (superior from the viewpoint of cost-minimizing or profit-maximization) in other economic circumstances, may be seen (in David, 1986) to underlie the entire class of microeconomic equilibrium models of innovation diffusion based on the presence of heterogeneity in the population of potential adopters.

7. See, for example, Hayami and Ruttan (1971) on the US federal agricultural research programmes. Hough (1975), examines the experience of other government agencies as well, notably in the public health and defence fields.
8. It is striking to notice that this whole line of thought and programmatic action re-emerged in a new context in the 1980s, when publicly funded universities in the US were charged with, or volunteered themselves for, the mission of fostering private-sector technological innovation by 'transferring' scientific and engineering knowledge. The necessity of involving university scientists in a fuller collaboration with industry if this was to be commercially successful has had numerous implications that lie beyond the scope of the present discussion. See, however, David and Steinmueller (forthcoming in 1997).
9. See Teece (1976) and Mansfield *et al.* (1982).
10. On the emergence of so-called 'techno-mercantilist' thinking in some of the advanced industrial societies during the 1980s and its relationship to the concept of national innovation systems', see David and Foray (1995).
11. On Baumol (1986) and other contributions to the empirical study of macroeconomic 'convergence', see Abramovitz and David (1996).
12. On spillovers and convergence, see Baumol (1986, pp. 1072–85); Barro (1991). For technology gap models of trade and growth, see, for example, Goglio (1991); Grossman and Helpman (1989); Grossman and Helpman (1991, pp. 86–91).
13. I offer it in the spirit of the remark attributed to Samuel Clemens, the American novelist and essayist who acquired fame under the *nom de plume* Mark Twain: 'When a man rids the world of a cancer, he is not obliged to put something in its place.' But perhaps taking fresh inventory of the recent literature on technological knowledge and the practical problems of its transfer will lay a foundation for new and better formal modelling exercises.
14. A somewhat different rationale might have been offered for regimes of weak intellectual property protection in the developing countries' markets, but was not advanced at the time. It is this: their markets, in most cases, were not those at which the patent- and/or copyright-holders had targeted their innovations, so that profits deriving from sales there would represent pure economic rents and would not be needed to sustain the rate of innovation in the future. If so, although it might be debated as a matter of *equity* that being beneficiaries they should pay, or that being poor they should not be asked to pay, the important point remains that it would not much matter from an *efficiency* standpoint; the developing countries' adoption of a 'free-riding' policy would not be likely to lower the rate of innovation elsewhere. The growth of consciousness of global marketing possibilities more recently, however, would tend to vitiate this line of rationalization.
15. See Contractor (1984); OECD (1987); Mansfield (1993, Table 5-5) reports survey results in which 20–40 per cent of US firms (in five industries, and higher proportions in the chemicals and pharmaceuticals) said that the protection of intellectual property in India, Taiwan, Brazil, Thailand, Nigeria and Indonesia was too weak to permit them to license the use of their 'newest or most effective technology' to non-subsidiaries.
16. For much of the following I draw upon material presented with full source citations in David (1993). See also David (1994).
17. Such was the case of the letters patent given to the Flemish weaver, John Kempe, by Edward II in 1331, and of the protection granted to two Brabant weavers to settle at York in 1336, and of the similar grant conferred in 1368 upon three clock-makers from Delft.
18. And it did so during the early eighteenth century rather as an afterthought, when in the course of a movement to free the English economy and polity from the abuses of royal grants of monopoly privileges, an exception was made in the Statute of Monopolies (1623) to permit royal patents to be awarded 'to the first and true inventor' of a new manufacture. But that is another story, which need not be further pursued here.
19. Even the duration of these early English patents – fourteen years, with seven-year extensions possible – was not fixed arbitrarily. The term of service of an apprentice was seven years, and so the protection afforded was to last at least for two generations of trainees. Inasmuch as this was the conventional term of apprenticeship irrespective of the trade or craft, there was some considerable logic to fixing the term of the patent award uniformly

across all branches of industry, even though modern economic analysis finds this aspect of the contemporary patent system difficult to rationalize.

20. The point is demonstrated rigorously in David and Olsen (1986).

21. This little-noticed facet of the patent system has been further clarified by David and Olsen's (1992) analysis of a model of interdependent diffusion and learning, showing that an overall gain in social welfare may or may not be attainable by the creation of a monopoly franchise, depending upon the exact form of the learning function, and on conditions governing the demand for the new product. Because a 'learning' monopolist initially will want to set a higher level for the current flow of production than the competitively organized industry would establish, the existence of a positive time discount rate implies that there will be a gain in social benefits from accelerating the diffusion of the new product and the reduction in its production costs. But, on the other side of the ledger, the learning monopolist will want to stop producing when the new good is still less-extensively diffused than it would be under conditions of competitive supply, which would entail some welfare loss. The point at which it is privately optimal for the monopolist to cease producing will always occur prior to the end of the time period for which the exclusive patent right has been granted. Indeed, the best strategy for the monopolist may be to shut down production long before the point at which the expiration of the patent/franchise would allow competitors to enter into free use of the knowledge gained through previous production experience. Permitting this lull is, in a sense just the social cost of using monopoly to correct the problems caused by the externalities in learning-by-doing.

22. On hysteresis effects and path-dependence in technological evolution, see, for example, David (1975, Introduction, ch. 1); David (1988); David (1993). David (1994) deals with path-dependence in the evolution of organizations and institutions, as well as in informal norms and social conventions.

REFERENCES

Abramovitz, M. and David, P.A. (1996), 'Convergence and deferred catch-up: productivity leadership and the waning of American exceptionalism', in R. Landau, T. Taylor and G. Wright (eds), *The Mosaic of Economic Growth*, Stanford, Cal.: Stanford University Press.

Arora, A. (1991), 'The transfer of technological know-how to developing countries: technology licensing, tacit knowledge, and the acquisition of technological capability', unpublished economics PhD dissertation, Stanford University, November.

Barro, R.J. (1991), 'Economic growth in a cross-section of countries', *Quarterly Journal of Economics*, 106 (2), 407–43.

Baumol, W.J. (1986), 'Productivity growth, convergence and welfare: what the long-run data show', *American Economic Review*, 76 (5), 1072–85.

Chin, J.C. and Grossman, G.M. (1990), 'Intellectual property rights and north–south trade', in R.W. Jones and A.O. Krueger (eds), *The Political Economy of International Trade*, Oxford: Basil Blackwell.

Contractor, F.J. (1984), 'Licensing versus foreign direct investment in US corporate strategy: an analysis of aggregate US data', in N. Rosenberg and C. Frischtak (eds), *International Technology Transfer: Concepts, Measures and Comparisons*, New York: Praeger.

David, P.A. (1975), *Technical Choice, Innovation and Economic Growth*, New York: Cambridge University Press.

—— (1986), 'Technology policy, diffusion and industrial competitiveness', in R.

Landau and N. Rosenberg (eds), *Positive Sum Strategy: Harnessing Technology for Economic Growth*, Washington, D.C.: National Academy Press.

—— (1988), *Path-dependence: Putting the past into the future of economics*, Institute for Mathematical Studies in the Social Sciences Technical Report 533, Stanford, Cal.: Stanford University, November.

—— (1993), 'Intellectual property institutions and the Panda's Thumb: Patents, copyrights and trade secrets in economic theory and history', in M. Wallerstein *et al.* (eds), *Global Dimensions of Intellectual Property Rights in Science and Technology*, Washington, D.C.: National Academy Press.

—— (1993), 'Path-dependence and predictability in dynamical systems with local network externalities: A paradigm for economic history', in D. Foray and C. Freeman (eds), *Technology and the Wealth of Nations*, London: Pinter Publishers.

—— (1994), 'Why are institutions the "carriers of history"? Path-dependence and the evolution of conventions, organizations and institutions', *Structural Change and Economic Dynamics*, 5 (2), 205–30.

—— (1994), 'The evolution of intellectual property institutions', in A. Aganbegyan, O. Bogomolov and M. Kaser (eds), *Economics in a Changing World*, Vol. 1: *System Transformation: Eastern and Western Assessments*, London: St Martin's Press, for the International Economic Association.

—— and Foray, D. (1994), 'Dynamics of competitive technology diffusion through local network structures: The case of EDI document standards', in L. Leydesdorff and P. van den Desselaar (eds), *Evolutionary Economics and Chaos Theory: New Directions in Technology Studies*, London: Pinter Publishers.

—— and —— (1995), 'Accessing and expanding the science and technology knowledge base', *STI Review – Science, Technology and Industry*, No. 16, 14–68.

—— and Olsen T.E. (1986), 'Equilibrium dynamics of diffusion when incremental technological innovations are foreseen', *Ricerche Economiche*, XL (4), 738–71.

—— and —— (1992), 'Technology adoption, learning spillovers, and the optimal duration of patent-based monopolies', *International Journal of Industrial Organization*, 10, 517–43.

—— and Steinmueller, W.E. (eds) (1997, forthcoming), *A Productive Tension: University–Industry Research Collaborations in the Era of Knowledge-based Economic Growth*, Stanford, Cal.: Stanford University Press.

Goglio, A. (1991), '"Technology gap" theory of international trade: a survey', in *United Nations Conference on Trade and Development: ITP/TEC/28*, Geneva, 17 April.

Grossman, G. and Helpman, E. (1989), 'Endogenous Product Cycles', National Bureau of Economic Research Working Paper no. 3099, Cambridge, Mass.: NBER.

—— and —— (1991), 'Trade, innovation, and growth', *American Economic Review*, 80 (2), 86–91.

Hayami, Y. and Ruttan, V.W. (1971), *Agricultural Development: An International Perspective*, Baltimore, Md: Johns Hopkins University Press.

Hough, G.W. (1975), *Technology Diffusion*, Mt Airy, Md: Lomond Press.

Mansfield, E. (1993), 'Unauthorized use of intellectual property: Effects on investment, technology transfer, and innovation', in M. Wallerstein *et al.* (eds), *Global Dimensions of Intellectual Property Rights in Science and Technology*, Washington, D.C.: National Academy Press.

——, Romeo, A., Schwartz M. *et al.* (1982), *Technology Transfer, Productivity, and Economic Policy*, New York: W.W. Norton.

Mody, A. (1990), 'The new international environment for intellectual property rights', in F.W. Rushing and C.G. Brown (eds), *Intellectual Property Rights in Science, Technology, and Economic Performance: International Comparisons*, Boulder, Col.: Westview Press.

Ohkawa, K. and Rosovsky, H. (1972), *Japanese Economic Growth*, Stanford, Cal.: Stanford University Press.

Organization for Economic Co-operation and Development (OECD) (1987), *International Technology Licensing: Survey Results*, Paris: OECD.

Rogers, E.M. (1962), *The Diffusion of Innovations*, Glencoe, Ill.: The Free Press; 2nd edn, 1971.

—— and Kincaid, D.L. (1981), *Communication Networks: Toward a New Paradigm for Research*, New York: The Free Press.

Salter, W.E.G. (1960), *Productivity and Technical Change*, Cambridge: Cambridge University Press.

Sherwood, R.M. (1990), *Intellectual Property and Economic Development*, Boulder, Col.: Westview Press.

Steinmueller, W.E. (1989), 'Four observations on the creation and protection of intellectual property', *Technology and Productivity Workshop Paper*, Stanford, CA: Stanford University Department of Economics, December.

Teece, D. (1976), *The Multinational Corporation and the Resource Cost of International Technology Transfer*, Cambridge, Mass.: Ballinger Books.

United Nations Conference on Trade and Development (UNCTAD) (1991), *Transfer and Development of Technology in a Changing World Environment: The Challenges of the 1990s*, Report by the UNCTAD Secretariat, TD/B/C.6/153, Geneva: United Nations, April.

Vernon, R. (ed.) (1970), *The Technology Factor in International Trade*, New York: National Bureau of Economic Research.

Westphal, L.E., Kim, L. and Dahlman, C.J. (1984), 'Reflections on the Republic of Korea's acquisition of technological capability', in N. Rosenberg and C. Frischtak (eds), *International Technology Transfer: Concepts, Measures and Comparisons*, New York: Praeger.

2. Technology and competitiveness in Asia: case studies in Japanese technology transfer with implications for the People's Republic of China

Christopher Howe

INTRODUCTION AND SUMMARY

Interest in the role of technology in development has undergone a considerable revival in the past decade or so. There are two important reasons for this. One is the prominence of technology issues in debates about trade performance and international trade frictions. The other is the search for new explanations of long-run variations in productivity performance and of periodic crises of adjustment that cannot be explained by failures of macroeconomic policy. In this search, a growing role is being played by economic historians, organizational theorists and other social scientists engaged in a detailed examination of the technological dimension of economic experience.

The study of Japan must play a fruitful, even central, role in these endeavours; for what particularly interests large developing countries today is Japan's obvious and rapid success in technology transfer, not only in industries where its comparative advantage naturally lay, but in those where initially it did not.

Traditional Japan had a long history of technology transfer that included limited contact with Europe and, more important, intra-Asian transfers, particularly from China.[1] The early Tang dynasty contributions of China and Korea to Japan are relatively well known. Less well known are the surges of technology transfer in textiles and agriculture in the seventeenth and eighteenth centuries. In the modern era, however, the dominant transfers have been those from the west to Japan, and from Japan to other parts of Asia. It is with these latter paths and patterns that we are concerned here.

Japan's modern phase of technology transfer was a response to the combination of commercial and military aggression from the west in the 1840s. This *combination* was symbolized by the activities of the English East India

Company which, in pursuit of trade development, constructed the world's first iron gunboat, purpose-built for transcontinental naval warfare and operations in Chinese coastal waters. Thus, whereas a Chinese admiral in the seventeenth century could still envisage the destruction of Dutch fleets off Taiwan, after the naval engagements of the Opium War it was said that 'a single gunship is worth a thousand junks'. All this was observed and reported to the Japanese, who began almost immediately with new efforts in modern iron-making, steam engines and gun construction (Bernard, 1844).

In an important sense this first phase of technology transfer could be said to have been completed by 1914; for by that year Japan had substantially completed import substitution in textiles, and had demonstrated the capacity to compete in Asian markets with the most technologically advanced economies. It had also achieved capabilities in the heavy industry and armaments sectors that put the economy close to the contemporary frontier in shipbuilding, civil engineering and railway construction; and had made a start in the chemical and electrical industries and in the metallurgical sector.

By the late 1930s Japan had advanced to a position of commercial dominance in large segments of the world textile market and, in a much more limited way in markets such as India, had even begun to convert technological capabilities in the heavy sector into commercial exporting success (Indo-Japanese Association, 1939).

Although the Pacific War was itself a surprising indicator of Japanese technological progress, its end result was, paradoxically, the opening of a wide gap between best practice in Japan and the frontier of best practice, at the time largely located in the United States. The opening of this gap reflected the limitations of the Japanese industrial and innovation systems in the sense that, unlike the American, it lacked the resources and organization to create, develop and mass-produce new technologies under wartime conditions.

In the immediate aftermath of 1945 the technology gap widened further during the phase that Japan devoted to the basic rehabilitation of industry and agriculture. However, the postwar technology 'gap' created the potential for Japan's era of high-speed growth, generally defined as lasting from 1955 to the oil shock of 1973–74. During this era, public technology policies were directed towards technological inflow and the achievement of full competitiveness in the heavy industries. By the 1970s Japan had achieved competence in a whole range of new products and processes, and international competitiveness was generally based on high productivity and low prices for standardized goods – notably chemicals, metals and household electrical products.

The oil shock marked the beginning of the final and current major phase of Japanese technology history. Faced with the structural implications of the oil price change and with new environmental considerations and other factors, the Japanese private sector embarked on a growth path that was heavily dependent on research and development. The purpose of this was partly to further enhance productivity and cost reduction, but much more important was the use of technology to improve competitiveness by innovation and product differentiation (Kanemori, 1984, ch. 2). Differentiation and innovation were also consciously pursued in response to trade restrictions (voluntary and otherwise), since these tended to be most severe in clearly defined product categories. As an inherently heterogeneous sector, machinery has played a particularly important role in this process, which it was able to do since the timing was ripe for the accelerated integration of electronic and mechanical technologies in a new generation of machine tools and other devices (Keizai Kikakucho, 1986, ch. 2).

This 150-year experience of technology transfer is interesting for two related reasons. One, already alluded to, is that although a latecomer, Japan accomplished its technology objectives in a way that quickly fulfilled nationalistic aspirations for strategic industry capability. The other, now to be examined in detail, is the successful interplay of technology and market. For the strategic technologies had to be transferred and learned in cost-conscious ways, and then converted either almost simultaneously (shipbuilding) or later (vehicles, optics) into market-oriented activities; while the non-strategic sector had to achieve commercial success in import substitution almost immediately.

To pursue these issues further I propose now to examine the experience of two Japanese companies which between them illustrate many aspects of Japanese technology experience since the late nineteenth century.

COTTON TEXTILES AND THE CASE OF THE OSAKA BOSEKI COMPANY

Prior to the opening of trade with the west, Japan had a large, traditional textile industry. The industry was based on indigenous raw cotton and silk and had a long history of technological borrowing. By the mid-nineteenth century it was highly diffused, employed complex machinery made mainly with natural materials (especially wood and bamboo), and served all segments of society through well-developed, market-sensitive channels.

The arrival of machine-made cotton textile imports threatened to destroy the domestic industry. Imports also led to fears of national bankruptcy, since foreigners forbade the use of tariff protection before 1899, and Japan had no coherent exchange rate policy or currency system until well into the Meiji era. Moreover, the very sophistication of the traditional system became a liability since imported goods that were cheaper and regarded as qualitatively more attractive by consumers flowed easily along the dense trading networks developed by merchants to serve the indigenous industry. This was in contrast to the contemporary experience of China, where poor transport, local taxes and administrative obstacles 'protected' the nineteenth-century traditional sector from foreign competition much more successfully.[2]

The threat posed by foreign textiles was judged by the Meiji government to be as great as that posed by foreign warships. Its first reaction was to build a small sector of state-supported enterprises using imported machinery. In the early 1880s, however, the initiative was passed to the private sector in the form of the Osaka Boseki Company (Osaka Boseki Kabushiki Kaisha). This was established in 1882 and eventually merged in 1911 to form the modern Toyo Company (Toyo Boseki Kabushiki Kaisha).[3]

The company was an almost immediate success and the performance of its shares could be said to have created the Osaka Stock Exchange, opening the way for rivals to join the industry using equity finance. During the 1890s the industry leaders moved from import substitution in yarn to exporting, and by the end of the decade were well-established exporters in the China market. By 1914 the Japanese industry was poised to take advantage of the opportunities offered by war to supplant western exporters throughout most of Asia. What role did technology play in this transformation?

Before looking at activity in the company we must note the contribution of the state to the technological environment. This took several forms: one was the creation of a bureaucratic structure specifically charged to designate priorities and to facilitate and subsidize technology transfer; another was the establishment of an educational system that sought to provide (in the long term) a floor of universal literacy and numeracy, with secondary and tertiary education geared closely to vocational requirements. Prominent among vocational studies were foreign languages, commercial skills and all branches of engineering. The establishment of engineering, in particular, was an unprecedented undertaking; and yet by the late 1870s W.E. Ayrton (a pupil of Kelvin's) could remark that the Japanese had already established in Tokyo the largest academic institution in the world dedicated to engineering education (Armytage, 1961). Tokyo University, as it became, has played an important role in the public–private alliance for the transfer of foreign technologies to Japan ever since. In the early years, the University was especially prominent in marine and civil engineering and in the electrical and optical industries.

The most important thrust of government policy in textiles was the determination to develop an economically viable, transitional system in which *three* levels of textile technology were operative. Under this the still-large traditional weaving sector was kept competitive by drawing its supplies of yarn not only from imported and, later, domestic machine-made sources, but also from establishments using the *garabo* machine. The *garabo* was an example of intermediate technology: less-productive than imported machines, but six to eight times as productive as traditional hand-spinning. The development and diffusion of this machine was a direct result of state encouragement in the form of prizes, a patent system, non-material rewards for innovators, and the use of industrial fairs (*naikoku kangyo hakurankai*) and 'competition exhibitions' (*kyoshinkai*) to stimulate adoption among the large number of textile producers (Kiyokawa, 1995).

Now let us turn to the technology issues as seen from the perspective of the Osaka Boseki Company. The lack of competitiveness evident in the early public-sector companies reflected the difficulties of learning the installation, operation and maintenance techniques required for western textile machinery.[4] A major factor in this was the lack of expert technical advice and shortages of Japanese managers and senior technical staff. To remedy the first, Shibusawa Eiichi, the company's first head, recruited Yamanobe Takeo. Yamanobe was a student of political economy in London and was to play a crucial role in the company's (and the industry's) history. He was persuaded to abandon political economy in favour of the study of contemporary textile technology, which he did by a combination of self-help and shop-floor experience in the mills of Lancashire. He communicated his progress and observations in letters to Shibusawa who, on the basis of his advice, settled in 1880–81 upon the following strategy for the Osaka Boseki:

1. Plant size was to be raised to 10,000 spindles – five time the size of the first generation of imported plants.
2. Steam was to replace water power.
3. The machinery was to be supplied by Platt of Oldham, and Platt would send its own engineers for the setting-up process.

Remarkably, within four years of the new plant coming on stream the Osaka Boseki switched from the mule originally installed to the ring system of spinning. Ring systems had just become commercially available after fifty years of development, and their rationale in Japan was their appropriateness to Japanese factor proportions (i.e. relatively well endowed with inexpensive, unskilled female labour). Further, the low-quality (count) output associated with rings was appropriate to both domestic Japanese and Asian export markets. The adaptation and refinement of this system over the next five decades was to be the basis of the long-run trends in quality and cost improvement that made the Osaka Boseki – and the industry generally – such a powerful international force by the 1930s.

Thus, within less than a decade the Osaka Boseki had demonstrated the capacity to acquire technology from a remote foreign source with no loss of national control; to make bold, large-scale decisions; and to switch to radically different technologies with speed and little concern for sunk investment costs as soon as this decision seemed appropriate for Japanese factor- and product-market conditions. In the longer run, the particular skill exhibited by the Osaka Boseki and follower companies was that of optimizing the trade-off between price and quality in ways that maximized Japanese competitiveness against foreigners. For several decades the foreign competition retained a technological superiority in the industry, but consumers found (and can still find) that Japanese textiles more than compensate with price what they lack in quality.

I have summarized the role of government and company in the first major phase of textile development. The other party to this success was the textile trade association, the *Bokyo* (or *Boren* as it is also called). The *Bokyo* was established in 1882 as part of the institutional infrastructure provided by government to launch the infant private sector into the competitive world. Other parts of this package included subsidized shipping and government-supported banking, insurance and trading companies.

According to the *Bokyo's* charter, technology transfer, development and dissemination were among its direct responsibilities. This was illustrated by its role in the dissemination of the ring system, which it did partly through its monthly newsletter and partly through nationwide exhibitions and demonstrations not dissimilar to those used by government to disseminate the *garabo* in the 1870s (*Bokyo hyakunenshi*, 1982).

Once the industry had been placed in the private sector, however, technology, investment and programmes for skill development all became dependent on the industry's financial health, and it was here that the *Bokyo* made an important indirect contribution to technological progress.

Fluctuations and crises were a common feature of Japanese textile history and in bad times the *Bokyo* responded, first, with arrangements for short-time working and temporary spindle retirement; second, by planning export drives in which domestic prices were manipulated to subsidize those of exports; and third, by leadership in programmes of rationalization and merger. These programmes ensured that companies could obtain the full economies of scale and utilization offered by the best contemporary technology, together with such types of vertical integration between sectors as was deemed optimal for exploiting the technology available. Since by the 1900s Japan's understanding of the technological issues was becoming very advanced, the latter was increasingly a judgement about the future rather than the application of present knowledge.

The interplay of all these factors is illustrated in the industry's campaign to gain competitive advantage in the Manchurian markets, where the Americans were particularly well entrenched in the early 1900s. To do this, the modernization of weaving and its integration with spinning were deemed essential. On the basis of the cost advantages gained and with the help of subsidized rail tariffs and the support of an alliance of banks and trading companies, the industry leaders, known collectively as the 'actively managed' companies (*omowaki keiei kabushiki kaisha*) did quickly capture the Manchurian market. Moreover, in the course of the rationalization undertaken during the 1900s the stock market ceded to the banks the central role in the provision of company finance.

The Osaka Boseki was itself a major actor in this phase of the industry's history, through its merger in 1911 to form the Toyo Company. The merger document specifically identified the need for companies to draw on ever-larger *internal* stocks of technological expertise as a prime motive for the merger; and the new company's first chief executive was none other than Yamanobe Takeo. The engineer had finally displaced the financier.

As the private sector expanded and became more concentrated in the 1900s the role of the public-sector technology bureaucracy declined. After the First World War, however, new challenges led to a revival of active, state-led intervention for technological improvement. Japan's early achievement in catching up had been overtaken by the spread of mass-production techniques in the war economies, and was further threatened by the rise of new technologies in the electrical, chemical, car, vehicle and consumer-durable industries in the 1920s.

To the Japanese these changes appeared to be associated (especially in America) with the emergence of very large companies, cartels and ever more highly concentrated industrial structures. The message received was that the 'competitive stage' of world economic development was over. Future industrial power would depend on a combination of giant enterprises and industrial groupings, with active government intervention both to guide and support technology policies and to provide the discipline needed to avoid abuse of monopoly power.[5] Thus the main thrust of national technology policy in the 1920s was a widespread programme of standardization and restructuring (rationalization), designed to facilitate the speedy retirement of old plant and the diffusion of current best practice in new plant. A crucial role was to be played in these processes by voluntary trade associations.

Nowhere was rationalization, investment renewal and technical progress more important than in textiles. The industry had over-expanded in the easy conditions of the war, and in the 1920s was faced with serious productivity challenges dictated by external factors. One factor was the over-valuation of the yen and the intention to return to the prewar gold standard parity. Another was the International Labour Office timetable for the abolition of night work – always regarded by the Japanese managers as providing the crucial margin of cost advantage required during their learning phase because of the more intensive plant utilization it allowed. The upshot of the latter was that most companies faced the requirement of an improvement of company productivity of 40 to 50 per cent within five to six years – a target which, when first formulated, few regarded as feasible without a significant contraction in plant numbers.

One favourable condition enjoyed by the industry was the vast accumulation of wartime trading profits, which came both from selling textiles and from speculation in raw cotton. Unlike Lancashire, where wartime profits were cashed in corporate restructuring, the Japanese used these windfalls to finance the retirement of old capital stock and to re-equip with new technology.[6]

The Toyo Company was a leader in the rationalization of the 1920s, embarking on a major programme of internal reorganization and re-equipping and then moving on to intensive efforts in technological adaptation and innovation. Several features of this programme are worth comment. First, its purpose was not simply the cost-reduction targets referred to above, but also some highly specific commercial objectives as well, since the markets now within sight of the company's strategists ranged from the low-income colonial nations of Asia and Africa, through the 'middle-income' economies of Latin America and the white colonies (especially Australia), and on up into the heartland of high-income consumer markets in Europe and America. Success in these markets was seen to require intensive investigation of consumer demand, combined with new levels of technological versatility, to meet these demands in the most effective way.

In the case of the low-income economies (especially India, the Dutch East Indies and Africa) the Japanese were pioneers in their attention to the detail of consumer requirements. Their conclusion was that the key to such markets (where literacy was low) was consistency of product quality, packaging and delivery, all to be associated with attractive and iconographically powerful brand symbols.[7]

The Toyo was in no doubt that competitiveness called for enhanced integration, not only between spinning and weaving, but also embracing dyeing, finishing and packaging. Only in this way could new technologies be developed and applied with consistent standards across all relevant operations in the industry. In other words, competitiveness with low-income customers was seen to require sophisticated, integrated technology supply conditions.[8]

The scale of the merged company was now very large and its plants and offices spread out not only across Japan, but increasingly to other Asian locations as well. Further, whereas before 1914 adaptation and innovation had been essentially the task of western specialists working with a very small number of Japanese experts and in-house older, experienced workers, by the 1920s the western role was in sharp decline and the company was in a position to recruit large numbers of Japanese graduates. All this gave rise to strategic decisions relating to the location and control of R&D activity. The strategy adopted was to decentralize and locate R&D units at the major plants, while ensuring a strong flow of information within the company. A key role in this was played by the new cohorts of Japanese graduates whose academic, more radical approach to technical problems differed sharply from the adaptive incrementalism of the old workers.[9]

The new research centres were charged with raising the range and quality of output, lowering fault rates, and increasing labour and machine productivity; and the fact that research was mainly internal to the firm ensured a close relationship between technical investigations on the one hand and shop-floor and market realities on the other.

Particular emphasis in the 1920s was placed on the new high-draft spinning technologies, the introduction of automatic looms and the full use of the potential created by the electrification of Japan. The Japanese textile machinery industry grew rapidly after the war, but although the Toyoda and other automatic looms were increasingly recognized as being at the frontier of loom technologies, there was no chauvinism in the investment policies of the Toyo Company, which continued to implement joint trials of Japanese and foreign looms. One other feature of this decade was the attention paid not only to machines, but to factory layouts, training, environmental problems and the applicability of Taylorian and standardization techniques.

These programmes were dramatically successful. Maximum spinning counts in the Toyo rose to over 200 and the product range and quality of cloth and clothing were greatly extended. These successes not only reinforced the company's competitiveness in export markets, but also provided the supply flexibility that enabled the company to navigate the abolition of nightwork intact, and to respond to the enormous surge of demand that followed Japan's 50 per cent devaluation of the yen in 1931.

Throughout these programmes, technical improvements were not only tied to specific marketing objectives, but were integrated with new systems of internal cost accounting. These systems had been pioneered by the old Mie Company (the Osaka Boseki's merger partner of 1911) and they eventually enabled the company to evaluate, on a common basis, the performance of both spinning and weaving plants with very different characteristics and histories. Highly successful plants were rewarded with non-material incentives; poor performers were descended on by teams of specialists to analyse what the problems were and to ensure, through intra-firm technology transfers, that they were solved.

Finally, mention must be made of the importance of cotton purchasing and blending technologies in Japanese textile competitiveness. Cotton supplies suitable for highly competitive manufacturing processes come from a widely scattered but limited number of sources, mainly America, the Middle East and India. Raw cotton varies greatly in its physical characteristics and the output of some producers is notoriously erratic, reflecting year-to-year meteorological variations. The combination of these two factors makes prices unstable and cotton purchasing a complex, information-intensive task. In the factory, moreover, the potential for blending different varieties in yarn manufacture is considerable. Thus a company with full market information, large financial resources and extensive technological capabilities in blending can integrate these skills to gain significant competitive advantage in yarn costs.

The Japanese companies were helped in this by their close links with specialist cotton trading companies and banks, and by their successful development of secret blending techniques evolved during their early struggles with raw materials from China and India. So unprecedentedly successful were Japanese blending techniques, that western companies wrongly insisted that they were selling yarn below cost. Thus here, too, we see the close integration of technical with commercial and financial skills that gave the Japanese industry its competitive power.

By the mid-1930s the Japanese textile industry held joint leadership of the world industry with Britain. But whereas the British industry was clearly in decline (especially because of its failure to compete in India) the Japanese industry was still rising.

The contribution of technological factors to Japanese textile progress may be summarized as follows:

1. At the national level success reflected:
    - the establishment of a government structure charged with formulating technological priorities and strategies; allocating public funds to stimulate technological advance in ways appropriate to the various phases of Japanese development; disseminating information and providing special incentives (including non-monetary ones) in the small-scale, traditional sector where market mechanisms and information flows were exceptionally weak;
    - the provision of human skills through the formal educational system and (especially in the early years) by direct hiring of foreigners;
    - the support of a wide-ranging service sector in the form of trading companies and banks, which themselves had a special relationship with government, and which played an important role in supporting technological initiatives and seeking out technological and market information;
    - the toleration of high levels of industry concentration and associated levels of profitability;

- government support in the form of intensive technological and commercial intelligence-gathering by Japanese diplomatic services, which worked in conjunction with chambers of commerce and trade associations for purposes of dissemination.
2. At the company level the keys were:
   - entrepreneurial boldness in going rapidly for the most advanced, large-scale plants;
   - flexibility in switching to new technologies as soon as these had decisive advantages in terms of Japanese factor endowments, supply conditions and product-market realities;
   - the ability to adapt and improve foreign capital goods and, eventually, to establish a self-sufficient textile machinery industry with innovative and exporting capabilities. Adaptation and improvement of foreign equipment was exceptionally effective because it conceived of 'technology' in the broad sense, i.e. of seeking productivity enhancements by analysis of machinery operation in its full environmental, factory, social and human setting;
   - entrusting firm-level R&D to internal research centres located at major plants, thus ensuring close links with production practicalities, but also ensuring diffusion through strong intra-company information flows;
   - consistent linking of technical to commercial objectives. Particularly original was the study of the markets in low-income countries and the dedication of R&D efforts to serving these most competitively;
3. At the industry level:
   - The development of trade associations – pre-eminently the *Bokyo*. This encouraged companies to achieve the gains available from stable, long-term relationships and from economies of scale in the creation and diffusion of both technical and commercial information. The *Bokyo* also enabled companies to form effective alliances against foreigners without losing a strong element of domestic competitiveness. It therefore helped establish a system that was neither the invisible hand of markets nor the visible hand of corporate organization.[10]

Although it is appropriate to leave this analysis of the textile industry at the point where it was at the apogee of international competitiveness, it is worth noting that this was by no means the end of the story. During the 1930s the industry also took a strong position in the man-made fibres sector and reappeared in postwar markets as a formidable competitor, with a continuing role for MITI and *Bokyo* guidance.

Thus, although the history of Japan's post-Second World War development is usually written in terms of the growth of heavy industry, remarkably Japan remained a net exporter of textiles and clothing until 1993. Like Germany (still the world's largest textile exporter), Japan has an enormous two-way trade in what is in reality a hierarchy of industries. Therefore, notwithstanding Japan's imports of increasing quantities of labour-intensive textiles (and clothing) from developing countries, especially China, by continued restructuring and the application of intensive R&D in production methods (especially man-made fibres), Japan retains a significant export business.

THE OPTICAL INDUSTRY AND THE NIKON COMPANY

The technology issues facing Japan in the optical industry were completely different from those in textiles. One reason for this was that large sectors of the industry, including cameras, rangefinders and military applications, were only developed in the west in the late nineteenth century; hence the technological objectives for contemporary emulators were less clear, changed all the time, and were very much dominated by Zeiss, a highly innovative and commercially aware company.

Second, the industry was highly intensive, not only in capital but also in a wide range of skills extending from those needed by factory operatives to the advanced mathematical techniques used by lens designers. Further, while the normal pattern for Japanese technological transfer in new industries was for learning to be subsidized during a period while a protected home market was created, civilian markets for optical goods were minute at first, and even military and public-sector markets were small and unstable for many years. Thus in terms of both comparative advantage considerations and of congruence with established patterns of Meiji technology transfer, the optical industry's problems were severe prior to the emergence of large-scale military demand in the late 1920s.

In spite of the problems, interest in optical technologies was intense. Japan had three centuries of lens-making experience (for spectacles and telescopes) although Meiji lens-makers were still dependent on optical 'blue' glass imported from Holland.

The opening of Japan coincided almost exactly with the invention of photography in France and Britain and this created a small retail industry, mainly serving foreigners, but quickly linking backwards to the manufacture of wooden plate cameras.

By 1896 the army had begun to take a serious interest in the manufacture of gunsights and rangefinders. Awareness of these instruments was heightened by the naval and land battles of the Russo-Japanese War, and this led to various technology scouting expeditions to Europe. During the First World War, not only did the military significance of these technologies become all the more obvious – extending now to air as well as land and sea warfare – but Japan suddenly found itself cut off from imported supplies of optical glass. The strategic implications of this led the Imperial navy to establish an optical glass foundry in 1915.

Although this public-sector initiative was understandable, much of the skill reservoir in optics was in small companies and, as demand grew, more of these appeared. Nikon, formed in 1917 from three small companies but supported from the outset by Mitsubishi and the navy, was to be by far the most important firm in the private sector – although it was preceded by Konishiroku (Konica) and followed by Olympus and Canon in the 1920s.[11] Nikon retained its close contacts with the navy, and after the navy's own foundry was destroyed in the Kanto Earthquake of 1923 it supplied Nikon with a replacement.[12]

During the 1920s an intensive public–private drive for optical technology transfer began. This included study of all non-proprietary knowledge, travel abroad to scout for information, and the recruitment to live in Japan of eight Germans specialized in lens-making and the mathematical techniques required for lens design.

The major problem of the 1920s was that the Washington Naval Agreements of 1922–23 led to a sharp reduction in Japanese military demand and for many years Nikon was close to insolvency, kept afloat only by short-term contract work for the public sector. None the less, lens-making skills increased and in 1931 the company manufactured the first Japanese-designed camera lens: a highly significant landmark.

During the 1930s military demand expanded rapidly. This reflected army requirements following the invasion of Manchuria in 1931 and naval requirements flowing from Japan's decision to embark upon a massive (and secret) programme of warship construction. Between 1925 and 1936 Nikon's sales increased threefold while research expenditure increased eighteen-fold. This intense research activity was reflected in patents, for whereas the company obtained only twelve patents between 1917 and 1927, between 1927 and 1937 the number grew by a further ninety-three. To aid lens computation in this era, Nikon designed and made a remarkable mechanical analogue computer.

It is difficult to measure the precise standards reached by Nikon manufacturing in the 1930s and 1940s. The official postwar history of the optical industry was written specifically to prove that prewar Japanese optical manufacturers had reached and surpassed world standards of lens and prism design and construction, although this had been concealed for security reasons.[13]

By the 1940s Nikon was certainly producing an astonishing array of equipment, including land and air cameras, gunsights, periscopes, binoculars, telescopes and navigational instruments. Even the US War Department admitted that Japanese optics were 'outstanding'.[14] Among the many extraordinary landmarks of the company's output was the 28-metre-high 'land' telescope for viewing over forests, a 5-metre, lorry-mounted telescopic camera for long-distance reconnaissance photography, and Nikon's crowning prewar achievement: the batteries of 15-metre rangefinders for the battleships *Yamato* and *Musashi*. These instruments required a sixty-fold improvement in conventional prism accuracy, and although the battleships themselves proved a strategic failure, the rangefinders demonstrated their unparalleled qualities by enabling the *Musashi* to score a direct hit at 35 kilometres in the Battle of Leyte in October 1944.

The end of the Pacific War was potentially disastrous for Nikon since output in 1944 and 1945 had been almost entirely for the armed forces and public sector. As a private-sector company, therefore, an urgent and difficult reorientation was necessary and had to secure approval of the occupying Supreme Command Allied Powers (SCAP) administration.

The company took into the new era two major assets. One was its immense reservoir of research experience and manufacturing expertise. Within this, four innovations in particular proved critically valuable in the civilian market:

1.   multi-surface lens coating developed for submarine periscopes;
2.   prism-making, also developed for periscopes;
3.   mass-production techniques developed to enable the company to meet demand for binoculars in the latter part of the war when skilled labour was unobtainable;
4.   early experimentation with the integration of optical, mechanical and electrical techniques.

Of these four, lens-coating techniques were particularly important. They had been developed to minimize the losses that occurred as light passed through the thirty-two elements of the standard periscope. It was later discovered that the same techniques were highly effective in lenses with as few as four elements, and coating was probably the single most important reason why Nikon lenses were discovered in the early 1950s to be markedly superior to Zeiss and Leica rivals.

Similarly, prisms, also a critical component of periscopes, were to be the key to the reflex camera – the form of technology in which Japan added superiority in camera body and viewfinding capabilities to its lens superiority.

The other inheritance was the prewar experience in the markets for civilian products. The development of these had started as early as 1918, and products for these markets included binoculars and opera glasses, small lenses for

Canon and other camera manufacturers, microscopes, and a magnificent 8-inch reflecting telescope for the Imperial observatory, an instrument which functions to this day.

The speed with which Nikon adapted after defeat in 1945 was extraordinary and is illustrated by the following timetable:

14 August	Japan surrenders.
1 September	The company establishes fifteen committees to examine groups of possible products for the civilian market.
20 September	Report issued identifying a preliminary batch of possibilities including watches, cotton spindles and medical and scientific instruments of all kinds.
29 September	The first production plan made.
12 October	Permission to convert to civilian production sought from SCAP occupation authorities.
16 October	Permission granted for eight products.

At this stage the list of proposed products did not include cameras, since no market for such an expensive product was immediately foreseen. Also, the company's experience of large military cameras was remote from the requirements of the potential civilian buyer. The company thus began its postwar business by concentrating on the equipment needed in public and private sectors for the rebuilding of Japan and the Japanese economy (surveying and scientific equipment of all kinds) and on *essential* consumer products (spectacle lenses).

Research was put in hand immediately, however, for the camera market, spurred on by the realization that a large market was actually to hand in the shape of camera-mad GIs and foreign occupation officials. Although at first the company experimented with plans for Rolleiflex-type cameras, they quickly settled on developing a rival to the Contax/Leica 35 mm type of camera. Permission was given to produce for export, and trial models were produced by April 1946. After experimenting further in the local GI market, in 1951 the company finally produced the Nikon S series, which marked the breakthrough to international recognition.

The successors to the Nikon S went on to dominate the market in the late 1950s. Technologically, this series could be said to consist of derivative products that took the design concepts of Leica/Contax as their basis and created a trajectory of highly competitive products by combining and developing the best body features of both rivals, equipping with better lenses and, finally, creating a total *system* of lenses and accessories that surpassed anything being offered by rivals to the main market, which at that time was made up of professionals and relatively affluent amateurs.

Thus by 1960 (the date of the last model in this series) Nikon could be said to have achieved a high degree of integration of technological excellence and marketing skills in the development of a single model of a single product. By the same date, the company was ready to sweep the world with a totally innovative product: the fully fledged reflex camera, a product that owed so much to the wartime submarine commanders who pressured Nikon to make their periscopes safe for low-light use. As living standards in America and Europe rose, this product was able to develop a new, mass market and this in turn called for a revolution in production methods and quality control. By the 1970s the company was ready to integrate electronics and optics in ways that finally enabled it to establish a leading role in the professional/scientific market and in the mass consumer market.

Today, the company is faced with a situation where the integration of market thinking and technology is total in the sense that the store of technological capability now available to it is so large, and the capacity to achieve new objectives once identified so great, that conventional technological objectives such as improved lens performance by standard criteria are no longer the issue. The main issue now is how to identify what consumers will buy, what trajectories will be followed by production costs and market prices, and how competitors will behave. The company has always been very R&D intensive, but in the contemporary market place this factor is greater than ever before in peacetime. Nikon's R&D expenditure as a percentage of sales increased from 1 per cent in 1963 to 3 per cent in 1982, and had reached 6 per cent in 1992.

What is so striking about the long-run history of Nikon is the belief that, whatever the market environment and whatever the stage of Japan's economic development and technological level, absolute technological supremacy must be part of the objective – but in order to enjoy the satisfaction that such supremacy provides intrinsically, the company now also understands that this objective has to be related to the realities of its markets.[15]

SOME LESSONS FOR CHINA?

A number of caveats must be entered before any attempt can be made to draw lessons for China from the experiences outlined above. First, the successful development of a company (or even an industry) is not necessarily coterminous with the successful development of a whole economy. Care must therefore be taken in drawing conclusions from partial evidence. Second, Japanese policies and organization for technology have been part of a total system evolving in response to a variety of structural and historical factors, many unique and unrepeatable.

The textile industry, for example, began as clusters of small-scale spinning and weaving activities and into this traditional, largely household environment, modern systems of mechanized spinning were implanted, and imported yarn was made available to the weaving sector. As the industry matured, private companies took over and grew in size and degrees of integration until, by the 1920s, the industry was largely dominated by a small number of highly integrated, oligopolistic firms. The interplay between technology factors and this evolution was changing all the time. Thus no timeless, static blueprint can be obtained.

Further, while there is much to admire in the Japanese system, it is none the less a system with problems. Its strengths have been associated with particular forms of government leadership and highly concentrated, internally co-operative industrial structures. The latter facilitate strong inter- and intra-company flows of tacit and codified information. These are favourable to the efficiency not only of search and initial learning but, above all, of dissemination. However, the structures required as the economy graduates from being a follower to being a leader may be very different. In particular, the mixture of competitive and non-competitive elements is not an easy one to hold in satisfactory long-term equilibrium and may eventually fall into a state of atrophy or serious inefficiency (Boisot, 1983; Schumpeter, 1950).

Finally, in drawing comparative lessons we must bear in mind the extraordinary enlargement of the role of foreign investment and aid in technology transfer during the last three decades, since this implies that the development path taken by Japan is now much less viable than it was earlier in the century.[16]

Having said all this, however, as China emerges from public ownership and bureaucratic planning into a state of semi-marketization, because technology issues are so important and the guidelines and current Chinese policy remain so unclear, some study of Japan must be worthwhile. Indeed, we should bear in mind that China already owes much to Japanese companies since in the textile industry, in particular, there was a significant learning benefit derived from the Japanese direct textile investments in prewar Shanghai. Unfortunately for China, much of this benefit was then exported by the migrant textile entrepreneurs who became the foundation for the extraordinarily fast, textile-based industrialization of Hong Kong in the 1960s and 1970s (Nishida, 1990; Howe, 1996, ch. 4).

More recently, we find that the contemporary relevance of Japanese industrial experience is a subject that is clearly preoccupying Chinese scholars (Ran Zhan-ping *et al.*, 1993).

Against this background, I would sum up the Japanese lessons for China in the following suggestions:

1. Planning, financial and other arrangements should encourage industrial structures that can accommodate a wide range of enterprise scales but, as marketization proceeds, the state should not worry dogmatically about concentration if this seems to have dynamic benefits.

2. The state should continue to encourage the outflow of technical personnel from institutes and semi-independent organizations into productive enterprises and local government. Enterprises should be encouraged to locate R&D and technology transfer efforts at the level of the plant and invest in the shop-floor training necessary to reap the benefits of this approach. In this way technological resources can be focused on market-oriented learning and adaptation in sectors where China is, or is potentially, competitive.

3. The problems of economies of scale and dissemination of R&D remain generally serious, but particularly so for small-scale and township industries – although these are precisely the sectors where the gains are potentially great and could strengthen still further international competitiveness. Part of the answer must lie with a continuing government role in searching and in the preliminary development and dissemination of new techniques, as well as in the provision of the basic skills necessary to enable codified knowledge to penetrate to the less-modernized strata of the economy. For larger firms, collaborative strategies should be encouraged.[17]

4. For industries that are highly intensive in technical knowledge and dependent for competitiveness on exceptional levels of R&D, the fairly autarkic Japanese example is to some extent now a negative one, because contemporary opportunities for technology transfer through foreign direct investment are now so important and are, for most industries, the obvious route. Even this difference, however, should not be exaggerated. Japan has relied heavily on joint ventures and FDI down to the present day, and the skills required to learn through these frameworks are not so different from those needed to get a strong overflow of technological capacity from foreign direct investment, even where wholly foreign owned.

5. Skill-intensive sectors in China are, in most cases, producing goods that are militarily important or at least dual purpose. The government has not only emphasized the need to unlock the technological capabilities of the military sector so that they can flow to the civilian, but has also encouraged the military sector to marketize its output. These policies are expected to continue, although fears that business efforts will impede military efficiency may be some form of brake on them.

6. In conclusion, I would suggest a thought rather than a prescription. Japan's technological modernization has been driven, supported and disciplined to a considerable extent by non-economic objectives and values.

Meiji military aspirations and the post-Second World War policy of national rehabilitation through economic success both defined and justified Japan's industrialization and technology objectives.[18] In different contexts, they also strengthened the willingness to support technologies during learning phases when by market criteria they would not have been viable; and they even may have played some role in the disciplining of monopolies, thus enabling Japan to gain some of the benefits without all of the costs associated with these market forms. Social values may also have been of significance in the development of networks of trust and information vital to technological acquisition and diffusion, and one may take this view without subscribing to any exclusively cultural theory of economic development.[19] So much is all this the case that many Japanese see the economic crisis of the 1990s as arising in part from the erosion of this underlying value base during the epochs of high-speed growth and the 'bubble boom' (Mizusawa, 1994).

Values and non-economic factors may yet prove vital to China's economic future. On present evidence, although there are some signs among both Chinese Party intellectuals and capitalists (home and overseas) of a Confucian nationalism similar to that which inspired the Meiji entrepreneurs, these sentiments are effectively restricted to a small élite and seem no match for the tide of short-termism, greed and corruption that has swept away the Maoist altruism ('serving the people') of the pre-reform epoch.

Predicting the future of these trends is far beyond the scope of this essay, but there is no doubt that their direction will have an important bearing on the quality of economic relationships, and hence on the character of China's technological future. For while there must be an important role for personal incentives, the current thrust for unconstrained personal gain may, on its own, do more harm than good.[20] And if relationships both between and within companies are infused by personal anxieties and collective stress, China is unlikely to become the kind of environment needed to produce the 'learning company' and will be unable to transform itself into a truly innovative society.[21]

NOTES

1. 'Traditional' is defined here to refer to the period before the opening of Japan in the 1850s.
2. The key sources for the history of the Japanese textile industry from the 1850s to the 1930s are Takamura (1971, 1982). Also very detailed, with citations from primary sources, are MITI (1968, 1972). Other sources used are cited in the bibliography.
3. Detailed histories of the company and its transformations are: *Toyobo nanajunenshi* (1953) and *Hyakunenshi Toyobo* (1986).
4. See also n. 10 in the Introduction.

5. These issues are discussed in MITI (1961), especially valuable is the editor's hundred-page introduction. For western materials on rationalization and standardization, see Urwick (1929); Marshall (1919); Schumpeter (1939).
6. The failures of the British textile companies in the 1920s were fiercely criticized in Utley (1931) and elsewhere.
7. British manufacturers complained that the Japanese stole their brand symbols. However, the Japanese rapidly developed their own brands which feature prominently in the company histories.
8. The issue of integration versus disintegration was the source of much debate and dispute in Western theory. Following Marshall, Sidney Chapman (1904) tended to the view that the highly disintegrated character of the British industry was a reflection of the exceptional division of labour appropriate to world leadership. Later, however, critics of this view concluded that integration was necessary to improve information flows and avoid the excesses of short-termism and the ruthless use of market power by minor actors in the web of market relationships.
9. These comments are based on material in the two Toyo company histories cited.
10. See the related and much fuller discussion in the study by Michael Gerlach (1992). Cheng-Tian Kuo has also recently thrown important light on the role of Trade Associations and their dynamic impact. Although his analysis is set in the context of a study of postwar Taiwan, much of his argument can be retrospectively applied to Japan, from whom the Taiwanese learned much about economic organization (Kuo, 1995).
11. The early name of the company was Nippon Kogaku (lit. Japan Optical) – later abbreviated to Nikon. I have used the latter throughout.
12. This section is based on the Nikon company histories cited in the bibliography. Of the four company histories, the most important are the first (1942) and the last (1993). The first is particularly valuable for the early and wartime history of the company. The last has a high quality of analysis and a very useful statistical supplement. I am grateful to the Nikon Corporation for supplying me with copies of all these histories.
13. Kogaku Kogyoshi Henshukai (1955). This vast compendium is a goldmine of data, photographs and qualitative information on all the major prewar companies and their products. It deals in detail with military applications.
14. The main official survey of Japanese war materials and their characteristics is US War Department (1944). In general, this handbook is critical and patronizing of Japanese manufacturing standards.
15. The 1942 Nikon history emphasizes the national strategic significance of technological superiority. The postwar histories focus on the interplay of technical strength and market factors.
16. This is certainly the Japanese view expressed, for example, in aid policies and advice to developing economies.
17. The MITI still has an important role in the technological upgrading of small firms in Japan. For the role of the state in securing strong overflow effects from foreign direct investment and the problems of the small-scale sector in Taiwan, see Howe (1996) and Simon (1994).
18. The hidden, nationalist agenda of Japan's early industrialization is particularly well analysed in the writing of Morikawa Hidemasa (see Morikawa, 1973, 1974). In the Meiji period, theorists had the greatest difficulty reconciling their wish to adopt western notions of *laissez-faire* and free trade with their instinctive notions of what was needed in the interests of social order and national advantage. This conflict was particularly pronounced in the case of Fukuzawa Yukichi. His and two related cases are the subject of an important recent work of intellectual history (Sakamoto, 1991).
19. Charles Sabel (1994) has argued that cultural predisposition is an inadequate explanation for the success of some economies in developing the institutions for collaborative learning, but there is no reason why his own analysis should entirely preclude this factor, or indeed why values may not be learned through experience.
20. The problems posed by the evaporation of socialist morality were the particular preoccupation of the late, Soviet-era planner Chen Yun. For recent penetrating comment, see Pye

(1995). World Bank advice emphasizing privatization and incentives has encouraged this trend in China.

21. The social and political environment within which companies develop has undoubtedly changed radically since the time when visitors such as myself (in 1974) could observe directly the paralysis and violent factionalism inflicted by political dispute. However, behavioural patterns formed over decades cannot just evaporate and may, if circumstances change, revive. On the theory and implications of the learning company, particularly in its Japanese form, see especially Nonaka and Takeuchi (1995).

BIBLIOGRAPHY

Materials in Japanese and Chinese

Bokyo hyakunenshi [The Hundred-year History of the Japan Cotton Spinners Association) (1982), Osaka: Nihon Boseki Kyokai.

Fujii Mitsuo (1987), *Senkanki Nihon seni sangyo kaigai shinshutsu no kenkyu* [Researches into the History of the Overseas Advance of the Interwar Japanese Textile Industry], Tokyo: Minerva Shobo.

Hyakunenshi Toyobo [The One Hundred Year History of Toyobo], (1986), 2 vols, Osaka: Toyobo.

Hayashi Katsuya (1957), *Nihon gunji gijutsushi* [A History of Japan's Military Technology], Tokyo: Haruki Shoten.

Ishii Kanji (1972), *Nihon sanshigyoshi bunseki* [An Analysis of the History of Japan's Silk Industry], Tokyo: Tokyo Daigaku Shuppankai.

—— (1976), *Nihon keizaishi* [Economic History of Japan], Tokyo: Tokyo Daigaku Shuppankai.

—— (1989), *Kaikoku to Ishin* [The Opening of the Ports and Restoration], Tokyo: Shogakukan.

—— and Sekiguchi Hisashi (eds) (1982), *Seikai shijo to Bakumatsu kaiko* (The World Market and the Opening of the Ports at the End of the Tokugawa Period), Tokyo: Tokyo Daigaku Shuppankai.

Isobe Kiichi (1985), *Dento sangyoron* [The Theory of Traditional Craft Production], Tokyo: Yuhikaku .

Kanemori Hsiao (1984), *Nihon keizai daitenkan no jidai* [The Era of Great Change in the Japanese Economy], Tokyo: Nihon Keizai Shinbunsha.

Keizai Kikakucho (1986), *Keizai hakusho 1986* [Economic White Paper 1986], Tokyo: Okurasho Insatsukyoku.

Kimura Masato (1991), *Shibusawa Eiichi*, Tokyo: Chuo Shinsho.

Kiyokawa Yukihiko (1995), *Nihon no keizai hatten to gijutsu fukyu* [Japanese Economic Development and Technology Diffusion], Tokyo: Toyo Keizai Shimposha.

Kogaku Kogyoshi Henshukai (1955), *Nihon no kogaku kogyoshi* [The History of the Japanese Optical Industry], Tokyo.

Koyama Koken (1972), *Nihon gunji kogyo no shiteki bunseki* [An Historical Analysis of Japan's Military Industries], Tokyo: Ochanomizu Shobo.

Minami Ryoshin and Kiyokawa Yukihiko (eds) (1987), *Nihon no kogyoka to gijutsu hatten* [Japanese Industrialization and Technological Development], Tokyo: Toyo Keizai Shimposha.

MITI (1961), *Shoko seisakushi* [A History of Policy Towards Commerce and Industry], vol. 9: *Sangyo gorika* [Industrial Rationalization], Tokyo.

—— (1962), *Shoko seisakushi*, vol. 3: *Gyosei kiko* [Administrative Structures], Tokyo.

—— (1965, 1971), *Shoko seisakushi*, vols 5–6: *Boeki* [Foreign Trade], Tokyo.

—— (1968, 1972), *Shoko seisakushi*, vols 15–16, *Seni kogyo* [Textiles], Tokyo.

—— (1985), *Shoko seisakushi*, vols 1–2, *Sosetsu* [Summary], Tokyo.

Mizusawa Kei (1994), *Heisei daifukyo no kenkyu* [Research into the Great Heisei Depression], 2 vols, Tokyo: Sanichi Shobo.

Morikawa Hidemasa (ed.) (1973), *Nihongata keiei no genryu* [The Sources of Japanese Style Management], Tokyo: Toyo Keizai Shimposha.

Morikawa Hidemasa *et al.* (eds) (1974), *Kindai Nihon no keieishi no kiso chishiki* [Basic Knowledge of the History of Modern Japanese Management], Tokyo: Yuhikaku.

Nakaoka Tetsuro, Ishii Tadashi and Uchida Hoshimi (eds) (1986), *Kindai Nihon no gijutsu to gijutsu seisaku* [Technology and Technology Policy in Modern Japan], Tokyo: Tokyo Daigaku Shuppankai.

Nawa Toichi (1949), *Nihon bosekigyo no shiteki bunseki* [An Historical Analysis of the Japanese Textile Industry], Tokyo: Choryusha.

Nihon keizaishi jiten [A Dictionary of Japanese Economic History] (1940), 3 vols Tokyo: Nihon Hyoronsha.

Nikon nanajugonenshi [The Seventy-Five-Year History of the Nikon Corporation] (1993), Tokyo.

Nippon kogaku kogyo kabushiki kaisha gojunen no susumi [Fifty Years of Progress of the Nikon Company] (1967), Tokyo.

Nippon kogaku kogyo kabushiki kaisha nijugonenshi [The Twenty-Five-Year History of the Nikon Company] (1942), Tokyo.

Nippon kogaku kogyo kabushiki kaisha yonjunenshi [The Forty-Year History of the Nikon Company] (1957), Tokyo.

Nishikawa Hiroshi (1987), *Nihon teikokushugi to mengyo* [Japanese Imperialism and the Cotton Industry], Kyoto: Minerva Shobo.

Odaka Konosuke (1993), *Shokunin no seikai kojo no seikai* [The World of the Craftsman and the World of the Factory], Tokyo: Libro Porto.

—— and Yamamoto Yuzo (eds) (1988), *Bakumatsu Meiji no Nihon keizai* [The Japanese Economy in the Late Tokugawa and Meiji Periods], Tokyo: Nihon Keizai Shinbunsha.

Ran Zhan-ping *et. al.* (eds) (1993), *Zhong-Ri guanli sixiang bijiao* [A Comparison of Japanese and Chinese Management Thinking], Beijing: Science and Technology Materials Publishing House.

Sakamoto Takao (1991), *Shijo. Dotoku. Chitsujo* [Markets, Morals, Order], Tokyo: Sobunsha.

Sampei Takako (1941), *Nihon mengyo hattatsushi* [A History of the Development of the Japanese Textile Industry], Tokyo: Keio Shobo.

Showa sangyoshi [A History of Industry in the Showa Period] (1952), 3 vols, Tokyo: Toyo Keizai Shimposha.

Takamura Naosuke (1971), *Nihon bosekigyoshi no josetsu* [An Introduction to the Japanese Cotton Textile Industry], Tokyo: Hanawa Shobo.

—— (1982), *Kindai Nihon mengyo to Chugoku* [The Modern Japanese Textile Industry and China], Tokyo: Tokyo Daigaku Shuppankai.

Toyobo nanajunenshi [The Seventy-Year History of Toyobo] (1953), Osaka: Toyobo.

Materials in English

Armytage, W.H.G. (1961), *A Social History of Engineering*, London: Faber & Faber.

Baird, J.R. (1990), *The History of the Japanese Camera*, Yakima, Washington: Historical Camera Publications.

Balfour Committee (1928), *Report on Trade and Industry*, Part 3: *The Textile Industry*, London: HMSO.

Bernard, W.D. (ed.) (1844), *Narrative of the Voyages and Services of the Nemesis from 1840 to 1843, and of the Combined Naval and Military Operations in China*, 2 vols, London: Henry Colburn.

Boisot, M. (1983), 'Convergence revisited: the codification and diffusion of knowledge in a British and a Japanese firm', *Journal of Management Studies*, 1, 159–90.

Burstall, A.F. (1963), *A History of Mechanical Engineering*, London: Faber & Faber.

Chapman, S.J. (1904), *The Lancashire Cotton Industry*, Manchester: Manchester University Press.

Chaterji, B. (1992), *Trade, Tariffs, and Empire: Lancashire and British Policy in India, 1919–1939*, Dehli: Oxford University Press.

Crouzet, F. (1982), *The Victorian Economy*, London: Methuen.

Dosi, G., Pavitt, K. and Soete, L. (1990), *The Economics of Technical Change and International Trade*, New York: Harvester.

—— *et al.* (1988), *Technical Change and Economic Theory*, London: Frances Pinter.

Farnie, D.A. (1979), *The English Cotton Industry and the World Market 1815–1896*, Oxford: Clarendon Press.

Freeman, Christopher (ed.) (1984), *Design, Innovation and Long Cycles in Economic Development*, London: Design Research Publications.

Fruin, W.M. (1992), *The Japanese Enterprise System: Competitive Strategies and Co-operative Structures*, Oxford: Clarendon Press.

Gerlach, Michael L. (1992), *Alliance Capitalism: The Social Organization of Japanese Business*, Berkeley, Cal. University of California Press.

Howe, Christopher (1996), *The Origins of Japanese Trade Supremacy: Development and Technology in Asia, 1540 to the Pacific War*, London: C. Hurst.

—— (1996), 'The Taiwan economy: the transition to maturity and the political economy of its changing international status', *China Quarterly* (no. 148, December).

Hubbard, G.E. (1935), *Eastern Industrialization and its Effects on the West: with Special Reference to Great Britain and Japan*, Oxford: Oxford University Press.

Indo-Japanese Association (1939a), *A Glimpse of Japan's Business and Her Trade with India*, Tokyo.

—— (1939b), *The Indo-Japanese Business Directory 1939–40*, Tokyo.

Kao, Charles K. (1991), *A Choice Fulfilled: The Business of High Technology*, Hong Kong: Chinese University of Hong Kong.

Kindleberger, Charles P. (1987), *The World in Depression, 1929–1939*, London: Penguin Books.

Kulkarni, V.B. (1979), *History of the Indian Textile Industry*, Bombay: Bombay Millowners' Association.

Kuo, Cheng-Tian (1995), *Global Competitiveness and Industrial Growth in Taiwan and the Philippines,* Pittsburgh, Penn.: University of Pittsburgh Press.

Marshall, A. (1919), *Industry and Trade: A Study of Industrial Techniques and Business Organization, and their Influences on the Conditions of Various Classes and Nations,* London: Macmillan.

Martelli-Chautard, M. (1934), *L'Expansion japonaise en Afrique*, Paris: Comité de l'Afrique française.

National Science Council Review 1990–91 (1991), Taipei: National Science Council.

Nishida, Judith M. (1990), 'The Japanese influence on the Shanghaiese textile industry and implications for Hong Kong', unpublished MPhil thesis, University of Hong Kong.

Nonaka, Ikujiro and Takeuchi, Hirokata (1995), *The Knowledge-creating Company: How Japanese Companies Create the Dynamics of Innovation,* New York: Oxford University Press.

Obata, Kyugoro (1937), *An Interpretation of the Life of Viscount Shibusawa*, Tokyo: Daiyamondo Jigyo Co.

Pearse, Arno S. (1929), *Japan and China: Cotton Industry Report*, Manchester: International Federation of Master Cotton Spinners and Manufacturers.

—— (1930), *The Cotton Industry of India*, Manchester: International Federation of Master Cotton Spinners and Manufacturers.

Pye, L.W. (1995), 'Chinese politics in the late Deng era', *China Quarterly*, no.142, June, 573–83.

Rosenberg, Nathan (1982), *Inside the Black Box: Technology and Economics*, Cambridge: Cambridge University Press.

Rotolin, Robert (1983), *The Nikon Rangefinder Camera*, Brighton: Hove Foto Books.

Sabel, Charles F. (1994), 'Learning by monitoring: the institutions of economic development', in L. Rodwin and D.A. Schon (eds), *Rethinking the Development Experience: Essays Provoked by the Work of Albert O. Hirschman,* Washington, D.C.: Brookings Institution, 231–74.

Sandberg, Lars (1974), *Lancashire in Decline: A Study in Entrepreneurship, Technology, and International Trade*, Columbus: Ohio State University Press.

Schumpeter, Joseph A. (1939), *Business Cycles: A Theoretical, Historical, and Statistical Analysis of the Capitalist Process*, 2 vols, New York: McGraw-Hill.

—— (1950), *Capitalism, Socialism, and Democracy*, 3rd edn, London: George Allen & Unwin.

Seki, K. (1956), *The Cotton Industry of Japan*, Tokyo: Japan Society for the Promotion of Science.

Shindo, T. (1961), *Labour in the Japanese Cotton Industry*, Tokyo: Japan Society for the Promotion of Science.

Simon, D.F. (1994), 'The orbital mechanics of Taiwan's technological development: an examination of the "gravitational" pushes and pulls', in G. Klintworth (ed.), *Taiwan in the Asia-Pacific in the 1990s*, Canberra: Allen & Unwin, 195–216.

Staley, E. (1939), *The World Economy in Transition: Technology vs. Politics, Laissez-faire vs. Planning, Power vs. Welfare*, New York: Council on Foreign Relations.

Stinchecum, Amanda M. (1984), *Kosode: 16th–19th-century Textiles from the Nomura Collection,* New York: Kodansha.

United States War Department (1944), *Handbook on Japan's Military Forces*, Washington, D.C.: Government Printing Office.

Urwick, L. (1929), *The Meaning of Rationalization*, London: Nisbet.

Utley, Freda (1931), *Lancashire and the Far East*, London: George Allen & Unwin.

Uyeda, Teijiro (1936), *Small-scale Industries of Japan: The Electric Light Industry*, Tokyo: Institute of Pacific Relations.

White, Fifi (1988), *Japanese Folk Textiles*, Kyoto: Shikosha.

3. Technical progress and technology transfer in a centrally planned economy: the experience of the USSR, 1917–87

Charles Feinstein[1]

INTRODUCTION

The outstanding feature of the technological history of the USSR is its low rate of innovation and diffusion, and the consequent failure to close the gap which separated the Soviet economy from its foreign rivals. Despite advances in a few sectors during the late Tsarist period, the Russian economy was relatively very undeveloped when the Bolsheviks seized power in 1917. Seventy years later, when the era of state ownership and central planning was drawing to a close, Soviet industry was still technologically backward compared with the leading market economies. Seven decades of state socialism had produced large numbers of highly proficient scientists and engineers and had financed huge outlays on research and on investment. But it had not succeeded in generating either a successful economy-wide rate of domestic invention and innovation or a dynamic process of technological advance based on the acquisition, adaptation and diffusion of leading-edge technology from abroad. There were a few important exceptions, most notably in the defence and space sectors, but taken as a whole Soviet socialism proved unable to promote technical progress at the rate which it desired and required.

The aims of this chapter are to examine how the USSR attempted to exploit new technology, to review the evidence which provides the basis for the judgement that it was unable to do so at a satisfactory rate, and to explain the reasons for this failure. The next section examines the undistinguished accomplishments of indigenous innovation, and this is followed by a summary of the various methods adopted to acquire technology from abroad. The two subsequent sections are devoted to an assessment of the technological standard attained by the Soviet Union, and an analysis of the reasons for the very modest level of performance. The chapter concludes with a summary of the main findings.

THE FAILED QUEST FOR DOMESTIC INNOVATION

Russia has a long history of acquisition of technology from abroad, stretching back to Peter the Great's tour of western Europe at the end of the seventeenth century. When the process of industrialization gained speed in the late nineteenth century Russia again looked to foreign technology to lead the way. French, British, Belgian and German entrepreneurs and technicians were encouraged to enter the country. They initiated revolutionary changes in the new iron and steel industries established in the south, and also played a major part in modernizing the mining, metalworking, textile and other industries.[2]

When the Bolsheviks took power they were conscious of their weakness in the face of the external threat to the revolution, and were eager to make themselves more independent, in technology as in other spheres. From an early date they gave priority to the expansion of technical and scientific education, to expenditure on research and development, and to the encouragement of technical progress (Lewis, 1994). The scope for these developments was initially severely constrained by the general lack of resources in a very poor economy, but steady progress was made in the 1930s and continued after the Second World War. By the mid-1960s the USSR had reached parity with the USA in the number of scientists and engineers engaged in R&D, and also in the percentage of GNP devoted to R&D (Table 3.1). It should, in principle, have been in a position to make a commensurate contribution to the international innovation process. In practice it proved incapable of doing this.

The most extensive investigation of the extent to which the USSR relied on western technology in the interwar and early postwar period is the three-volume study by Sutton (1968, 1971, 1973). His conclusions (1973, p. xxv) were utterly dismissive of Soviet performance: 'No fundamental industrial innovation of Soviet origin has been identified in the Soviet Union between 1917 and 1965.'

In a concluding summary of his research, Sutton (1973, pp. 365–70) listed the technological origins of seventy-five of the main industrial processes used in the USSR. Prior to 1930 there was, in his view, no Soviet innovation. In the period 1930–45 he identified two processes which were Soviet in origin and a further five in which the Soviet Union made an important contribution. In the final period, 1945–65, he found three processes which originated in the USSR, and five others in which the element of domestic innovation was significant.[3] Later studies have broadly sustained Sutton's verdict on the

Table 3.1　Resources devoted to R&D, USSR and other countries, 1950–75

A.　*Scientists and engineers employed in R&D (000s)*

	USSR	USA
1950	125	159
1955	173	254
1960	273	381
1965	474	494
1970	662	546
1975	874	535

B.　*Expenditures on R&D as % of GNP, selected countries*

	c.1967	1975
USSR	2.9	3.7
USA	2.9	2.2
UK	2.7	2.1
France	2.2	1.5
West Germany	1.8	2.2
Japan	1.8	2.0
Italy	0.6	1.0

Source:　Bergson (1983, pp. 54–5)

period to the mid-1960s, though with some qualifications which show Soviet innovation in a marginally more favourable light.[4]

It might have been expected that the independent innovation capability of the USSR would have increased as the resources available for R&D moved closer to USA levels, but this did not happen. On the contrary, according to a later study by Amann, Cooper and Davies (1977, p. 65): 'Soviet reliance on foreign technology has on the whole tended to increase in the course of the past 20 years.' This conclusion was based on case studies of eight high-priority industries. In four of these (space rocketry, weapons, nuclear power, and electricity transmission) the authors found that domestic innovations predominated; and in two others (iron and steel, and machine tools) they were important although imports from abroad also made a crucial contribution.

In the two remaining industries, both research-intensive, Soviet dependence on foreign technology was 'very high'. In computers virtually all innovations were transferred from the west; while the chemical industry was found to be 'the outstanding example of Soviet dependence on foreign technology'. One striking finding was that the Soviet Union was the only one among seven advanced industrial countries which 'has never been the original innovator of a major plastic material or chemical fibre'.[5]

The case studies did not cover the large number of low-priority sectors, but it is well known that they suffered from persistently substandard technology. The judgement that the Soviet performance in generating and applying new processes and products was inadequate could thus be extended to include the consumer durables, clothing, footwear, medical and food-processing industries, as well as agriculture, coal mining, road and rail transport, construction, distribution and other services.[6]

Further corroboration of the inferior indigenous contribution of the USSR and other centrally planned economies is provided by other studies. One consists of a listing of the country of origin of over fifty revolutionary modern products ranging from supersonic aircraft, programmable robots and Xerox copiers to penicillin and oral contraceptives (Kornai, 1992, pp. 296–300). Socialist economies contributed only three products to this list (satellites, plastic foil tents, and lasers), two of which were developed simultaneously in other countries. Another revealing study compared the contribution of the USSR and six other centrally planned economies with that of twenty OECD countries. The former's share of patents registered abroad was only about one-thirtieth of the latter's; and the value of the licences imported by the former in the 1970s was ten times greater than the value of their exports.[7] The very low share of the USSR (and other centrally planned economies) in imports of manufactures by the advanced OECD countries is another telling indicator of technological backwardness. The share was small in the 1970s and declined over time as the newly industrialized Asian economies expanded their exports of manufactures.

THE TRANSFER OF TECHNOLOGY FROM ABROAD

This inability to make a significant independent contribution should not, in itself, have constituted a serious economic handicap. As a late starter the USSR lagged well behind the advanced economies of Europe and the USA and so had enormous scope for acquiring more advanced technologies from abroad. Japan and many other countries had been similarly dependent on foreign technology and had successfully industrialized.

The USSR exploited the opportunity to import foreign processes and products on a substantial scale from the early 1920s onwards. Of course, designs or machines could not simply be acquired from abroad and utilized in the

Soviet Union without adjustment. It was necessary to adapt the plant and equipment to suit the different skills, attitudes and customs of the Russian labour force, as well as other specific features of the economy, especially the relative scarcity of capital. This need for adaptation complicated the process of transfer but did not seriously impair the huge potential gains to be made by massive borrowing of the most suitable innovations from the world's technological leaders.

There were frequent reservations by Soviet leaders about the desirability of such dependence on foreign technology; and by foreign governments about the wisdom of strengthening their communist opponents. But the mutual benefits – technical advance on the one side, exports, profits and job creation on the other – were usually sufficient to overwhelm any such doubts. The only significant exceptions on the capitalist side were the restrictions imposed for military reasons by the United States through the Co-ordinating Committee for Multilateral Export Controls (COCOM).

Numerous different methods were used to effect the transfer. Those which were normally most effective involved a high degree of participation by the transferor; in particular, concessions to foreign companies which allowed them to operate in the Soviet Union, purchases of complete plant and equipment (turnkey factories), and employment of foreign experts. Purchases of machinery or payments for licences to acquire designs, drawings, plans, patents and prototypes were also useful modes of transfer when accompanied by appropriate training by the seller. More passive types of transfer were also utilized but were typically less effective, for example, ordinary commercial imports of machinery, or payments for designs, patents and so on, without accompanying contacts, sending Soviet personnel to observe foreign firms, subscriptions to foreign scientific and technical journals, and various forms of covert acquisition and industrial espionage.

In the 1920s concessions were the most common method of technology transfer.[8] In their pure variant foreign companies undertook a specific project, accepting responsibility for everything from finance and equipment to the organization and operation of the activity, and receiving in return the right to any surplus or profit after payment of royalties and taxes. In mixed concessions the foreign partner provided finance, technology and organization, but the actual work was done by a Soviet enterprise. The principal use of concessions was in the extraction of raw materials, but they were applied in other sectors and played an important part in the initial revival of economic activity under the New Economic Policy (NEP). However, the rights obtained by foreigners were fundamentally incompatible with the move to centralized state ownership and control at the end of the 1920s. No new concessions were granted, and almost all existing ones were terminated in the early 1930s.

It was precisely at this time, however, that the Soviet need for foreign assistance was accelerating as Stalin forced the pace of his industrialization campaign, and there was a massive increase in the acquisition of foreign know-how and equipment in the years 1929–32. The dominant form of the technology transfer in this crucial period was the construction and initial operation of complete plants by foreign companies. In some sectors whole plants were purchased abroad, in others they were constructed by Russian management and labour using foreign designs and equipment and working under the close supervision of foreign engineers and technicians. Many of the most highly publicized developments associated with the First Five-Year Plan were of this type, including the electric power supply from the Dnieper dam, the Magnitogorsk iron and steel works, the Stalingrad tractor factory, the Gorki automobile plant, two giant machine-building plants, and several oil refineries and chemical works.

The peak years of transfer at the beginning of the 1930s were followed by a lengthy process, lasting for the remainder of the decade, while this unfamiliar imported technology was painfully assimilated and brought into full production and millions of Russian workers gained their first experience of industrialization. The USSR then gained further opportunities to acquire advanced foreign equipment, first under the wartime Lend Lease programme, and again immediately after the war when vast quantities of machinery and equipment were transferred to Russia in settlement of the reparations exacted from Germany and other countries. In addition, some 10,000 German scientists and technicians were deported to the Soviet Union.[9]

In Stalin's final years and for a short time immediately after that the USSR relied mainly on the more passive types of transfer; for example, 'reverse engineering' and reading foreign technical literature. By the end of the decade the new leadership appear to have recognized that they would be unable to catch up with the west on this basis and that more energetic and effective policies were needed. From the 1960s there was once again a strong emphasis on the more active forms of transfer, especially the purchase of complete production systems, notably the huge Fiat-Togliatti car-making complex and the Kama River truck plant, and other massive projects for the chemical, ferrous metallurgy and machine-building industries. There was also a rapid expansion of machinery imports and of co-operative industrial agreements to obtain the involvement and assistance of western specialists. The overall scale of the programme was large in the 1960s and expanded even further in the 1970s. The agreements both benefited from and contributed to the period of *détente*.

The USSR thus sustained a substantial long-run programme of foreign technology acquisition with only minor interruptions. The critical questions to which we now turn are how effectively the Soviet Union was able to absorb and diffuse this imported technology, and how far it was able to progress on this basis towards the technological standards of its capitalist competitors.

AN ASSESSMENT OF THE TECHNOLOGICAL PROGRESS OF THE USSR

The previous section demonstrated that the Soviet Union was not good at domestic innovation. Our primary concern here is with its capacity to exploit the technology to which it gained access, regardless of where that originated. We have thus to appraise its ability to move from research and experimental development to commercial production, to bring innovations into full-scale, efficient operation, and to disseminate best-practice techniques and products throughout the economy. Because of the enormous diversity and complexity of modern technologies it is extremely difficult to measure these elements of performance, even in a single industry, and assessment of the overall level of attainment of an entire economy is still more problematic.

Two principal methods have been adopted by those who have attempted to assess the technological performance of the Soviet Union. Both encounter formidable problems of methodology, measurement and interpretation, and both must be used critically and with caution. Fortunately, however, almost all the studies which have been made, whatever their particular method, have pointed to the same broad conclusion and are confirmed by the views expressed by Soviet planners and economists observing the system from within.

Microeconomic Case Studies

The microeconomic approach is based on comparative studies of specific products and processes. The aim is typically to determine the date at which commercial production of a specific innovation was first introduced, the rate at which new processes and products were diffused through the economy, and the technical standards attained in production, for example, the accuracy of machine tools.

The general conclusions which emerge from these case studies give a rather negative impression of Soviet performance.[10] Even in the high-priority sectors the Soviet Union appears to have achieved its best results in long-established industries with a relatively low R&D content, notably iron and steel, machine tools and electricity transmission. There were shortcomings even in these sectors, illustrated by the neglect of processes for the manufacture of alloy and high-quality steels and in steel rolling. Where a Soviet lead existed it was frequently based on scaling up existing technologies (for example, construction of very large open-hearth furnaces or mass production of standard machine tools), not on radical innovation, though there were some exceptions to this. It is also significant that in the ultra-high-priority weapons sector, represented in the case studies by tanks and intercontinental ballistic missiles, the USSR lost its initial technological superiority in the 1960s and had to compensate for this by relying on massive quantities of less-sophisticated technologies.

In the modern, research-intensive, civilian industries performance was extremely poor. In chemicals and control instruments the twenty years after the mid-1950s saw no diminution whatsoever in the considerable lag behind the more advanced countries; the gap may even have widened. In computers there was similarly no reduction in the lag which had existed since the 1950s in hardware, although there was a substantial improvement from a very low base in software. Two particularly bad cases may be quoted from the chemical industry: in 1972, the USSR was some nineteen years behind the USA in per capita production of plastics and synthetic resins, and seventeen years behind in synthetic fibres.

Studies of the diffusion of new products and processes, measured in terms of the number of years taken to reach some specified share of output, found that: 'In spite of some exceptions, it may be safely concluded that ... the rate of diffusion was lower in the USSR than in the other industrialized countries' (Amann *et al.*, 1977, p. 58). Evidence was found of technical conservatism which could not be justified by shortages of capital (ibid.):

> In the control instruments industry, for example, it would be difficult to find an adequate economic justification for the continued production of ... systems some of which are antiquated even by the standards of the most advanced Soviet production, which has itself been basically unchanged for 10 years.

Over vast areas of the economy the USSR was thus a technological laggard, and the studies highlighted especially long delays in catching up with the leaders in major 'revolutionary' innovations such as computers, microcircuits, plastics, man-made fibres and float glass.

A study by Martens and Young (1979) of the implementation of domestic patents in the early 1970s found that after two years only one-quarter of Soviet inventions were implemented, whereas in the USA and West Germany the comparable proportion was two-thirds. An authoritative appraisal of the acquisition and use of imported technologies by Hanson concluded:

> On the whole, the picture is not very impressive; assimilation takes longer than in Western Europe; in the case of the chemical technology ... there was no sign of a systematic reduction in lead-times with experience; subsequent manning levels tended to be on the high side and output levels on the low side, at least in the

chemical industry; and successful domestic diffusion and modification appear to be very limited. (Amann and Cooper, 1982, p. 448)

Other studies of foreign-assisted projects provide similar evidence of long delays from initial negotiations to start-up, low levels of performance once the plant was in operation, and slow dissemination of the imported technology. Some exceptions are noted, but the general impression is unfavourable.

Macroeconomic Measurement of Technical Progress

The second approach to evaluation of Soviet technological performance attempts to make explicit estimates of the contribution of technical progress to the growth of output. These estimates are derived by distinguishing between that part of the growth of output which can be attributed to increased use of the inputs of labour and capital, and that part which represents the contribution of other sources of growth. The contribution of these other sources, known as total factor productivity (TFP), is taken as a measure – albeit a very imperfect one – of the impact of technical progress.

This contribution can be calculated by the technique known as growth accounting. The growth rate of total factor inputs (TFI) is calculated as a weighted average of the growth rates of the individual inputs, with the weights

Table 3.2   *Output, factor inputs and total factor productivity, Soviet industry, 1951–82 (average annual rates of growth, per cent per annum)*

	Industrial production (1)	Labour (man-hours) (2)	Capital (3)	Total factor inputs (4)	Total factor productivity (5)
1951–55	10.6	4.2	11.7	7.8	2.8
1956–60	9.8	2.1	11.2	6.4	3.4
1961–65	6.5	2.9	11.4	6.9	−0.3
1966–70	6.3	3.1	8.8	5.7	0.5
1971–75	5.9	1.5	8.7	4.9	1.0
1976–80	3.2	1.6	7.7	4.5	−1.2
1981–82	2.3	0.8	7.3	3.8	−1.5

Note: Cols (1) and (2) are western estimates; col (3) is the official Soviet series. The weights used in col (4), taken from Bornstein (1985), are 52.4% for labour and 47.6% for capital.

Source: Weitzman (1983, pp. 179–83); Bornstein (1985, p. 31)

given by each factor's marginal contribution to output (its output elasticity). The TFP growth rate is then derived as the difference between the rates of growth of output and of TFI. The main drawback to this approach is the need to assume that the USSR was a competitive economy in which factors were paid their marginal products so that the weights can be taken as equal to the (imputed) factor shares.

Illustrative results for the industrial sector from 1951 to 1982 are given in Table 3.2. Two features stand out prominently. The first is the precipitate decline in the growth rates for both production and labour input. The second is that the growth rates for total factor productivity were relatively good in the 1950s, but then declined sharply and were very low or even negative for the remainder of the period.

These results are broadly consistent with those for all material sectors of the economy over the period from 1950 to 1975 presented in an authoritative study by Bergson (1983). He also attempted to go one step further, and estimated that part of TFP growth which might be attributed to other factors, for example, improvements in the quality of the labour force as a result of education and training; sectoral shifts from agriculture (where productivity is low) to industry (where it is higher); and economies of scale. This adjusted series for Soviet technological progress again shows a respectable annual growth rate of 2.9 per cent in the 1950s, but then falls away to only 1.0 per cent in the 1960s and a bare 0.2 per cent in 1971–5.

Bergson also made comparable factor productivity estimates for six other countries for the period 1955–70 (Table 3.3). These show that TFP growth in the Soviet economy was poor relative not only to advanced capitalist countries such as France and Germany, but also to countries such as Japan and Italy, which were at broadly the same stage of development as the USSR and thus had roughly comparable opportunities to benefit from the 'advantages of backwardness'.

Table 3.3 *Total factor productivity, USSR and other countries, 1955–70*
              (average annual rates of growth, per cent per annum)

Japan	5.9
Italy	4.4
France	3.9
Germany	3.4
USSR	2.4
UK	1.8
USA	1.6

Source: Bergson (1983, p. 41)

This growth-accounting approach was challenged in the 1970s by a number of writers. They suggested a significantly different interpretation of the post-war Soviet experience based on an alternative econometric approach.[11] According to this analysis the primary cause of the retardation in growth of output was diminishing returns to capital because of the increasing difficulty encountered in substituting capital for labour (cf. cols (2) and (3) of Table 3.2). The rate of technological progress was not declining and was not exceptionally low.

However, this alternative approach was itself criticized by Bergson (1979) on the grounds that it implied an improbably high rate of return to capital at the beginning of the period. Weitzman (1983) reconsidered the issues and compared the two procedures over a longer period. His econometric estimates of a constant elasticity of substitution (CES) production function yielded a constant annual rate of technical change for Soviet industry of less than 1 per cent, compared to a declining trend with an average rate of 1.75 per cent using the growth accounting procedure.[12] He adopted an agnostic attitude to these differences, saying that without further information it was not possible to decide on statistical grounds alone between the two approaches.[13]

There are severe conceptual and statistical limitations to these estimates of total factor productivity and to their interpretation as indicators of Soviet technological performance. However, the different estimates all broadly support the proposition that the post-1960 pace of technical change in the USSR was relatively modest.[14] They thus lead to the same disparaging assessment as the case studies, and both sets of external judgements are supported by numerous highly critical comments made within the USSR. In the view of a Russian official, the average technological gap compared with the west in major industries was ten to fifteen years in the mid-1950s, and increased to twenty to thirty years by the mid-1980s, with the greatest retardation in the advanced high-technology sectors.[15]

When all the available evidence is considered there can thus be little doubt that overall Soviet performance in this critical field was consistently poor. We turn now to consider the possible reasons why this was so.

THE FAILURE TO ACHIEVE A SATISFACTORY RATE OF INNOVATION

The failure of the command economy of the USSR to make significant progress in the introduction and development of new technology might be attributed to a lack of the necessary resources, in particular of high-calibre scientists, engineers and technicians; to a failure on the part of the system's directors to allocate the necessary priority to this task; or to fundamental weaknesses in the Soviet system of central planning and management which precluded the achievement of these objectives even though they were forcefully pursued by those in control of the system.

The lack of scientific and technological resources was obviously important in the early phase of Soviet economic development, and would be a major part of the explanation for the dependence on foreign technology in the 1920s or during the period of the First and Second Five-Year Plans, but it cannot have much relevance to the position after the Second World War. By the 1960s the expansion of Soviet education had transformed the position, and the stock of qualified personnel was comparable to that in western Europe and the USA.

It seems equally clear that little or no weight can be given to the second possible explanation. Modernization of the economy was one of the dominant objectives set by the Bolshevik leaders. Lenin's famous aphorism in 1920: 'Communism is Soviet power plus electrification of the whole country', was an early indication of the importance attached to technological progress, and the need to improve its contribution to the performance of the Soviet economy remained a central priority for all his successors.

After the recovery from the devastation of the Second World War the urgency of this task was greatly enhanced. In earlier decades the Soviet Union had followed a path of extensive growth under which the expansion of output was achieved primarily by increasing the inputs of materials, labour and capital. By the late 1950s it became increasingly evident that this pattern of growth was reaching its limits: reserves of underemployed labour were largely exhausted, it was no longer feasible to drive up the share of national income devoted to capital investment by forcing the population to sacrifice present for future consumption. High rates of growth would be sustained only if the economy could make efficient use of scarce resources.

The crucial condition for the success of this alternative pattern of intensive growth was more effective exploitation of science and technology, and the shortcomings of the Soviet performance in this respect became a major motif in the speeches and writings of the leadership. But the rate of growth of output declined remorselessly, both in industry and in the wider economy. The slower the pace became, the greater was their anxiety to boost the rate of innovation.

The failure to make significant progress notwithstanding the powerful pressure for improved performance – and frequent efforts to reform the system – suggests strongly that the forces which frustrated this were intrinsic and rooted deep in the economic system; a proposition which is reinforced by the parallel failures in other centrally planned economies (Kornai, 1992; Holliday, 1984). What were these systemic barriers to innovation?[16]

The economic system devised under Stalin and continued by his successors succeeded in allocating scarce resources to the branches and sectors to which the planners gave priority, but it did so at the expense of inordinate shortages, hoarding, waste and misuse of resources. These problems were caused by a variety of factors including the prevalence of 'taut planning' and the permanent seller's market in a shortage economy, the informational deficiencies of central planning and allocation of supplies, and the procedures for fixing prices with little or no regard to the balance of supply and demand.[17]

Within this overall economic context the four major sources of Soviet technological weakness were the separation of research and development from production, the rigid and restrictive nature of the bureaucratic (non-market) relationships of enterprises with both their administrative superiors and their suppliers; the lack of appropriate income and price incentives; and the absence of competitive pressures. These deterrents to innovation operated both within existing enterprises and also, though to a lesser extent, where the central planners attempted to promote technical change by constructing completely new plants.[18]

The first of the organizational problems was created by the Soviet practice of establishing separate R&D institutions with responsibility for invention and innovation. In general this lack of integration did not prove effective. The proposals made by the R&D agencies were frequently regarded by the enterprises as impractical or inappropriate, and the former paid insufficient attention to development work and the preparation of prototypes. There was very little incentive for them to worry about the difficult transition from invention to commercial application, since they fulfilled their plans simply by creating proposals, regardless of what happened subsequently. There were also lesser problems, such as the lack of competition between R&D institutions, and bureaucratic obstacles to collaboration among personnel located in different ministries.[19]

The difficulties encountered by potentially progressive firms in obtaining the necessary inputs of materials and equipment represented an even more fundamental obstacle to change. The inability of the centralized system of supply to ensure the regular and timely flow of supplies was a persistent and frustrating problem for enterprises even when they were following a conservative path and seeking to obtain the same materials from the same suppliers. Since innovation by definition involved either a new method of production or alterations to the nature and quality of the goods produced, corresponding changes in the materials and equipment used were almost always an essential precondition. The greater such changes, the more difficult it was to obtain the new supplies, and the problems were especially acute if the new materials or machinery required some co-operative experimentation from the supplier in order to 'get it right'. From the point of view of the prospective suppliers all such requests were an unwelcome and unwanted burden: as long as they were satisfactorily fulfilling their plan targets they had little or no incentive to change their output.

Problems arising at the interface between an innovating firm and its suppliers and customers are not, of course, unique to a centrally planned economy, but in a market economy they are usually overcome by appropriate incentives. Why was the command economy not able to do this? The major part of the answer is that the overriding goal of the Soviet economic system was to increase output. Other objectives were specified at various times, for example, reduced costs or greater product variety, but these were always subordinate in the minds of both planners and enterprise directors. One highly conspicuous and powerful manifestation of this priority was the very large proportion of directors' incomes which was paid as a bonus for fulfilment of the output targets. Another was the role which this indicator played in determining promotion.

If a prospective innovation failed (or succeeded only after prolonged disruption), the enterprise would be unable to meet its targets. The managers and other workers would lose a substantial fraction of their pay; in some circumstances they might face even more severe penalties. Conversely, however, if the innovation was successful any benefits to the directors and workers were likely to be at best temporary. If, for example, the change increased output, a 'ratchet effect' operated to ensure that the increment was rapidly incorporated into subsequent annual plans. It became the new baseline from which further additions were to be made, and thus gave the firm no respite from the ceaseless pressure for increased production and fulfilment of plan targets.

Innovation and risk are inextricably related but the Soviet system combined high penalties for failure and low rewards for success, an arrangement almost guaranteed to discourage radical technological change. It is thus not surprising that under these conditions enterprises preferred to make minor adjustments to known systems rather than introduce 'discrete' revolutionary innovations. Incremental progress is necessary and can be very effective (as indicated, for example, by John Enos in Chapter 6 in this volume) but it is not enough. It cannot compensate for slowness in developing radical discoveries or in responding to those introduced in more dynamic foreign economies.

The barriers to innovation created by these deficiencies in organization and incentives were reinforced by the pricing system. Under the standard Soviet procedures wholesale prices in each branch of the economy were effectively set by adding a standard mark-up to planned average cost of production. A technically progressive enterprise which introduced cheaper processes was likely to find that this simply led to reductions in output prices and thus diminished the value of its sales and profits. Attempts were made to meet the deterrent effects of this system by introducing special mark-ups for new products. However, this created additional profits which were rapidly deemed to be excessive by superior agencies searching feverishly for ways to reduce costs, and so the mark-ups did not survive long enough to give enterprises a real incentive to innovate.

The final factor serving to inhibit innovation was the lack of competitive pressure. In a market economy innovating is risky but so too is not innovating; a firm which stagnates faces the threat of competition from more dynamic rivals, and failure to change can lead to bankruptcy. Soviet firms were under no such compulsion. There was no threat from domestic rivals in an economy with a permanent seller's market, and so-called 'soft budget constraints' (Kornai, 1980) effectively ensured that the authorities would almost always keep an enterprise afloat, no matter how outmoded and inefficient its methods and technology or how great its losses. Furthermore, control of foreign trade, together with the exclusion of direct inward investment, effectively eliminated the potentially powerful stimulus that foreign competition would have provided.[20]

The planners could attempt to circumvent some of the inherent systemic problems faced by existing enterprises by imposing the introduction of new technology from the top and ordering the construction of completely new plants. This met with some notable successes, but many factors operated to frustrate innovative progress even in these circumstances. This was demonstrated with stunning clarity during Khrushchev's struggle to implement his crash programme for the expansion and modernization of the chemical industry in the 1960s. The chemicalization drive was impeded to an appalling extent by bureaucratic inertia and by hostility from vested interests (Amann and Cooper, 1982, pp. 146–54). The most important of the many difficulties encountered

> was the relative inability of the chemical industry to command much needed supplies. ... despite the repeated exhortations of Khrushchev many influential political leaders and economic officials found it inconvenient to adjust. ... the so-called 'command economy' did not respond to commands.

The many disadvantageous features of the Soviet system were widely recognized. As early as 1955 Liberman had complained that it constituted 'a system for rewarding technical stagnation', and every leader from Khrushchev to Gorbachev attempted to reform and improve it. There was endless tinkering with organizational structures, the supply system, the formulae for fixing bonuses, the pricing of new products, and much else. But as long as centralized planning and administration was sacrosanct and expansion of output remained the highest priority there could be no fundamental change and no significant improvement. In Bergson's caustic phrase (1983, p. 58): 'reform in the USSR has again and again only been a prelude to more reform'.

There is, however, one striking exception to these generalizations: the Soviet success in the development of new weapons, although even here they eventually fell well behind the United States.[21] Why were the military industries not afflicted by inimical systemic factors to the same extent as other sectors? There are basically three reasons. First, unlike the civilian industries, they were subject to competition and were very aware of how much was at stake if they failed to maintain rough parity with the NATO countries. Second, they were always given the highest priority, and typically had, for instance, the information and authority to impose their requirements on their suppliers or to ensure that they obtained scarce materials, and other resources, regardless of any adverse effects this might have on other industries. Third – and this is probably the most important factor – there is a crucial difference in the nature of the task set for the military scientists and engineers. R&D in this sector is essentially designed to achieve a well-specified technical objective, regardless of cost or other economic considerations. In a command economy operating with inconsistent performance indicators and arbitrary prices it is far easier for scientists and engineers to fulfil a technical mission than for planners and managers to choose and diffuse the innovations which would be economically most beneficial in the civilian sector.[22]

This is not the whole story. There were some strengths in the socialist system; for example, the ability to mobilize resources on a massive scale for a desired end and to 'order' innovation by constructing new plants; a high rate of investment and of economic growth; the planned co-ordination of investment decisions; the avoidance of duplication between competing enterprises; and the absence of commercial secrecy. Some Soviet specialists (I am thinking, for example, of Maurice Dobb) thought such factors would be decisive in the economic competition with capitalism. In the event they were greatly mistaken, and the negative features of the socialist system outlined above ultimately proved far more powerful. Moreover, some of the potential advantages of socialism were dissipated; for example, ministerial empires proved to be as least as bad as capitalist companies in their duplication of production facilities or their unwillingness to share information with rival firms. In the decades after the Second World War the technological level of the market economies repeatedly surged forward, while the performance of the Soviet Union with respect to the adoption and diffusion of innovations remained, in general, sluggish, inefficient and unsatisfactory.

CONCLUSION

The results of this survey thus show that the command economy established in the Soviet Union never succeeded in creating an all-round capacity to discover and absorb new technology through domestic research and development. There were a few notable successes, but in general these occurred either in weapons production and the closely related aviation and space industries, or in long-established, high-priority sectors such as ferrous metallurgy and electric power which were not research-intensive. Furthermore, where innovation was successful it usually took the form of scaling up existing technologies, not of radical changes.

Throughout its seven decades the USSR was thus forced to rely on the acquisition of foreign technology for its crucial dynamic element. Borrowing from abroad was a good strategy for a relatively backward country, but the potential benefits were severely restricted by serious shortcomings in the Soviet economic system. Examination of the pace at which the innovations acquired from the international technological leaders were assimilated shows a rather undistinguished performance. The socialist enterprises in the Soviet Union were slow off the mark in obtaining the new technologies from abroad, slow to bring the new processes into full operation, and slow to promote their diffusion throughout the economy.

Initially technical progress was held back by lack of resources and experience, but after the Second World War this ceased to be a valid explanation. The primary obstacle to effective technological progress was the centrally planned socialist economy with its chronic seller's market and soft budget constraints. The specific systemic barriers which hindered technological advance included the division of responsibility between R&D institutions and the productive enterprises; the rigid and bureaucratic relationships between planners and producers and between enterprises and their suppliers; the absence of adequate incentives in a system which desperately needed innovation but consistently attached greater priority to fulfilment of taut output targets; the deficiencies of the arrangements for fixing prices; and the absence of competitive pressures.

In successful market economies a dynamic firm envisages the prospect of large profits; a stagnant firm must contemplate the threat of competition and bankruptcy. In the USSR the planners created a risk-reward environment in which repetition and routine typically seemed more attractive than the introduction of new processes and products. All these features of the Soviet system severely impeded technological advance and the USSR was unable to sustain a satisfactory rate of growth or to close the gap which separated it from its market-economy rivals. The leadership diagnosed the symptoms of the disease but could not deliver the cure. In the end it proved fatal.

NOTES

1. I should like to thank Chris Davies, Mark Harrison and Nick von Tunzelmann for very helpful comments and references.
2. See, for example, McKay (1970), Cooper and Lewis (1990).
3. Harrison and Simonov (1996, p. 3) criticize Sutton for concentrating on machinery products and neglecting other fields where 'technological leadership belonged to the Soviet Union'. One area where Sutton fails to give credit to the USSR for successful innovation in the 1930s is the military sector, notably the design for the famous T-34 tank; see Amann and Cooper (1982, pp. 370–86).
4. See, for example, the comments in Amann *et al.* (1977, pp. 276, 284 and 498) and in Amann and Cooper (1982, pp. 141–2 and 421).
5. Amann *et al.* (1977, pp. 63–6).
6. See, for example, Davis (1989, pp. 453–5) for an analysis of the 'low technological level and slow pace of technological innovation' in the low-priority medical sector.
7. Slama (1982) quoted in Gomulka and Nove (1984, p. 17).
8. Information in this and the following paragraphs about the Soviet acquisition of foreign technology is largely drawn from Sutton (1968, 1971, 1973) and Hanson (1981).
9. For a detailed evaluation of the contribution of the German specialists in the development of postwar Soviet jet propulsion technology, see Harrison and Simonov (1996).
10. The most detailed and thorough of the microeconomic studies of Soviet technological performance are described in Amann *et al.* (1977) with further discussion in Amann and Cooper (1982). The summary in the following paragraphs are based largely on the overview by Davies in Amann *et al.* (1977, pp. 35–82), and on other studies reviewed in Hanson (1981), Holliday (1984) and Bornstein (1985).
11. See Weitzman (1970), Desai (1976) and Gomulka (1976). The alternative approach specifies different forms of production function, and then derives both the output elasticities and the elasticity of substitution, as well as the rate of growth of TFP, by econometric estimation. A variety of statistical tests are used to establish which form and specification of the function gives the best results. The two standard forms normally employed are the Cobb-Douglas and the CES; the latter does not require returns to scale to be constant or the elasticity of substitution to be unity. The disadvantage of this approach is that the econometric techniques on which it relies are usually neither definitive nor robust in the face of small changes in specification, estimation procedures or time-period.
12. Weitzman's figure of 1.75 per cent per annum for 1961–78 is considerably higher than the corresponding TFP growth rate in Table 3.2 because his (arbitrary) weights of 75:25 give greater weight to the slower-growing labour input.
13. Desai (1987) retained confidence in the econometric approach, but reversed her previous finding and concluded that the Cobb-Douglas was superior to the CES function. Her estimates show that TFP growth was very low in the 1950s and negative from the mid-1960s, but seem to be the result of implausibly high input coefficients for capital.
14. A Russian economic statistician, G.I. Khanin, has recently published an independent and original set of estimates of Soviet output and factor inputs. For the period since 1950 these show a lower rate of growth of the stock of fixed assets than the estimates used by western scholars. However, the implied contribution of TFP to overall growth remains very low, with a sharply declining trend in the period after 1950, and becomes negative from 1975 to 1985; for a detailed and very perceptive analysis, see Harrison (1993).
15. This estimate by the then Russian Minister for Foreign Economic Relations is quoted by von Tunzelmann (1995, p. 294) from Glaziev and Schneider (1993, p. 238).
16. The following analysis draws heavily on the subtle and illuminating study of these problems by Joseph Berliner (1976).
17. For further discussion of this fundamental and pervasive weakness of the Soviet system, see standard accounts such as Berliner (1957), Nove (1977) and Kornai (1980).
18. Other systemic shortcomings of the Soviet economy were not an integral part of the innovation process but also had a deleterious effect on technological progress, notably the

chronic delays in completion of construction projects, pressures for ministerial self-sufficiency, and the misleading nature of the information conveyed by fixed, bureaucratically determined prices.

19. Cocks (1983) gives a very full account of the attempts made since the late 1960s to eliminate these structural weaknesses and of the reasons why relatively little was achieved.

20. Poznanski (1988) argues that the limits on foreign competition were the most important explanation for the lack of innovation.

21. Davis (1990) quotes a CIA report (US CIA, 1986) which argued that the Soviet weapons industry 'has a technologically unsophisticated production base, lags the West in most important production technologies (e.g. computer-aided design, industrial robots, numerically-controlled machine tools), maintains old and technologically obsolete machinery in service, and has a low level of capital productivity'.

22. Concorde, the technologically superb but economically disastrous supersonic aeroplane developed for civilian flight by Britain and France, is a valuable reminder that market economies are not immune from similar problems when their governments choose to ignore economic considerations.

REFERENCES

Amann, R. and Cooper, J.M. (eds) (1982), *Industrial Innovation in the Soviet Union*, New Haven, Conn.: Yale University Press.

——, —— and Davies, R.W. (eds) (1977), *The Technological Level of Soviet Industry*, New Haven, Conn.: Yale University Press.

Bergson, A. (1978), *Productivity and the Social System: The USSR and the West*, Cambridge, Mass.: Harvard University Press.

—— (1979), 'Notes on the production function in Soviet postwar industrial growth', *Journal of Comparative Economics*, 3, 116–26.

—— (1983), 'Technological progress', in A. Bergson and H.S. Levine (eds), *The Soviet Economy: Toward the Year 2000*, London: Allen & Unwin.

Berliner, J. (1957), *Factory and Manager in the USSR*, Cambridge, Mass.: Harvard University Press.

—— (1976), *The Innovation Decision in Soviet Industry*, Cambridge, Mass.: MIT Press.

Bornstein, M. (1985), *East–West Technology Transfer: The Transfer of Western Technology to the USSR*, Paris: OECD.

Cocks, P. (1983), 'Organizing for technological innovation in the 1980s', in G. Guroff and F.V. Carstensen (eds), *Entrepreneurship in Imperial Russia and the Soviet Union*, Princeton, N.J.: Princeton University Press.

Cooper, J.M. and Lewis, R.A. (1990), 'Research and technology', in R.W. Davies (ed.), *From Tsarism to the New Economic Policy*, London: Macmillan.

Davis, C. (1989), ' Priority and the shortage model: the medical system in the socialist economy', in C. Davis and W. Charemza (eds), *Models of Disequilibrium and Shortage in Centrally Planned Economies*, London: Chapman & Hall.

—— (1990), 'The high priority military sector in a shortage economy', in H.S. Rowen and C. Wolf (eds), *The Impoverished Superpower: Perestroika and the Burden of Soviet Military Spending*, San Francisco: Institute for Contemporary Studies.

Desai, P. (1976), 'The production function and technical change in postwar industry: a reexamination', *American Economic Review*, 66, 372–81; reprinted in Desai (1987, 63–77).

—— (1987), *The Soviet Economy: Problems and Prospects*, Oxford: Blackwell.

Glaziev, S. and Schneider, C.M. (eds) (1993), *Research and Development Management in the Transition to the Market Economy*, Luxembourg: IIASA.

Gomulka, S. (1976), 'Soviet postwar industrial growth, capital–labour substitution and technical change: a reexamination', in Z.M. Fallenbuch (ed.) *Economic Development in the Soviet Union and Eastern Europe*, vol. 2, New York: Praeger.

—— and Nove, A. (1984), *East–West Technology Transfer: Contribution to Eastern Growth. An Econometric Evaluation*, Paris: OECD.

Hanson, P. (1981), *Trade and Technology in Soviet–Western Relations,* London: Macmillan.

Harrison, M. (1993), 'Soviet economic growth since 1928: the alternative estimates of G.I. Khanin', *Europe–Asia Studies*, 45, 141–67.

—— and Simonov, N. (1996), 'Invention, imitation and Soviet rocketry after 1945', University of Warwick, Department of Economics, Working Paper series no. 9601.

Holliday, G.D. (1984), *East–West Technology Transfer: Survey of Sectoral Case Studies*, Paris: OECD.

Kornai, J. (1980), *Economics of Shortage,* Amsterdam: North-Holland.

—— (1992), *The Socialist System: The Political Economy of Communism*, Oxford: Clarendon Press.

Lewis, R. (1994), 'Technology and the transformation of the Soviet economy', in R.W. Davies, M. Harrison, and S.G. Wheatcroft (eds), *The Economic Transformation of the Soviet Union, 1913–1945*, Cambridge: Cambridge University Press.

Martens, J.A. and Young, J.P. (1979), 'Soviet implementation of domestic inventions: first results', in Joint Economic Committee, Congress of the United States, *Soviet Economy in a Time of Change*, vol. I, Washington, D.C.: US Government Printing Office.

McKay, J.P. (1970), *Pioneers for Profit: Foreign Entrepreneurship and Russian Industrialization, 1885–1913,* Chicago: Chicago University Press.

Nove, A. (1977), *The Soviet Economic System*, London: Allen & Unwin.

Poznanski, K.Z. (1988), 'The CPE aversion to innovations: alternative theoretical explanations', *Economics of Planning*, 22, 136–45.

Slama, J. (1982), 'Technologietransfer zwischen Ost und West in den 70er and 80er Jahren', *Ost Europa-Wirtschaft*.

Sutton, A.C. (1968, 1971, 1973), *Western Technology and Soviet Economic Development*, vol. 1: *1917 to 1930*, vol. 2: *1930 to 1945*, vol. 3: *1945 to 1965,* Stanford, Cal.: Hoover Institution.

US Central Intelligence Agency (CIA) (1986), *The Soviet Weapons Industry: An Overview*, Washington, D.C., DI 86-10016.

von Tunzelmann, G.N. (1995*), Technology and Industrial Progress: The Foundations of Economic Growth*, Aldershot, Hants.: Edward Elgar.

Weitzman, M.L. (1970), 'Soviet postwar economic growth and capital–labour substitution', *American Economic Review,* 60, 676–92.

—— (1983), 'Industrial production', in A. Bergson and H.S. Levine (eds), *The Soviet Economy: Toward the Year 2000*, London: Allen & Unwin.

4. China's international technology transfer: the current situation, problems and future prospects

Xu Jiangping

INTRODUCTION

Since implementing the policies of economic reform and opening to the world (1980), China has achieved a series of remarkable successes in technology improvement, reflecting the high priority placed upon such work during this period. The technical innovation process set in motion has given a strong impetus to economic growth.

Technological improvement is normally thought of as taking place in three ways: invention and adoption of new techniques; transactions that diffuse technology among domestic enterprises; and the introduction of technology from abroad. The last of these is the main mode of improvement in China today.

The great success of China's open door policy has been, to a large extent, attributed to the import of technology. The introduction of the operational skills and production lines needed to produce colour TVs, refrigerators, steel and chemical fibres has contributed much to the qualitative improvement of consumer goods and to the output of raw and semi-finished materials. Some of these goods have filled gaps in the domestic market. This makes it all the more important to carry out studies relating to China's introduction of new technology.

Unfortunately, it is very difficult to obtain complete sets of statistical data for a full analysis of these issues. This is because of the complicated administration of technology introduction in different regions and ministries in China. In this chapter, therefore, I shall focus on major technology projects that have been centrally approved through the State Economic and Trade Commission (SETC) and the Ministry of Foreign Trade and Economic Co-operation (MOFTEC). These are all projects at the core of China's programme of technology imports.

By internationally acknowledged agreement, we may define the import of technology as the transfer of the scientific knowledge and production technology related to a certain good. It does not strictly include equipment imports. The Chinese government adopted this concept in its 'Administrative Regulations of the People's Republic of China on Contracts Involving the Import of Technology', promulgated in 1985. However, in practice, many Chinese recipients of foreign technology believe that the import of technology includes not only patents, patented technology and technological services, but also imports of equipment. The former is regarded as the 'software' of technology and the latter as the 'hardware'. Both 'software' and 'hardware' are imported by Chinese policy-makers, and both aspects of the problem are considered in this chapter.

THE CURRENT SITUATION WITH REGARD TO CHINA'S IMPORTS OF TECHNOLOGY

China's introduction of technology since the 1980s can be divided into three phases: the first, from 1981 to 1987, was the stage of large-scale introduction of technology, while the second, from 1988 to 1991, was a time of stagnation in new technology introduction. During the third stage, from 1992 to the present, market-oriented enterprises have been the main investors in imported technology, and the value of imports has tended to fall. The following is a summary of these developments.

1981–87: Large-scale Imports

First, as to scale, the import of technology grew throughout the whole period. Between 1981 and 1984, about 726 technology import projects were introduced, with a total contract value of some US$2 billion. Between 1985 and 1987, the number decreased somewhat, but their annual value increased to a total of almost US$3 billion (see Table 4.1).

With regard to the structure of such imports, there was an important improvement with a decline in the share of whole-plant imports and an increase in co-production projects. Thus by 1985 imports of whole plant (complete sets) had reached their peak. This peak in fact triggered government institutions to take a series of measures to control the import of equipment and whole plants. They did this through new systems of strict procedures for examination and approval of such imports. The effects of these measures are clearly visible in Table 4.1. In contrast, the share of co-production projects increased from 16 per cent in 1985 to 70 per cent in 1987. Moreover, the share of licences and technical services decreased in the total import of technology.

If we look at the foreign partner structure set out in Table 4.2, we find that a very large part by value of technology imports came from three countries:

Table 4.1 China's technology imports by category, 1981–87

Category of imports	1981–84				1985				1987			
	Contracts		Value		Contracts		Value		Contracts		Value	
	No.	%	US$ m	%	No.	%	US$ m	%	No.	%	US$ m	%
Whole plant	309	43	1,145.7	57	295	44	2,234.3	75.4	235	41	350.8	12.0
Licences	294	40	368.5	18	291	43	219.8	7.4	30	5	16.0	0.5
Technical services	59	8	391.5	20	30	5	12.9	0.4	24	4	10.2	0.3
Consultancy	28	4	16.2	1	21	3	8.9	0.3	25	4	509.9	17.0
Co-production	36	5	70.8	4	34	5	485.4	16.5	267	46	2,097.9	70.0
Total	726	100	1,992.7	100	671	100	2,961.4	100	581	100	2,984.9	100

Source: Zhongguo jingji nianjian [Alamanac of China's Economy], Beijing: Alamanac of China's Economy Publishing House, various years

Table 4.2 Sources of China's technology imports, 1981–87

Source of imports	1981–84				1985				1987			
	Contracts		Value		Contracts		Value		Contracts		Value	
	No.	%	US$ m	%	No.	%	US$ m	%	No.	%	US$ m	%
Japan	163	23	656.5	33	175	26	550.8	19	138	24	706.1	24
United States	181	25	532.9	27	138	21	692.3	23	119	21	673.4	23
W. Germany	143	20	256.6	13	124	19	794.8	27	109	19	288.8	10
Italy	62	9	114.4	6	34	5	124.5	4	47	8	212.8	7
Britain	51	7	52.4	3	41	6	79.8	3	31	5	295.6	10
France	24	3	135.3	7	34	5	326.2	11	30	5	116.5	4
Total[a]	726	100	1,992.7	100	671	100	2,961.4	100	581	100	2,984.9	100

Note: [a] Including imports from other countries.

Source: As for Table 4.1

Japan, the United States and the former West Germany; and that most of the remainder was obtained from Italy, France and Britain. These six developed countries accounted for 89 per cent of China's technology imports in 1981–84 and for 78 per cent in 1987.

Most technology imports were for the energy, raw materials, machinery, electronics, light and textile industries. For instance, in 1987 the contracted value of imported technology for the electric power, metallurgy, oil, petrochemical, motor vehicles and textile industries alone was over US$100 million.

Thus the 'golden age' of Chinese technology imports was 1981–87. In this period, state-controlled imports of technology focused on two major programmes: the '3,000 item plan' and the 'twelve production lines plan'. The former project was carried out in 1983–85 at a cost to the state budget of about US$3 billion and was aimed at the renovation of technology in existing enterprises. The latter project started in 1986 and imported twelve lines to develop domestic production of colour TVs, numerically controlled lathes, special iron and steel product casting, ships and ocean-going vessels for export, electric locomotives and diesels, synthetic industrial equipment, coal excavators, cement, open-ended spinning and arrow shaft looms, clothes, beer and lean meat pigs.

With the co-operation and assistance of academic research institutions and universities, the production enterprises digested and absorbed the new technology of these two big programmes, which contributed significantly to a general improvement in China's technological level.

Features of the Period of Stagnation, 1988–91

From the second half of 1988 to 1991, China implemented a contractionary macroeconomic policy with the result that imports of technology were strongly affected. The number of technology imports in this phase declined consistently. As Table 4.3 shows, the number of contracts in 1988 was only 437: 25 per cent below the previous year. There was a further reduction to 328 in 1989 and to 232 in 1990. It was not until 1991 that the number recovered, but even then it was well below the 1987 level.

However, comparison of Tables 4.1 and 4.3 shows that this was associated with an increase in the average value of the contracts, and that the position in terms of the aggregate value of technology imports was one of stagnation rather than decline. Despite the reduced number of contracts their total value was US$500 million higher in 1988 than in 1987. After a fall in 1989 and 1990 the value recovered in 1991 to regain, but not surpass, the 1988 level of US$3.5 billion.

As can also be seen from Table 4.3, the structure of technology imports in this period changed strongly in favour of hardware (whole-plant imports) and

Table 4.3 China's technology imports by category, 1988–91

Category of imports	1988				1989				1991			
	Contracts		Value		Contracts		Value		Contracts		Value	
	No.	%	US$ m	%	No.	%	US$ m	%	No.	%	US$ m	%
Whole plant	212	49	3,019.9	85.0	194	59	2,723.6	93.0	217	61	2,911.0	84.0
Licences	169	39	476.6	13.0	96	29	148.4	5.0	116	32	478.0	14.0
Technical services	27	6	14.3	0.4	13	4	38.4	1.0	10	3	13.0	0.4
Consultancy	19	4	27.5	1.0	14	4	6.2	0.2	8	2	4.0	0.1
Co-production	10	2	10.0	0.3	11	3	6.6	0.2	8	2	53.0	1.5
Total	437	100	3,548.3	100	328	100	2,923.2	100	359	100	3,459.0	100

Source: As for Table 4.1

away from software. The proportion of imports in this form was well over 80 per cent in these years, markedly above the level of the early 1980s. This switch back to whole-plant imports caused considerable difficulties for enterprises wishing to renew plant and import components.

The distribution of imported technology focused mainly on primary industries, energy, oil and petrochemicals. In 1989, the share of these industries was 56 per cent of the total. In addition, changing political and economic relations between China and other countries had an effect on the country structure of technology imports. The economic sanctions of some western countries against China made the Commonwealth of Independent States and Italy the main sources of China's imported technology, replacing Japan, the United States of America and Germany.

In sum, the contractionary macroeconomic policy, to which were added the effects of sanctions, created many difficulties for China's import of software technology. The import of hardware technology took the dominant percentage in this period, with no fundamental improvement in the pattern of technology imports.

The Main Features of Technology Imports since 1992

In 1992 China entered a new phase of high-speed growth, during this phase the establishment of the socialist market system was set as the main objective of institutional reform. In the transitional economy that developed, the challenge of new problems and difficulties had to be faced. These challenges extended to the work of importing technology. The changing role of the government was crucial in this.

In the 1980s, the government was the main actor in the import of technology, and enterprises accepted or adopted passively whatever the government introduced. In recent years the roles of the government and enterprises have been changing: enterprises are becoming independent economic entities that have to be responsible and assume the risks involved in the import of technology. This is in contrast to the 1980s, when the government had authoritative power in decision-making on imported projects of technology and enterprises did not concern themselves with the economic effects of the new technology. In the 1990s, enterprises have been given much more autonomy to import technology, and the role of the government is diminishing: its main task is now to set macro targets for technology imports, not to seek micro-control of the structure and content of such imports.

Against this background, the scale of technology imports by value has tended to decline. In 1992, there was a total of about 625 imported projects, with a total value of US$1.7 billion. In 1993, the number of projects fell to 385, with the contracted value declining to US$1.4 billion. The underlying causes for this decline were many, including the continued effect of contractionary macroeconomic policies and a growing sense among enterprises of their responsibility or the risks relating to technology imports.

The structure of imported technology in these two years focused on electronics, textiles, motor vehicles, machinery and light industry. Furthermore, the import of software technology in the form of technical licences, technical services, consultancy and information accounted for 18 per cent of expenditure in 1992 and decreased to 11 per cent in 1993. The import of hardware (equipment) reached 82 per cent in 1992 and remained at about 89 per cent in 1993. The industry structure reveals that the key industries were the good economic performers, i.e. the car, electronics and textile industries, since these industries had the funds and foreign exchange as a result of continuing decentralization. The high share of hardware in technology imports reveals that enterprises put more emphasis on the direct economic benefits brought by hardware and still doubted whether the costs of investment in assimilating and absorbing technology were worthwhile.

It should be pointed out that since 1992 inward foreign direct investment (FDI) has become a strong force in the development of China's economy, and this has created a new channel for the import of technology. It is certain that with a high growth rate, inward FDI will become the main form of China's technology imports.[1]

THE COSTS AND BENEFITS OF TECHNOLOGY IMPORTS

It is obvious that large-scale imports of foreign technology since the 1980s have contributed to the high growth rate of the national economy, to the upgrading of industrial structures and to the development of new products and goods. More specifically, a group of new industries has been established as a result of upgrading and changing the industrial structure.

Before the 1980s, China had an irrational industrial structure, in three senses: first, light industry was quite backward and failed to grow on the scale called for by the demands for a rising standard of living. The technology of light industry was far behind or, at best, was kept at the level normal in the developed countries in the 1950s and 1960s. Second, heavy industry was on a track of technological repetition with no secular trend of progress. Third, the newly developed industries were moving too slowly to form a critical mass. All these problems restrained the growth rate and healthy development of China's economy.

With large-scale imports of technology since the 1980s, the capital stock of the machinery, electronics, petrochemical, light, transportation and communication sectors has been renovated, and this has increased the productivity of these sectors. In addition, the transfer of technology has promoted structural change. Thus on one side, the processing industry has increased its share in the gross national product, while on the other, a fundamental change of structure inside the processing industry has led to the gradual formation of a network of closely connected industries producing raw materials, processed and final consumer goods. Meanwhile, a new group of industries, including electronics, optical communication and biotechnology, has emerged. All this has laid a foundation for narrowing the technological gap with the developed economies and for continuing rapid and healthy growth.

In addition, several large and medium state-owned enterprises have become the main force in economic development through the renovation of technology. Before the 1980s, most Chinese enterprises suffered from obsolete machinery and equipment, backward technology and poor management. It was a tough task for most of them to face the challenge of foreign enterprises in China's domestic market, and the import of technology was an effective way for Chinese enterprises to improve their competitiveness.

Since the 1980s, over 50 per cent of the large and medium state-owned enterprises have imported technology, equipment and technical services through various channels to improve their technical level and management skills. As a result, the quality of their products has been improved, and this has led to an expansion of both their share in the domestic market and their capacity to export. Many of these enterprises can now work to high international standards and produce internationally marketable goods. Typical products in this category include colour TVs, refrigerators and washing machines. China's achievement in exporting ships is also particularly noteworthy, and the unquantifiable learning effects of all these changes are also important.

However, in spite of great achievements, problems still exist in our technology importing. One aspect of this is that weak macro-control and poor administrative instruments have allowed excessive duplication of some technology imports. These problems have become worse under the open door policy and there are many underlying causes for this. In particular, after enterprises and local governments were given more autonomy, they all sought to import projects with high economic returns and, as a result of such indiscriminate profit-seeking behaviour, much duplication occurred. One obvious example was that over a hundred production lines for colour TVs and dozens of refrigerator production lines were imported in the late 1980s. In spite of their positive role in the development of our national production, these lines were imported at extremely high cost. Similar patterns in the import of technologies for non-oxygen coppermaking, tins with easy opening devices, silicon steel cutters and video tapes led to oversupply, overstocking and waste.

There has also been too much emphasis on the importance of the hardware form of technology. This has led to poor assimilation of the technology introduced, and there has been no improvement in China's self-sufficiency rates for key commodities. But although in the short term the direct import of technology can achieve quick economic results, strictly speaking, this kind of equipment import has been a tool to enhance productivity rather than to transfer technology. In the long run, this kind of technology importing will simply make us consumers of foreign high-technology products rather than proprietors.

For a developing country, the import of technology, its assimilation and absorption should be integrated parts of a single process. The experience of Japan and South Korea has shown that the ratio of absorption to initial purchase costs for imported technology should be of the order of 3:1. In other words, one yuan spent on the import of technology needs three yuan for its assimilation and absorption. Unfortunately, Chinese enterprises have paid too much attention to the import of technology and have overlooked the absorption issue. Expenditures on absorption have typically been only 50 per cent of the initial import cost.

One of the underlying problems has been the short-termism of enterprises. In the early 1990s, China introduced the responsibility system under which enterprises contracted for certain plans with various incentives incorporated (that is, instead of receiving mandatory plans from bureaucrats). But managers' terms of office were too short for them to take care of the assimilation and absorption problems. Also, although funds for the import of technology were included in the state annual budget and guaranteed by every possible means, funds for absorption were not provided. Thus there were no funds for absorption, let alone improvement and innovation on the basis of the imported technology. A third problem is that lack of adequate preparation has led to undesirable economic effects from technology imports. Many Chinese enterprises were not fully prepared for the import of technology. They were mainly concerned with the advance of technology itself, neglecting the issue of the marketability of the products. Without careful, comparative analysis, some premature technologies were introduced and these failed to meet their targets.

Finally, many imports of technology were closely related to inward foreign direct investment (FDI). Many foreign investors set up joint ventures in China, supplying the necessary equipment and technology. In some joint ventures the value of the foreign-partner contributions in the form of equipment and technology was overestimated, with consequent harm to investors and the Chinese partner. Furthermore, some of the foreign equipment supplied under these deals incorporated out-of-date techniques. The problem of controlling these unsatisfactory contracts has become an urgent one for the supervising administrative organs.

FUTURE STRATEGIES FOR CHINA'S IMPORT OF TECHNOLOGY

In the 1990s, China has entered a critical stage of economic development in which it will be essential to maintain a sustained, stable and rapid growth rate in order to join the ranks of the intermediate developed countries in the next century. Although many factors affected the development of the economy, the import of technology had been one of the important 'push' factors during the past fifteen years. It is believed that the import of technology will play an even more important role in the next ten years and in the longer run. It is important, therefore, that four basic principles are followed:

1. There must be adherence to government policies for the import of technology and for strengthening the dynamic impact of technical improvement. Despite recent advances, there is no doubt that China's technology is still at a relatively low level. The technology imported to date is far below the most advanced levels available in developed economies. Basically, we are still in the 1980s. Technology renovation is also badly needed in many Chinese enterprises. Much of the equipment still in use in China is out-of-date or obsolete by the standards of developed countries.

    Furthermore, we have a weak capacity for technological invention. Although some advanced technology and equipment has been imported, Chinese enterprises have failed to promote research and development in new technology. This is primarily due to lack of funds for assimilation and absorption of imported technology. Our capacity for research and development is still largely a capacity to imitate; and importing technology has not had the effect of strengthening our ability to develop new technologies independently. We must make great efforts to change this.

2. We must adjust the structure of technology imports to one that favours the less-tangible forms of technology transfer (i.e. licences, consultancy, etc.) and relies less on 'hardware' in the form of equipment imports. As noted earlier, the import of equipment has accounted for about 80 per cent of all expenditures on technology imports, leaving only 20 per cent for other forms of technology transfer. In the early 1990s, imports of equipment retained their dominant position. Although many factors contribute to this, one of the most important has been unclear government policy. Further, the role of FDI has made control of technology trends even more difficult.

    In these circumstances official policy must make its objectives absolutely clear and these should be as follows: first, the import of high-level technology should be required to account for 50 per cent of the total value of the contracts which use funds raised by enterprises (i.e. loans, retained earnings, etc., as distinct from government-allocated funds); second, in the case of foreign investment, these projects should have imports of pure technology, services, patents, etc., equal to equipment imports. Particularly in the coastal areas of south-east China, the technological level expected of foreign investment should be upgraded, ensuring that investment inflows and technological improvement are fully integrated.

3. We must strengthen macro-control of technology imports and ensure that all imports undergo similar procedures and are subject to common criteria. All the existing problems in the import of technology may be attributed to inappropriate overall macro-control; by macro-control in this context is meant control of the broad shape of the technology import programme. Problems created by lack of such control include duplication and the unthinking introduction of inappropriately low-level technologies.

   In China's market-oriented reform, market activity will play a more important role in the national economy. But in the import of technology, overemphasis on the market without proper macro-control will lead to bad results. It is absolutely necessary to strengthen this and to identify clear objectives, key projects and the overall structure of technology imports – bearing in mind particularly the problems of absorption and assimilation.

4. In selecting technology imports we must follow market-oriented principles, although this does not exclude a role for macro-control of the type mentioned above. Technology imports are now undertaken by many different industries and institutions and market prospects should be a key factor in choosing projects. However, some projects are closely related to national economic priorities and to the people's livelihood in ways that make purely market success an inappropriate criterion. Social factors must also be taken into account. Project selection by market principles requires that careful feasibility studies be made, that the technological advance in projects be evaluated, and that commercial considerations be taken fully into account.

The Need for Further Reform

To achieve all these objects will require further reform. First, we must re-model the main institutions involved in the import of technology through deepening the process of enterprise reform. Under the market principle, only when enterprises become fully independent economic entities, responsible for their profits and losses, will they be cautious in selecting and judging the feasibility of imported projects and be responsible for the risks and benefits in the import of technology. All these are the basic foundations for success in technology importing.

Great efforts should be made to deepen enterprise reform through establishing modern corporations, clarifying property rights, separating ownership from management rights, and nurturing a group of entrepreneurs. The success of the reform of large and medium-sized state enterprises and their conversion into modern corporations will have a direct impact upon the quality and efficiency of China's import of technology in future. For most enterprises, the joint stock company is a feasible form of organization for the reform.

The government will hold a majority of the shares of enterprises in all the major industries such as energy, electricity, transportation and communication, i.e. all sectors which have high priority in the national economy and are directly relevant to the people's livelihood. In other commercial and light industry enterprises, the government can give up its dominant position as the main shareholder and allow them to be transformed into joint-stock holding companies or privatized through leasing or auction. Only the realization of such enterprise reform will create the organizational structure needed for the import of technology.

Second, we must transform the function of the government in the import of technology. The government must improve macro-control, supervision and investment in major technology import projects. At present, governments at various levels interfere too much: they control the process through the allocation of funds, which leads to dispersion and waste of resources.

In future, government must concentrate on the big state projects and leave the rest to the enterprises themselves acting on their own initiative and using funds raised by themselves. Based on existing industrial policies, the manufacture of machinery, electronics, cars, petrochemicals and construction are the 'pillar' industries in the national economy; but their technology is remote from the standard that should be expected from them, and this must be changed by the policies outlined above.

Third, we must create a good environment for the import of technology through establishing intermediaries. Lack of intermediary services causes enterprises many difficulties since they are unable to target the technology that is badly needed. This problem has led some enterprises to suffer heavy losses due to inadequate feasibility studies and incorrect technology import choices. Without employing good services and the assistance of intermediaries, enterprises will not fulfil their technology import projects well. We need to use more private providers of services and consultancy for market surveys, data collection, information analysis and appraisal of technology and to act as agents for technology imports. In this way, the role of the government can be changed and the role of enterprises can be brought into full play as the real entities in the import of technology.

Lastly, we should have a policy to encourage inward foreign direct investment, together with the import of technology. With more foreign investment in China, more advanced technology will be imported. With FDI, full preparation and consideration will be given to the high cost that the Chinese enterprises will pay for any imports of technology, although foreign investors must also share certain risks. Usually, the excessive costs of technology imports to the Chinese side arise from two factors: one is the high valuation given to the foreign technology contribution in joint ventures, the other is the sharing of markets and profits. Therefore, when China introduces foreign investment in the car, pharmaceutical and electronics industries, government must give much more attention to the technology dimension of such transactions. Joint ventures by which foreign partners are either not bringing high-level technology or are unwilling to transfer the technology that they bring should be avoided.

By making great efforts during the past ten years, China has fulfilled its basic technology acquisition targets in a quantitative sense. What we have to do now is to produce a qualitative improvement. Our objective is clear and straightforward: it is to promote technological progress through foreign investment, and only by following the policies set out above shall we ensure that foreign investment does in fact enhance our technological level.

NOTE

1. For further discussion of the scale and effect of inward FDI, see Chapters 5 and 8 in this volume by Ding Jingping and Tang Shiguo.

5. Using imported technology to transform existing enterprises in China

Ding Jingping

INTRODUCTION

Before the period of reform, most of China's industrial enterprises were state-owned entities and the national economic system was highly concentrated and centralized. Government investment in this period was divided into two categories: funds for capital construction (i.e. for new or enlarged enterprises) and funds for technical transformation of existing enterprises. Before China embarked on policies of open door and reform, most of the investment funds for fixed assets were spent on building new enterprises, thus stimulating development in the extensive, quantitative sense. The result of this policy in the long run was that many existing enterprises failed to receive funds for their equipment renovation and technical transformation, and found themselves hampered by antiquated equipment, backward technology, reduced product quality and low profits.

Since 1979, China's open door and reform policies have been put into practice and imported manufactures have flooded into the Chinese market. Under these circumstances, the problems of China's existing enterprises became even more obvious. Their products were unable to compete with those from abroad due to problems of quality, variety, function and price, etc. Some enterprises even have no new products to enter the market with. The Chinese government was therefore forced to make a choice: either to let these backward enterprises go into bankruptcy or to assist them with funds for rapid transformation of technology and help them enhance their ability to survive and compete in the Chinese market. China was bound to follow the latter way, by providing more resources for the technical transformation of these enterprises.

The technical level of China's pre-1949 industry was low, and there existed a wide gap between Chinese industry and that of the developed countries. During the 1960s this gap became much wider as a result of frequent political movements and social instability. When Chinese enterprises were confronted with foreign competition in the 1980s, it was impossible for them to raise their level of competitiveness by using their own internal technological resources. The only effective way for them to narrow the gap of industrial technology as soon as possible was to introduce advanced technology from abroad. Thus, since the 1980s China has made use of imported technology to transform its enterprises on a vast scale.

This chapter will give a brief account of China's main practices and achievements in introducing new technology to transform existing enterprises, of the changing management system controlling the process of this introduction, and of the different viewpoints in China in relation to these issues. The term 'existing enterprises' is used here to distinguish the situation of older enterprises from that of newly established ones.

ACHIEVEMENTS AND PRACTICES USING IMPORTED TECHNOLOGY

The main period when China made use of imported technology to transform its existing enterprises on a vast scale was the 1980s, when efforts were exerted throughout the whole decade. These efforts produced great results, as is illustrated by the following facts. The government investment of funds in fixed assets allocated to technical transformation increased year by year. Prior to the 1980s, the proportion of the funds allocated to transformation and renovation was no more than 26 per cent of total national investment in fixed assets (see Table 5.1). This figure was much lower in the 1950s – at most 10 per cent. There were two reasons for the low figure at that time. On the one hand, China's prewar industrial foundation had been very backward and therefore many new enterprises were needed. On the other hand, the general thinking on industrial development at that time attached importance to establishing new enterprises while playing down the technical transformation of existing ones.

When China began carrying out its policies of openness and reform, Chinese enterprises began to realize the huge gap in technology and production standards compared to their foreign counterparts, and they began to pay attention to the transformation of technology. From 1981 to 1993, investment funds in national fixed assets allocated to capital construction increased by more than nine times from 45 billion yuan to 462 billion.[1] However, funds allocated to technical transformation and renovation increased by more than ten times from 19 billion yuan to 220 billion. The proportion of funds allocated to technical transformation in total investment increased step by step. In the 1980s, the average proportion was more than 30 per cent, the highest figure (in 1988) being 35.5 per cent (see Table 5.1 for details). An even higher proportion could be seen in some of the large-scale individual cases and

Table 5.1　Chinese government investment in fixed assets, 1953–93 (annual averages, billion yuan)

	Total investment (bn yuan)	Capital construction		Technical renovation and transformation		Other investment[a] (bn yuan)
		(bn yuan)	(% of total)	(bn yuan)	(% of total)	
1953–57	12.3	11.8	96.2	0.5	3.8	–
1958–62	26.1	24.1	92.3	2.0	7.7	–
1963–65	10.0	8.4	84.5	1.6	15.5	–
1966–70	24.2	19.5	80.7	4.7	19.3	–
1971–75	45.5	35.9	78.9	9.6	21.1	–
1976–80	63.7	46.8	73.5	16.9	26.5	–
1981	67.8	45.3	66.4	19.5	29.3	2.9
1982	84.5	55.6	65.7	25.0	29.6	3.9
1983	95.2	59.4	62.4	29.1	30.6	6.7
1984	118.5	74.3	62.7	30.9	26.1	13.3
1985	168.1	107.4	64.0	44.9	26.7	15.7
1986	197.9	117.6	59.4	61.9	31.3	18.3
1987	229.8	134.3	58.4	75.9	33.0	19.6
1988	276.3	157.4	57.0	98.1	35.5	20.8
1989	253.5	155.2	61.2	78.9	31.1	19.5
1990	291.9	170.4	58.4	83.0	28.2	38.5
1991	362.8	211.6	58.3	102.3	28.2	48.9
1992	527.4	301.3	57.1	146.1	27.7	80.0
1993	765.8	461.6	60.3	219.6	28.7	84.7

Note:　[a]　Before 1981 figures for 'other investment' are included in investment in technical renovation and transformation.

Source:　Zhongguo tongji nianjian, 1994 (1995).

many enterprises thereby not only enhanced their productive capacity but also improved their technical level and product quality.

Since 1990, China has put even more stress on technical transformation. In the three years from 1991 to 1993, the accumulated investment funds in national fixed assets allocated to technical transformation reached the high point of 468 billion yuan, which far surpassed the total of 398 billion spent during the period of China's Seventh Five-Year Plan from 1986 to 1990. The average increase in the rate of growth of the funds for transformation in these three years was 38.2 per cent. Investment in technical transformation has created 331 billion yuan of new accumulated fixed assets for state-owned enterprises.[2]

The policy in spending these funds has been to focus on relaxing bottleneck industries and encouraging export business to create foreign exchange; 281 billion yuan of the technical transformation funds were spent in this way, with funds for energy-saving projects and for projects to increase product variety and quality accounting for 60 per cent of the total. In 1993, 111 billion yuan of the transformation funds were allocated to developing energy resources, improving the conditions of traffic, transportation and telecommunications, and increasing production of raw materials. These funds accounted for 50.7 per cent of the total annual investment for technical transformation.[3]

In the meantime, more funds for technical transformation investment were arranged for projects in processing enterprises in the export trades to increase foreign exchange earnings. For instance, in the textile industry, special projects to help promote the export of high-quality textiles were provided with support from these funds. By the end of 1993, 404 technical transformation projects were carried out in line with these objectives, using a total of 4.90 billion yuan of technical transformation funds.

Another example in light industry was the special arrangement made for projects to encourage enterprises mainly engaged in export production. By the end of 1993, 108 such projects were completed and had started production, the total investment funds being 1.52 billion yuan. These investments resulted in valuable achievements and the foreign exchange earnings of light industry rose to account for a third of China's total exports. In addition, exports of machinery and electronic products for light industry earned a third of the foreign exchange earned by the machinery and electronic product sectors overall.[4]

If we turn to the regional dimension of this investment, we find that the emphasis of investment has been put on the technical transformation of six old industrial bases. Over quite a long period, these bases paid the state more in tax and profits than they received in investment funds. After forty years of this treatment their competitiveness had greatly deteriorated. Since 1990, the state has selected these six old industrial bases and supported them with special funds for technical transformation to improve their difficult situation. The six are: Shanghai, Tianjin, Shengyang, Harbin, Chongqing and Wuhan. From 1991 to 1993, 1,015 transformation projects were arranged in these cities with a total of 28.3 billion yuan invested. Of these, 674 were completed and production started. The transformation brought about 7.7 billion yuan in profits tax and US$500 million in foreign exchange.[5]

Acceleration of Technology Imports

Large-scale technology imports began in the early 1950s. At that time, the main object of the transfer was to import complete sets of equipment from the former USSR and East European countries for China's new enterprises. Between 1950 and 1959, China imported 215 sets of equipment from the USSR and three from East European countries. China also imported 122 individual items of equipment and production lines. The total cost was US$2.7 billion. In one decade, China used this imported equipment to create entire new industrial sectors and to lay the foundation of its industrial development.

In the 1960s, because of China's political turmoil at home, technology transfer was suspended. Between 1963 and 1968, China imported only 84 items of technology and equipment from Japan, Germany, Britain, France, Italy and some of the East European countries, the total cost being US$300 million. These imported items were mainly related to metallurgy, chemical engineering, textiles, machinery, oil extraction and processing and the electrical industry. Most of the imported equipment was installed in new enterprises.

In the 1970s, China's relations with western countries improved and the scale and scope of technology imports expanded. Thus, from 1973 to 1978 China signed 250 or more import contracts, totalling more than US$3.96 billion. These contracts included thirteen sets of chemical fertilizer equipment, the annual production capacity of each of which was 300,000 tons of synthetic ammonia or urea. Other items included four sets of chemical fibre manufacturing equipment, twenty-two petrochemical production lines, 1.7 metre steel rolling machines, and Spey (aero) turbines, etc. They were applied to newly established enterprises as well as to some established factories for technical transformation.

Since 1980, China has carried out its policies of openness and reform, and the scale of both economic development and technical transformation has grown remarkably. From 1979 to 1990, China spent US$17 billion for more than 7,000 items of technology imported from abroad. Local government planners used US$13 billion to buy more than 10,000 imported technology items.

After 1980, the work of importing technology gained new momentum in an attempt to help China narrow the technological gap with the developed countries as soon as possible. In 1982, the State Council instructed the State Economic Commission to import 3,000 items of advanced foreign technology and to accelerate the pace of imports during the last three years of the Sixth Five-Year Plan (1980–85). In September 1982, the State Economic Commission, following instructions from the Party Central Committee and the State Council, delivered its *Report on the Arrangement of Imported Technology to Reform Medium and Small Enterprises* and a *Draft Plan for Using $3 billion US Dollars of State Foreign Exchange to Import 3,000 Items of Advanced Technology from Abroad for Improving Existing Enterprises in the Last Three Years of the Sixth Five-Year Plan* (the *3,000 Items Plan*).

The report on the Sixth Five-Year Plan of the Fifth Session of the Fifth Chinese People's Congress also asked the State Economic Commission to 'implement the items one by one and guarantee the time of completion'. The plan was started in 1983. By the end of 1985 the State Economic Commission had signed 4,450 contracts with other countries worth more than US$4 billion. Thus, 660 items worth US$603 million were contracted in 1983; 1,562 items worth US$150 million were contracted in 1984; and 2,222 items worth US$2,004 million in 1985. Most of these projects were for technology classed as 'advanced level' by the international standards of the late 1970s and early 1980s. Thus the implementation of the *3,000 Item Plan* had a big impact on a variety of regions and sectors.[6]

Benefits of Large-scale Importation of Technology

Technology imports have promoted the adjustment of China's backward industrial and productive structures and improved their ability to compete. With technical transformation, China has swiftly developed or set up a great number of the industries that previously had poor or no foundations. These include particularly the consumer durable industries that manufacture colour TV sets, washing machines, refrigerators and vacuum cleaners, etc. These new products and developing enterprises have not only transformed China's original, backward technological structures in industry, but have improved their profitability.

Generally speaking, surveys of key point renovation projects suggest that for every 1 yuan invested, output value increased 1.5 to 2 yuan, while profit and taxes increased 0.4–0.5 yuan. In the light and textile industries, for each US$1 of investment an increase of $3 was obtained in foreign exchange. According to a number of investigations in provinces and municipalities, 60 per cent of the increased industrial output value since 1980 was achieved with the support of these special funds for technical improvement and renovation. From 1979 to 1988, China's total industrial output value increased by 3.5 times from 468 billion yuan to 1,822 billion and much of this is the result of these expenditures as well.

The competitive ability of Chinese products in international markets has been greatly enhanced, and this is reflected in increased exports. As the scale of China's imports of technology used to transform existing enterprises has grown, many Chinese industrial products have shown an enhanced ability to compete in world trade. In addition to strength in the light, textile and electrical industries, China's ship export business is now the third largest in the world, behind only Japan and South Korea. During the ten years from 1979 to 1988, 1,200 technical items were imported to enhance the technical level of the machinery industry and, after study and development, 70 per cent of these entered production and new products began to replace those previously imported.

Technical imports also have the effect of training a cadre of newly skilled personnel. In the process of importation, Chinese enterprises selected tens of thousands of senior managers, engineering and other staff to go abroad to observe and study foreign technology. This has broadened their vision and improved their business ability. The achievements in this respect are hard to value in monetary terms, but are very important.

Finally, many enterprises have taken the opportunity to use technical renovation to solve problems of environmental pollution, save energy and improve working conditions. For example, in the ten years from 1978 to 1988, Jiangsu Province invested 680 million yuan in technical transformation work to save energy resources. With these funds, more than 560 industrial boilers were improved and this saved 1.6 million tons of coal annually. In the whole decade, Shanghai used 350 million yuan to handle waste and effluent problems, and the city of Suzhou moved 381 enterprises in the course of technical transformation, thereby restoring the beauty of the most famous city in Jiangnan.

FOREIGN INVESTMENT AND INDUSTRIAL TRANSFORMATION

Foreign investment in China has not only brought large amounts of capital to China, but has also advanced management skills, technology and equipment. In this sense, the absorption of large amounts of foreign investment has been an effective way to import technology. Since 1979, China has enlarged its inflow of foreign investment year by year. In 1983, China actually used US$1.9 billion of foreign capital (see the first column in the lower panel of Table 5.2). In 1989, the amount exceeded US$10 billion, and it has continued to increase, reaching almost US$20 billion in 1992 and US$39 billion in 1993.

Direct investment has become the main form of foreign investment in China. In 1983, China absorbed only US$636 million in foreign direct investment, which was only one-third of the total amount of foreign investment in the country. In 1992, direct investment from abroad rose to US$11 billion and was half the total, and in 1993 it reached over US$27 billion and accounted for two-thirds of total foreign investment (see Table 5.2).

There are three main methods by which foreign direct investment enters China. The main form is Chinese–foreign joint ventures; the two others are wholly foreign-owned enterprises and co-operative operations. As Table 5.3 shows, the total amount of foreign direct investment in 1993 was US$111 billion, of which US$55 billion was for joint ventures, US$25 billion for co-operative operations, and US$30 billion was invested by foreign-owned enterprises.

The classification of investing countries and regions is shown in Table 5.4. Except for Hong Kong, the biggest investors in China are Japan, Taiwan and

Table 5.2   *Contracted and utilized foreign capital in China, 1979–93 (US$ billion)*

	Total		Foreign loans		Foreign direct investment		Other foreign investments
	Number	Value	Number	Value	Number	Value	Value
A.	*Total value of foreign capital in signed contracts or agreements*						
1979–82	949	20.55	27	13.55	922	6.01	0.10
1983	522	3.43	52	1.51	470	1.73	0.18
1984	1,893	4.79	38	1.92	1,856	2.65	0.22
1985	3,145	9.87	72	3.53	3,073	5.93	0.40
1986	1,551	11.74	53	8.41	1,498	2.83	0.50
1987	2,289	12.14	56	7.82	2,233	3.71	0.61
1988	6,063	16.00	118	9.81	5,945	5.30	0.89
1989	5,909	11.48	130	5.18	5,779	5.60	0.69
1990	7,371	12.09	98	5.10	7,273	6.60	0.39
1991	13,086	19.58	108	7.16	12,978	11.98	0.44
1992	48,858	69.44	94	10.70	48,764	58.12	0.61
1993	83,595	123.27	158	11.31	83,437	111.44	0.53
B.	*Total value of foreign capital actually used*						
1979–82		12.46		16.09		1.17	0.60
1983		1.92		1.06		0.64	0.28
1984		2.70		1.29		1.26	0.16
1985		4.65		2.69		1.66	0.30
1986		7.26		5.01		1.87	0.37
1987		8.45		5.80		2.31	0.33
1988		10.23		6.49		3.19	0.54
1989		10.06		6.29		3.39	0.38
1990		10.29		6.53		3.49	0.27
1991		11.55		6.89		4.37	0.31
1992		19.20		7.91		11.01	0.28
1993		38.96		11.19		27.51	0.26

Note: Because of rounding, components may not sum to totals.

Source: See Table 5.1

the United States. In 1993, total investment was US$39 billion dollars of which US$19 billion dollars came from Hong Kong, 48.5 per cent of the whole; US$5 billion from Japan (12.6 per cent); US$3 billion from Taiwan (8.2 per cent); and US$2.7 billion from the United States (6.8 per cent). These four countries and regions thus accounted for 76 per cent of total foreign investment in China. A further US$3 billion was invested by France, the United Kingdom, Italy, Germany and other European countries.

Table 5.3   Contracted foreign capital in China, by type of investment, 1992 and 1993 (US$ billion)

	1992		1993	
	No. of contracts	Value	No. of contracts	Value
1. Foreign loans	94	10.70	158	11.31
(a) Government loans	75	4.39	132	2.89
(b) Loans from international monetary organizations	19	2.17	26	3.81
(c) Others		4.14		4.61
2. Foreign direct investments	48,764	58.12	83,437	111.44
(a) Joint ventures	34,354	29.13	54,003	55.17
(b) Co-operative operations	5,711	13.26	10,445	25.50
(c) Co-operative developments	7	0.04	14	.31
(d) Foreign enterprises	8,692	15.70	18,975	30.46
3. Other foreign investment[a]		0.61		0.53
(a) Compensation trade		0.41		0.07
(b) Processing and assembly		0.12		0.27
(c) International rent		0.08		0.20
Total	48,858	69.44	83,595	123.27

Note: [a] Other foreign investment includes the value of equipment supplied by foreign businesses in transactions involving compensation trade, processing and assembly, and the value of equipment supplied in financial leasing transactions.

Source: See Table 5.1.

Table 5.4   Foreign capital actually used in China, by lending country, 1993 (US$ billion)

	Total foreign capital	Foreign loans	Foreign direct investment and other
Asia			
Hong Kong	18.893	1.448	17.445
Japan	4.906	3.545	1.361
Taiwan	3.139	—	3.139
Singapore	0.675	0.183	0.492
Macao	0.624	0.037	0.588
Korea	0.384	0.003	0.382
Thailand	0.234	—	0.234
Philippines	0.122	—	0.122
Kuwait	0.119	0.034	0.084
Malaysia	0.091	—	0.091
Other[a]	0.109	—	0.109
North America			
USA	2.662	0.595	2.068
Canada	0.362	0.225	0.137
Europe			
France	0.775	0.633	0.141
United Kingdom	0.571	0.350	0.220
Italy	0.362	0.262	0.100
Germany	0.274	0.212	0.062
Spain	0.245	0.236	0.010
Belgium	0.147	0.121	0.026
The Netherlands	0.134	0.050	0.084
Sweden	0.119	0.096	0.023
Switzerland	0.093	0.046	0.047
Other[b]	0.229	0.155	0.074
Australia	0.187	0.076	0.110
International organizations			
World Bank	1.905	1.905	—
Other[c]	0.364	0.364	—
Others[d]	1.214	0.613	0.600
Total	38.960	11.189	27.771

Notes:
a   Burma, Israel, N. Korea, United Arab Emirates, Vietnam and Indonesia
b   Denmark, Luxembourg, Austria, Finland, Hungary, Norway, Romania, Russia and Yugoslavia
c   Includes Asian Development Bank
d   Includes Latin America and Africa

Source: See Table 5.1.

These investments from developed countries and regions resulted not only in the introduction of advanced technology and equipment, but also of advanced management experience. For example, China set up joint ventures with Belgium, Germany and Japan to establish three enterprises for the manufacture of telephone exchange controllers, and the output of these projects now constitutes 90 per cent of the national output. Similarly, joint ventures with France, Germany and the United States in the auto sector now produce 80 per cent of the country's auto output. Thus joint-venture enterprises are playing an important role in several industries in China.

TECHNOLOGY IMPORTS AND REFORM OF THE SYSTEM OF TECHNOLOGY MANAGEMENT

Before 1979, the technical transformation of industrial enterprises, like other economic work in China, was entirely under the tightly centralized control of the government. Under this system, enterprises had to surrender all income, including depreciation funds, to the centre. All expenditures, including the cost of equipment renovation, had to be applied for to central or controlling bodies. Thus enterprises only controlled three kinds of technical transformation and development funds allocated by the planning authorities: the funds for general overhauls; funds for technical measures; and funds for new product testing. However, these funds were very limited in amount and function.

China's technology imports were also controlled by the central government. Generally speaking, they were under the control of the State Planning Commission on the basis of discussions with related industrial and foreign trading ministries. Enterprises, no matter whether newly built or existing, had no voice in planning. As for the connections between technical transformation and renovation, these were also controlled and balanced by the State Planning Commission and various industrial leading bodies. Enterprises themselves were essentially passive.

Since 1979, changes have taken place in the state management of importing technology to transform enterprises. The former State Economic Commission was abolished and because, even as early as 1978, the scale of China's import business was getting beyond the state's capability to plan, the State Commission for Imports and Exports was established. However, this and various other new arrangements failed because they were not consistent with decentralization and reform and because of the handing over of responsibilities to lower levels of government. They were also not in line with the requirement that enterprises should be given more autonomous rights.

In 1988, the government accelerated the transformation of state-owned enterprises in order to develop them in a vigorous way. Some enterprises belonging to central government ministries of various kinds were thus handed over to province- or municipality-level management. At the same time a number of government management branches were merged or simplified, including the State Economic Commission. After the State Economic Commission was abolished, its central management of technical imports and transformation was transferred to the State Planning Commission.

However, different provinces and cities adopted different methods; thus whereas some also merged the (local branches of the) Economic and Planning Commissions, others left them and their functions unchanged. At the same time, central and local levels implemented new systems that allowed localities to retain budgetary funds and foreign exchange above agreed limits (i.e. to provide localities with incentives to maximize revenues and foreign exchange earnings) and these new arrangements greatly enhanced local authority control over imports for technical renovation.

After these reforms, therefore, the management of national technical importing by the central government may be summed up as follows. First, the central government took back all authority to permit the use of foreign exchange from its various branches, and the State Planning Commission was put in charge of routine procedures for approval. When local governments needed to use their foreign exchange quota and the investment amount was below agreed limits, the central government took no steps to intervene. The limits were different in different regions: US$10 million in Shanghai, US$5 million in Tianjin and Beijing, and US$3 million in other provinces. In cases where local government did have to apply to use foreign exchange, every cent had to be approved by the central authority. In this way, a clear line of demarcation was drawn between the authority of central and local governments.

In the meantime, local governments had considerably more authority in the management of technology imports according to their own plans. Following the handing down (*xia fang*) of powers in this way, the enthusiasm as well as the power to import technology at local levels grew quickly – particularly in the coastal regions, where rising foreign exchange earnings and consequent increased foreign exchange retentions gave great scope for local initiatives. As a result, there was a growing inequality in opportunities for importing technology between coastal and inland areas.

The rise of self-management in the importation of foreign technology and the increase in the channels open for import business resulted in a serious problem of statistical co-ordination for central government. After 1988, it became difficult for government to obtain a clear picture of the national situation. Since 1988, the statistics for China's technology imports have been derived from the central foreign exchange record, and it has been difficult to get exact statistics from local governments. With the heightened speed of local economic development and the increased ability to earn and retain foreign exchange, the scale of local technical imports became much bigger. However, no single office is able to grasp the overall situation and deliver a reliable, comprehensive statistical picture of what is happening.

In 1992, the State Economic and Trade Commission was established, but this did not have much influence on the management of technical imports. The management of technology transformation was transferred from the State Planning Commission to the State Economic and Trade Commission, where it became one of the new body's major duties. The Bureau of Technology Transformation under the State Economic and Trade Commission was responsible for concrete arrangements to sponsor approval procedures and the practical application of important, large-scale projects of technology transformation. As state financial bodies increasingly changed the appropriation funds into loans for the state-owned enterprises, the State Economic and Trade Commission also changed its approach to that of controlling the scale of funds rather than controlling the technical transformation itself.

Thus every year the State Planning Commission allocates a certain quota of bank loans to the State Economic and Trade Commission for its use in support of technology transformation at the local levels. The latter then distributes the loans to the respective local units. This has been the outstanding change made by the State Economic and Trade Commission in the management of technology transformation.

However, this system has a weak point: the local governments and enterprises behave as if indifferent to the interest rate on the loans from the bank, and always try to obtain loans as if they were (interest free) appropriations, as indeed they were under the old system. The fundamental reason for this is that state-owned enterprises have not yet become independent entities, responsible for their production and marketing decisions in a real sense. They are not worried about the high rates which might bring the risk of loss to the enterprises. Their only concern is that they may fail to receive loans and may not be able to fulfil their grand investment plans.

On the other hand, swift changes are taking place in the ownership system of the Chinese economy. More and more non-state-owned enterprises, including collectives, township and rural enterprises, foreign invested businesses, private and joint ventures, etc., are appearing in the economy. The State Economic and Trade Commission is now facing the question as to whether or not loans for technical transformation should be restricted to state enterprises. The case against the old system is that many collective, township and rural enterprises make higher returns on their investment. And indeed, if there were a fully competitive system for fund allocation, many state enterprises could not successfully compete and hence would fall further and further behind. Thus in the discussion on the financial resources which the state controls for the enterprises' technology transformation, the question must be faced of how to make use of them in a fair and effective way.

Generally speaking, the present management system for technology transformation is much more flexible than before. More financial resources for technical transformation and more channels to select the technology are now available. The technical transformation of state-owned enterprises, however, is now just part of the task facing the whole nation. For with the growing proportion of non-state-owned enterprises, state enterprises are taking a declining share in national technology transformation projects. Thus, when we examine the issue of how China uses imported technology to transform its existing enterprises we need increasingly to see more than simply the work going on in the state sector.

DIFFERENT VIEWPOINTS AND EVALUATIONS

The use of imported technology to transform existing enterprises is playing an important role in rapidly raising the technical level of China's existing enterprises. It is quite clear that after a decade of openness and reform, China's economic strength is growing, and many enterprises have raised their technical level to a fairly high degree. Without imported technology to transform existing enterprises, these achievements could not have been made. However, there are differing views in China's academic and political circles about the precise way forward in implementing technology policies. The four main issues are summarized below.

First, which kinds of technology should be imported into China at the initial stage: 'hard' or 'soft'? By 'soft' technology is meant technical design, know-how, blueprints and other purely technological forms. 'Hard' technology refers to production lines and equipment. Most of the technology imports of the 1980s were of the hard type, and these amounted to 90 per cent of total imported technology. In recent years the proportion of soft items has risen somewhat, but not dramatically. This situation has led to acute disputes within China's academic, political and industrial circles. Debate has particularly focused on the *3,000 Items Plan*, implemented by the former State Economic Commission in the 1980s.

The main point of contention has been whether it is correct to import foreign equipment and production lines on a large scale and whether such imports count as technology imports in a fundamental sense. Those who have negative views do not consider such projects to be true technology imports, but merely forms of trade. The other side believes that such imports can be technology transfers, provided they embody technology new to China. They consider that as a developing country China is correct to continue to import new hardware, and they point out that this view is shared by UNIDO and the World Bank.

The second issue concerns the question of whether technical imports should focus on 'upstream' or 'downstream' products. Before the 1980s, little attention was paid to light industry in China and, as a result, the supply of ordinary consumer goods was limited. This was particularly true of consumer durables that were much in demand and freely available in western countries (e.g. refrigerators, washing machines, TV sets, tape recorders). In the early 1980s, the central government delegated part of their previously centralized investment authority to provinces and cities to enable them to speed up the transformation of enterprises with imported technology. These local governments immediately put their funds into manufacturing light industry products. Within a very short space of time, China imported more than 120 TV production lines, more than 100 lines for washing machine manufacturing and several dozen production lines for refrigerators. In order to meet the component and materials needs of these lines, a large quantity of parts and accessories had to be imported from abroad, especially from Japan, and assembled for the Chinese market.

This approach is known as the upstream strategy, and it is hotly debated. The advantages of this method are as follows: only a short period of time is needed before manufacturing begins and the markets are quickly supplied. The disadvantages are that because of the focus on upstream products and the low rate of component self-reliance, the foreign exchange costs of this approach are high and the learning process somewhat limited. In spite of these debates, many local authorities continue to follow the upstream policy. Which line is correct?

The next question involves the balance between central and local power in relation to the introduction of new technology. Before 1982 China's technology imports were managed under the leadership of central authorities. After that date the State Economic Commission decentralized part of this power over technology imports to provinces and cities at the same time as implementing the *3,000 Item Plan*. These decentralization arrangements varied in different places, leading to a situation of widely varying administrative arrangements by which technology could be imported. As a result, there was much duplication, especially of washing machine and television lines.

Critics argued that decentralization had been a mess and that central leadership should be strengthened. According to this view, this was the only way the country could avoid continuous unnecessary imports and save foreign exchange. Others held that some decentralization was necessary and that some duplication was an inevitable and worthwhile price for this. In their view the main trend was a good one and should be confirmed. It was also recognized that changing the planning system while undergoing rapid change was difficult, and that it was necessary to strengthen the quality of local management.

The final debate has dealt with the issue of whether imported or local technology should be adopted in transforming existing enterprises. In recent decades China has trained its own specialists in the fields of science and technology and of research and development. Apart from the Chinese Academy of Sciences, almost every industrial ministry, province and city had its own structure of professional R&D staff. However, for various reasons, most domestic technology and equipment remained at a low level or was unable to reach the standard required by modern industrial production. Thus, when China opened to the world and foreign technology and equipment were imported into this country, domestic technology was unable to compete effectively.

As growing numbers of users bought technology and equipment from abroad, Chinese machine and capital goods manufacturers and domestic R&D structures were threatened with extinction. Under these circumstances some argued for protection. Others, however, argued that openness had to be a two-way process of export and import expansion. Thus when users wished to import we should not interfere with their choices, although we should help domestic producers upgrade technically and improve their marketing. When the users are able to make choices, we should not control their wish to purchase. We should try to help our domestic producers to improve the quality of their production and marketing services.

Others have argued that to make the transition to market mechanisms in a single leap is too difficult and that we need a period of transition during which the environment in terms of prices, fiscal arrangements and so on is changed. Indeed, it is only very recently that we finally abolished the 'dual track' price system in which one set of prices was used for the planned component of the economy and another for transactions outside the planned arena.

The above account illustrates some of the major views on the debates relating to technology imports in our country. These are the kind of exchanges that occur after a long period of historical development that has mainly tended in one direction. Because of the burden of historically formed attitudes it is not easy to reach an immediate resolution of these issues, but as time passes things clarify, and this whole process must be regarded as an inevitable part of the development of China's opening up to the outside world. Somehow the needs of opening up and marketization have to be reconciled with the preservation of China's domestic technological capabilities and policies to integrate these with the productive sector of the economy.

THE PROSPECTS FOR CHINA'S FUTURE USE OF IMPORTED TECHNOLOGY

We have now enjoyed ten years and more of technology imports. From the policy viewpoint this is just the beginning, and because of the size of the technology gap between China and the outside world we have to maintain our policies for closing the gap, whatever the difficulties. We shall have to try new initiatives in technology transfer and implement the policy of using imported technology for a long time.

In future, however, the main change will be that power and initiative will have to shift from the government authorities to the enterprises themselves. In the case of some state-owned enterprises, the opportunity to exercise power in this way is still not available because authority over them remains with local planning organs. As the development of a market economy advances, power will have to be given to these large enterprises, and technical renovation will become a normal part of their routine.

It is no easy job to fulfil these targets. The transfer of authority from government departments to enterprises requires reform of the entire social and economic system. The following are the main lines of reform required. First, we shall need to reform and fully liberalize the foreign trade and foreign exchange control systems to allow decentralized choice and competition. Only by introducing the full market system will enterprises grasp the real costs of technology imports and adjust their behaviour accordingly.

Second, the state-owned enterprises will have to follow the road of separating the government from management, adopt the self-managing approach, and take sole responsibility for their own profits and losses. Up to the present, the overwhelming majority of state-owned enterprises are still under the control of government organs and have hardly any authority to make decisions. Their technology decisions are still decided externally and involve no real risks. The change of mechanism from loans to allocations has still not changed this.

Third, the suppliers of new technology in China – whether domestic or foreign – should have equal access to the market and opportunities to disseminate information. Thereafter, choices should be left to the users. Inevitably the international competition that results will have some negative effects on domestic suppliers, but in the long run this system will be beneficial. Protectionism is not the answer to China's problems.

China's plans to use imported technology started in the era of planning, continued in the era of mixed planning and market, and now continue as we move towards a more fully marketized system. This sequence must be appreciated if the changes we have made are to be properly understood. There is no point in attempting an abstract, ahistorical judgement about these issues. For the future, two major issues still require our attention: one is what role the government will play; the other is what function foreign technology will perform.

First, whereas the system previously gave government the key role in planning, in future under reform the government will have as its main responsibilities the overall shaping of the system, ensuring competition, undertaking macroeconomic management, welfare and environmental responsibilities, and providing appropriate support for R&D activities. In a socialist market economy all enterprises should be administered on the same basis. State-owned enterprises should have the same powers and face the same risks as other types of enterprise, and should not be directly controlled by the central government.

Second, as China's scientific strength and manufacturing ability grows, import substitution will increasingly take place. However, we have to take account of the fact that the world pace of technical change is extremely rapid and it will be impossible to achieve complete technological self-sufficiency. For this reason we shall remain active in technology trade, and foreign technology will find a broad market in China.

NOTES

1. The term billion is defined as a thousand million.
2. *Qiye jishu jinbu* (1994, p. 4).
3. Ibid.
4. Ibid.
5. Ibid., pp. 4–5.
6. *Zhongguo yinjin jishu gaizao xianyou qiye shinianjian, 1979–1988* (1994, p. 86).

REFERENCES

Dui dangqian guoyou qiye jishu gaizao qingkuang de diaocha fenxi [An Examination and Analysis of the Present Situation with Regard to Technical Transformation in Existing State Owned Enterprises] (1994), Beijing: China Industrial Economics Research Publishing House.
Qiye jishu jinbu [Technological Progress in Enterprises] (1994), Beijing, no. 6.
Wo guo jishu yinjin zhanliu yu zhengce yanjiu [Research on our Country's Policy and Strategy for Technology Imports] (1987), Beijing: State Scientific and Technology Commission and National Research Centre for Research and Development.
Zhongguo gongye jingji yanjiu [China Industrial Economics Research] (1994), no.11.
Zhongguo jishu yinjin sishinian, 1950–1990 [Forty Years of China's Technology Imports, 1950–1990] (1992), Shanghai: Huiwen Press.
Zhongguo tongji nianjian, 1994 [China Statistical Yearbook, 1994] (1995), Beijing: China Statistical Publishing House.

Zhongguo yinjin jishu gaizao xianyou qiye shinianjian, 1979–1988 [Ten Years of China's Technology Imports for Existing Enterprises, 1979–1988] (1994), Beijing: China Economic Publishing House.

6. The adoption of innovations and the assimilation of improvements

John Enos[1]

INTRODUCTION

A radical innovation, particularly if it is a process innovation, is likely to require a new plant for its assimilation. Moreover, it is likely to be many years before the full potential of the innovation is realized, the realization coming from a host of improvements, incorporated gradually over time. New plants constructed in the years subsequent to the initial innovation may well include in their design improvements that have accumulated, and almost certainly will if the improvements are additive. But what is the history of plants built early in the sequence, before many improvements have accumulated? Is their technology static, reflecting the state of the art as of the date of construction? Or can they be brought up-to-date, so as to incorporate at least some of the improvements secured in the intervals after their initial operation? If such bringing up-to-date is possible, is it worth while?

At any instant in time after the date of the radical innovation itself, one is presented with two alternatives: does one build a new plant incorporating the latest technology; or does one try to bring an old plant up-to-date, in the hope that it too may incorporate the latest technology? Or are the alternatives this simple? Perhaps the very latest technology is too complex to be absorbed, given the capabilities of the organization for which the new plant is to be constructed. Perhaps the old plant cannot be brought completely up-to-date, but only partly so. What does one do then?

These are the sorts of questions which this chapter will address. Its outline will be as follows: first, I shall elucidate the terms to be used, concentrating on four major elements in the analysis: (a) size; (b) costs; (c) capabilities; and (d) technological improvements. Second, I shall try to give some idea of how these elements evolve through time, taking as an historical example the petroleum refining industry (for the history, see Reichle et al., 1992; Shankland, 1954; Gary and Hardwerk, 1984; and Venuto and Habib, 1979). Third, I shall relate the elements one to another, taking as a unifying concept the phenomenon of the 're-vamp' encountered again and again in the refining industry. Fourth, I shall cite a few examples of re-vamping encountered in China. Finally, I shall draw the implications for those developing countries facing the alternatives of modernizing previously constructed plants or building new ones in industries with rapid technical change.

ELEMENTS IN THE ANALYSIS

The term 'innovation' is used in at least two different ways, the first to signify any novelty, the second to identify from among all novelties those few which have far-reaching consequences for an economy. In this paper, 'innovation' will be used in the second sense of a substantial and radical advance. When the term 'innovation' is used in the second way, the term 'improvements' is used to encompass the lesser novelties. (In a recent volume, Antonelli *et al.* (1992) assign the term 'Type 1' to the novelty with far-reaching consequences and 'Type 2' to the improvements made subsequently. They then speak (p. 11) of a 'Type 2' modernization as a 'catching up with a backlog in incremental improvements'. Their 'Type 2' modernization is equivalent of meaning to re-vamping, although I shall make more of the concept than they do.)

But once having defined the term, I shall conceive of the innovation as having already taken place, not inquiring into its origin. What transpired before the operation of the first commercial plant producing the novel product, or incorporating the novel process, or employing the novel arrangements, or so on, will not occupy me: I shall neglect the initial ideas, the research and development, the acquisition of funds and other inputs, the design and construction of the plant and its start-up. It is only subsequent events, leading to the exploitation of the potential inherent in the innovation, that I shall focus on. These events are not trivial; they may consume more resources than were used up in the innovation and may span many decades: these are phenomena I hope to illustrate, and things that will rank significantly in the analysis.

That the technological focus is on improvements to a given innovation is now agreed: it is time to introduce the first of the four major elements in the analysis – size. By size I mean both plant size and market size, and by the growth in size I mean growth in the size of the plant – that is, in the rates at which it consumes inputs and produces outputs – and in the size of the markets for its inputs and outputs. So 'size' is essentially a comparative term, the comparison being between internal (plant size) and external (market size) factors affecting the industrial firm.

The second term, costs, will also be essentially comparative in nature, but the comparison will not be between forces internal and external to the firm. Rather, the comparison will be between costs, both capital and operating, of a new plant incorporating the latest version of the technology and costs of an existing plant re-vamped to the fullest extent, so as to employ a technology as close as possible to the latest version. For existing plants, re-vamping costs will vary with its date of original construction and the state of the art then reached; to the extent possible I shall make allowance for these factors.

With the third term in the analysis, capabilities, I intend to introduce a matter of some consequence to the less technologically advanced firms in the industry. The most technologically advanced firms can profitably absorb innovations and subsequent improvements, for they employ the skilled persons – scientists, engineers, technically alert managers and others – needed to appreciate and assimilate advanced technologies, and can draw upon their previous experience in carrying out each successive task. The less-advanced firms lack these prerequisites to technological advance: even if they draw upon outside suppliers for the tasks of planning, design, engineering, construction and initial operation they are likely to be left incapable of operating the plant so as to exploit its full potential, let alone securing the mundane day-to-day improvements that so markedly increase its performance. It may take all the technical and managerial resources of the less-advanced firm to master the technology inherent in the plant as originally constructed; to master improvements as they come along may provide too great a challenge. The improvements themselves may not be technically more exacting than the original technology (whether they are or are not is an interesting question, but not one that I shall pursue here); the difficulty for the less-capable firm is that the productive task becomes more demanding if the need to master the improvements follows swiftly upon, or even occurs simultaneously with, the need to master the original state of the art.

With the fourth and final term, technological improvements, I come to the element that will tie the whole argument together. As in the case of the (radical) innovation, so in the case of improvement I do not intend to discuss here their initiation: I shall take for granted that all the activities underlying the improvements take place, and that they are presented, full-blown, to the firms. Like manna from heaven, they will appear gratuitously; although, like prepared food in packaged containers, their ingredients may have to be acknowledged if their effects are to be appreciated.

What I shall do is indicate at this early stage how improvements, on the one hand, come to be tied into size, costs and capabilities, on the other. The link between improvements and size is double: improvements in an existing plant may well, and often do, permit an increase in its rate of output; and the increase may be so substantial, compared to the rate of increase of sales of the product, that no additional new plant need be built. The link between improvements and costs is also double: exploiting improvements requires expenditures, capital and current; and having exploited improvements, running costs will fall in real terms. One link between improvements and capabilities has already been mentioned: the owner of the plant must have certain capabilities if the improvements are to be recognized and exploited; the other link is that, in the exploitation, those very same capabilities may be augmented. But all these matters will be discussed later, after the individual elements of the analysis have been portrayed in their progress through time.

THE HISTORICAL DEVELOPMENT OF SIZE, COSTS AND IMPROVEMENTS

In one industry I have chosen to study, petroleum refining, there is no better way of portraying simultaneously progress in sizes, costs and improvements than to recount the experience of two plants that encapsulate the entire history. These exemplary plants are the fluid catalytic cracking (FCC) units at the Baton Rouge, Louisiana, refinery of the Exxon Corporation. Designed in the year (1942) of the FCC process innovation, started up in the following year and almost immediately operated so as to produce aviation gasoline blending stock for the Second World War; converted to the production of motor gasoline after the end of the war; 're-vamped' again and again so as always to incorporate the latest state of the art; and still (in 1995, fifty-two years later) producing efficiently at large scale and at low cost, these plants illustrate perfectly the salient features of technological change. I shall now proceed to present the summary data of these changes.

The unit of inquiry is the 're-vamp', so the following tables will be organized around these periodic assimilations of improvements. The initial re-vamp of one of the two FCC units at Baton Rouge (designated by Exxon as PCLA-3, signifying Powdered Catalyst Louisiana, the third unit to be designed for the refinery, although the second to be brought on stream, on 21 June 1943) was undertaken in January and February 1945; the second (on PCLA-2, first brought on stream on 20 September 1943) in March 1945, immediately afterwards. Since both plants are chosen to illustrate the history of re-vamping in the petroleum refining industry, it is both dates in 1945 that are listed in Table 6.1 as the first observation in a fifty-year series.

Subsequent observations and a rough estimate of events in intervening years, bring the series up to the present. All told, there have been a total of roughly seventeen re-vamps, approximately one every three years. A detailed list of the improvements secured in some of the re-vamps will appear later (Enos, forthcoming), but for our purposes here it is enough that we provide summary measures of their magnitude.

Looking at the data in Tables 6.1–6.3 it is possible to discern several trends, one of which is surprising and another of which is most impressive.

Table 6.1   Characteristics of re-vamps to the fluid catalytic cracking units at Exxon's Baton Rouge refinery, 1943–92

Plant designation	Initial operation	Charge Rates[a]			Specific gravity of fresh feed
		Fresh feed	Recycle	Total feed	
PCLA-3	21 June 1943	15,100	1,500	16,600	31.3°API
PCLA-2	20 September 1943	15,100	1,500	16,600	31.3°API
	Date of re-vamp				
PCLA-3	Jan/Feb 1945	n.a.	n.a.	n.a.	n.a.
PCLA-2	March 1945	n.a.	n.a.	n.a.	n.a.
PCLA-3	February 1947	33,000	3,300	36,300	28.5°API
PCLA-2	August 1947	33,000	3,300	36,300	28.5°API
PCLA-3	February 1948	39,000	6,500	45,500	28.5°API
PCLA-2	October 1948	39,000	6,500	45,500	28.5°API
PCLA-3 (only)	March 1949	n.a.	n.a.	n.a.	n.a.
PCLA-3	1952	48,418	6,582	55,000	28.5°API
PCLA-2	1952	38,700	14,300	53,000	26.5°API
PCLA-3 and 2 (both)	1953–91 (approximately 12 re-vamps each)	n.a.	n.a.	n.a.	n.a.
	Current operation				
PCLA-3	1992	94,000	—	94,000	23.1°API
PCLA-2	1992	94,000	—	94,000	23.1°API

Note: [a] Raw material input after re-vamps, barrels per stream day.

Sources: *1943–52*: Enos (1962) and field notes collected 1954–6; *1953–91*: the author's guess, based upon the experience of FCC units re-vamped over the same interval by process design and engineering companies and operated by other international oil companies; *1992*: Reichle *et al.* (1992, pp. 41–8).

But these revelations will come later, for I intend to proceed through the tables systematically, considering each piece of evidence in turn. The first is the frequency of observations of my unifying element, re-vamps. One would expect the interval between successive re-vamps to vary quite considerably, for several reasons. First of all, the objective in re-vamping is to assimilate the bulk of the improvements that have emerged since the last occasion; and my evidence about the securing of improvements themselves (see Enos, forthcoming, chs 1–5) indicates that improvements in fluid catalytic cracking occur at a rate that can be approximated by a statistically random series, with a mean frequency more or less constant over time and a more or less constant

Table 6.2 Productivity indices for FCC units at Baton Rouge refinery, 1943–92

Year of re-vamp and plant designation	Productivity factors				Productivity indices (PCLA-2 in 1943 = 100)	
	Production intensity[a] (1)	Raw material quality[b] (2)	Gasoline yield[c] (3)	Octane rating[d] (4)	Fixed inputs[e]	Variable inputs[f]
1943 (initial operation)						
PCLA-3	0.582	100	0.436	86	70	100
PCLA-2	0.833	100	0.436	86	100	100
1945						
PCLA-3	0.903	n.a.	n.a.	n.a.	n.a.	n.a.
PCLA-2	0.873	n.a.	n.a.	n.a.	n.a.	n.a.
1947						
PCLA-3	0.892	105	0.436	86	244	105
PCLA-2	0.916	105	0.436	86	249	105
1948						
PCLA-3	0.916	105	0.436	86	314	105
PCLA-2	0.921	105	0.436	86	317	105
1949						
PCLA-3	0.920	n.a.	n.a.	n.a.	n.a.	n.a.
1952						
PCLA-3	0.930	105	0.494	85	384	118
PCLA-2	0.930	108	0.572	85	371	140

	1953–91	1992 (current operation)
	n.a.	0.981
	n.a.	115
	n.a.	0.631
	n.a.	87
	n.a.	693
	n.a.	168

Notes:

a   Ratio of yearly average charge rates, barrels per calender day divided by barrels per stream day.

b   The difference between the specific gravity of the fresh feed and the specific gravity of the feed in 1943, multiplied by 2 cents per barrel per °API; the product subtracted from 125 (the costs of feed in 1943) and the resulting number inverted; i.e. as a formula:

Raw Material Quality = $1.25/[1.25 - 2(°API \text{ in } 1943 - °API \text{ in year of estimate})]$

(2 cents per barrel per °API was the industry's traditional measure of the premium or discount applied to feed stocks of varying gravity: Frankel and Newton; 1969, p. 31.)

c   Gasoline yield on fresh feed.

d   Octane rating as the simple arithmetic average of research and motor octanes.

e   The ratio of charge rate of total feed (Table 6.1, column 4) to the charge rate of PCLA-2 in 1943; multiplied by production intensity (Table 6.2, column 1); given 1943 = 100.

f   The product of Table 6.2, columns (2), (3) and (4); i.e. $(2) \times (3) \times (4)$; given 1943 = 100.

Sources: 1943 (raw material quality, gasoline yield and octane rating), and 1992 (all columns): Reichle (1992, pp. 41–8); 1943 (production intensity), and 1945–1952 (all columns): Enos (1962), and field notes

Table 6.3   Fresh feed rates and overall index of improvement, 1943–92

Year of re-vamp and plant designation (1)	Fresh feed rate after re-vamp (bpsd) (2)	Overall index of improvement (3)
1943 (initial operation)		
PCLA-3	15,100	83
PCLA-2	15,100	100
1945		
PCLA-3	n.a.	n.a.
PCLA-2	n.a.	n.a.
1947		
PCLA-3	33,000	184
PCLA-2	33,000	188
1948		
PCLA-3	39,000	225
PCLA-2	39,000	227
1949		
PCLA-3 (only)	n.a.	n.a.
1952		
PCLA-3	48,418	271
PCLA-2	38,700	272
1953–91	n.a.	n.a.
1992 (both units)	94,000 (each)	469

Sources: Year of re-vamp and plant designation; and Fresh feed rate: Table 6.1, columns 1–3; Overall index of improvement: 0.573 times the productivity index for fixed inputs plus (1 – 0.573) times the productivity index for variable inputs, both indexes from Table 6.2. The proportions 0.573 and (1.0 – 0.573) are calculated from Enos (1962, Appendix Table 2, p. 305) (for a FCC unit of 15,000 bpsd in 1942)

variance. Second, just like new plants, re-vamps represent capital investments of considerable magnitude, and so will generally be undertaken in periods of buoyant demand and high profitability. During economic recessions, re-vamps tend to be postponed. Third, shifts in relative prices, both those of different raw materials and of different products, encourage re-vamps which permit the increased use of cheaper raw materials or the increased production of more valuable products, or both. That such shifts in relative prices have occurred in the last fifty years is well documented: particularly important in stimulating improvements in the FCC process, and consequently re-vamps in the plants incorporating the process, have been increases in the price of sweet, light crude oils, relative to the price of heavy, sour crudes, and increases in the price of high octane motor fuels, relative to the price of low octane fuels. (This latter phenomenon has appeared, because of competition among refiners, as a long-term increase in the average octane rating of marketed gasoline.) These shifts in relative prices have not occurred with anything like regularity, so the stimuli they have provided to re-vamps have not occurred regularly either.

There is one factor, however, that does tend to impose a regular temporal pattern on re-vamps: that is the periodic shut-downs of FCC plants (and all other continuously operated chemical process equipment) for inspection and maintenance. Shut-downs (called 'turn-arounds' in the petroleum industry) are scheduled in advance, usually immediately after the end of the previous shut-down, so as to allow sufficient time for organizing the necessary resources: teams of maintenance men, storage of intermediate products to enable the rest of the units in the refinery to maintain production during the shut-down, selection and negotiating of contracts with outside firms providing specialized services such as instrumentation.

Provided that shut-downs can be undertaken according to schedule, re-vamps can be planned. The gestation period for a re-vamp is approximately three years, from the decisions to undertake the task internally or to employ the offices of a process design and engineering firm, through to the start-up of the re-vamped unit. In the 1940s, the normal interval between shut-downs was two to six months, so substantial re-vamps were planned several shut-downs ahead; but the achievement of longer run lengths between successive shut-downs – one to two years in the 1950s, and two to three years in the 1970s – meant that a minor re-vamp might be planned for the next shut-down. Today, fluid catalytic cracking units can be run steadily, twenty-four hours a day, for three to four years before being turned around, which gives sufficient time to plan even a major re-vamp for the next occasion.

Thus, re-vamps could occur more or less regularly, at three-year intervals, were it not for the various exogenous factors – irregular intervals between improvements, fluctuating profitability of operations, and shifts in relative prices – which interfere. It is entirely possible that a re-vamp might be interjected during an emergency shut-down in order to take advantage of an unanticipated cessation of operations; it is also entirely possible, and happens quite often, that a scheduled shut-down might pass without any attempts to incorporated recent improvements. So the lack of any regularity in the intervals between re-vamps of the FCC units covered in Table 6.1 is not unexpected.

In the second, third and fourth columns of Table 6.1 there are figures representing capacities of the plants after successive re-vamps, expressed in terms of the maximum amounts of raw materials processed during a day's operation (so many barrels, of 42 gallons, per day that the plant is on stream:

abbreviated to bpsd). Looking down the figures in the columns 'Fresh feed' and 'Total feed' one cannot fail to be impressed by the increase over the half-century: taking the first of these columns, from a daily rate of 15,100 barrels to one of 94,000 barrels, a six-fold increase. And this is for a plant whose physical dimensions and external appearance are unchanged. Imagine what improvements must have been achieved, and assimilated, for these results to have been obtained.

Less impressive, perhaps, but more instructive is the path followed by the increases in capacity. In almost every one of the re-vamps there is an increase in the unit's capacity. And even in some of the re-vamps in which there is not apparent increase (e.g. that of 1952 for PCLA-2), there are increases lurking. Take, for example, the re-vamp of 1952: the improvements assimilated in PCLA-2 enabled a cheaper raw material (heavy gas oil) to be substituted for a more expensive one (light gas oil).

Moving on to Table 6.2, one finds the word 'productivity' in its title. This is meant to give a rough-and-ready indication of the extent to which the improvements in the FCC process have increased its overall performance. Rough it is because no single indicator could cover all the different sorts of improvements – in equipment, in process design, in process operation, in catalysts, etc. – that have been secured; ready it is because I have been able to calculate it for the first few re-vamps carried out on the FCC units at Baton Rouge, from data that were given to me when I conducted my initial research in 1955–7.

The components of the measure of productivity can be observed in Table 6.2. There are four: the first measures the intensity with which the plant is operated; the second, the quality of the chief raw material (that fraction of crude petroleum boiling at temperatures less than motor fuel and higher than very heavy fuel oil); the third, the yield of motor gasoline; and the fourth, the quality of that motor gasoline. In more detail, production intensity is measured as the ratio of the calendar rate of charge of raw material to the stream rate of charge. It is equal to the fraction of an entire year during which the plant is on stream: i.e. producing outputs from inputs. It is also equal to unity minus the fraction of the time the plant is shut down. As an example, a contemporary plant operating for three years at a stretch, and then subjected to a three week turn-around, is producing, on the average over the three years, fifty-one weeks out of fifty-two, and so has an average intensity of 51/52, or 0.981. Examining the figures in the column of production intensity of the FCC plants at Baton Rouge, one sees that the average has risen from 0.833 for PCLA-2 in 1943 to the figure already calculated, 0.981, in 1994. The first of these two ratios represents an average period of shut-down of sixty-one days in the year, compared to the current period of seven days. Thus, over the half-century of improvements to the FCC units, an additional fifty-four days of operation have been gained each year, or, looking at the change in a different manner, fifty-four fewer days have had to be spent in maintenance and modernization.

Again, in more detail, the measure of the quality of the raw material charged to the FCC units is estimated, beginning with its gravity. In the industry, the gravity of hydrocarbon liquids has long been recorded as probably the most useful single indicator of the nature, both chemical and physical, of the material. The scale used is that disseminated by the American Petroleum Institute; it is an affine transformation of specific gravity and is given in °API. (For example, the specific gravity of the feed stock which would have been charged to PCLA-2 and -3 in 1943, had the units been operated to produce motor gasoline, was 31.3°API, which is equivalent to 0.8692 times the weight of an equivalent volume of water. (This is the feed stock charged to the reactor of the innovative plant PCLA-1 before it was switched to aviation gasoline production; see Reichle, *et al.* 1992, p. 45.)

The chain of reasoning behind the use of gravity of the feed stock as the measure of its quality is as follows: the higher is the specific gravity, the greater is the average number of hydrogen and carbon atoms in the molecules comprising the feed. The larger are the hydrocarbon molecules, the larger is the amount of carbon deposited as coke on the catalyst during the cracking reactions. The more coke deposited, the more there is that must be burned off the catalyst during its regeneration. Since the overall capacity of FCC units is often constrained by their ability to regenerate catalyst, the higher is the rate at which coke must be burned, the lower is the rate at which raw material can be charged. So there is an indirect but close relationship between the specific gravity of the feed stock, on the one hand, and the effective capacity of the FCC unit, on the other: the higher the former, the lower the latter.

One of the incentives to R&D in petroleum refining has been to increase the industry's ability to process lower and lower quality feedstocks. The price differentials between high-quality feedstocks (in our simple term, feedstocks of low gravity) and low-quality feedstocks is substantial, the industry's rule of thumb in 1943 being that each °API lighter cost 2 US cents more per barrel. Any improvement that enabled a refiner to charge a heavier feedstock to his FCC unit was thus welcome. So the measure of the quality of the raw material is estimated as its gravity, relative to that of the material charged in 1943, multiplied by the 2 cents; the product of those two numbers represents the price differential in favour of the cheaper fuel (see note [b] to Table 6.2).

The third and fourth measures of quality improvement in the FCC process should be taken together: they are the yield of motor gasoline, as a fraction of the raw material charged, and the octane rating of that gasoline. The former measure is unambiguous, but the latter can be calculated by several test procedures, the most common being the motor method and the research method (see Nelson, 1949, pp. 31–2). Rather than cite one octane number, the current practice in the industry is to take a simple arithmetic average of the motor and the research number; I have followed this practice.

The reason for using both gasoline yield and octane number in the measure of improvement in FCC processing is that there is a trade-off between the two in catalytic cracking (Maples, 1993). If the refiner wishes to maximize the volume of motor gasoline from a given feed, he will do so at the expense of the octane rating of that gasoline: if he wishes to maximize the octane rating of the gasoline, he will do so at the expense of the yield. The trade-off has long been recognized, but it is in recent years, with the design and manufacture of highly selective catalysts, that the relationship has been explored systematically. Today there are yield-selective catalysts and octane-selective catalysts, but to focus on one, at the expense of the other, would be to admit a bias to the measure of product quality. This potential bias can be reduced by multiplying gasoline yield by octane rating; i.e. by considering quality in terms of barrel-octanes.

The trend in the quality of FCC products over time can be seen by reading down columns (3) and (4) in Table 6.2; both gasoline yield and octane rating have shown rises, the former considerably more so than the latter. Improvements were directed initially at increasing the yield of catalytic gasoline blending stock, while the octane rating fell slightly. With the advent of the crystalline catalysts, octane too has been raised.

In the last two columns of Table 6.2 two measures of technological improvements are obtained, each transformed into a more easily appreciated index, on the basis of 100 for the year 1943. The first measure is that of the increase in productivity of the fixed factors of production, defined as capital (the depreciation of plant) plus technology (implicit royalty) plus labour. Since the productivity of the fixed factors rises as the effective capacity of the FCC units rises, and since the effective capacity has risen substantially over time, this index shows a remarkable rise, from 100 in 1943 to 693 in 1992: essentially, the productivity of the fixed inputs to FCC has increased seven-fold.

The second measure is that of the productivity of the variable inputs to production. This is obtained by multiplying together the three components: raw material quality, gasoline yield and octane rating (occupying respectively columns (2), (3) and (4) of Table 6.2). The yield of motor gasoline from the feedstock and its average octane rating have already been explained; changes in raw material quality reflect the increased ability through improvements of the FCC process to handle more intractable feedstocks; the way in which the estimates of quality are obtained is given in note [b] to Table 6.2.

THE OVERALL ECONOMIC EFFECT OF IMPROVEMENTS

The two indices in the last columns of Table 6.2 can be combined into a single index of the overall increase in productivity in FCC by making allowance for the relative contributions of fixed and variable factors in total value-added in production. There is available a breakdown of costs of FCC for the year 1942 for a plant of equivalent size to PCLA-3 and -2 (Enos, 1962, Appendix Table 2, p. 305); in this the fixed factors of production (capital, technology and labour) account for 57.3 per cent of total value-added, and the variable factors (all others) for 42.7 per cent. Weighting the figures in the final columns of Table 6.2 by these percentages, the weighted averages take on the numbers in column (3) of Table 6.3.

From 100 for PCLA-2 in 1943 (and the lower value of 83 for PCLA-3), the overall index of improvement rises to a final value of 469 in 1992, an increase of a little over 4.5 times. It can be said, therefore, that the productivity of the plants in the half-century 1943–92 had increased between four and five times, all through the assimilation of improvements. Since these improvements were technical in nature, it can also be said that the rate of technological advance in FCC was such as to raise the average productivity of the factors of production by approximately 4.5 times. Over the fifty years, this works out to an average rate of increase of productivity of 3 per cent per year.

GROWTH IN PLANT SIZES AND MARKETS

But an average rate of growth of productivity is only part of the story; the other part is the capacity of the plant to produce output. This brings me back to the figures in Tables 6.1 and 6.3 and to the phenomenon of 'capacity swelling'. Each re-vamp augmented the ability of the FCC plant in Baton Rouge to process raw material; each re-vamp permitted production at a higher rate of output. From the original rate of 15,100 bpsd of fresh feed, the two re-vamps of 1945 and 1947 blew the rate up to 33,000 bpsd; from the rate of 33,000 bpsd in 1947, the next re-vamp in 1948 blew it up to 39,000 bpsd. And so on and so on, until 1992.

Thus, the capacity of a periodically re-vamped plant would tend to swell with each re-vamp, whereas a plant never re-vamped would remain frozen at its original capacity. Taking my example, within four years, an unre-vamped FCC plant would only be able to process one-half (actually, 15,100 bpsd, versus 33,000 bpsd: a little less than one-half) the amount of raw material of the re-vamped plant. By 1992 an unre-vamped plant would have been charging raw material at only one sixth the rate of its re-vamped rival.

It is at this point that I want to bring in the growth of the market for the produce of the plant. It would have been a strange industry indeed if the market for its products had not grown over the course of a half-century. There are some such markets, of course, but they are not markets for technologically progressive products; they are markets for products which are being supplanted by technically progressive products or products produced by technologically progressive methods. But if the market for technologically progressive products grows with time, so do the capacities of technologically progressive plants that produce these products. In an industry which continuously improves its technology and which continuously modernizes its existing plants, the rate of growth of capacity of each individual plant may approximate the rate of growth of the market. One may observe the industry's output growing, year by year, at an impressive rate, and yet the number and physical dimensions of its plants, and perhaps even their appearance, not changing at all. What is happening is that the modernization of the industry's plants is enabling their capacity to keep in step with the growth of the market. The growth of a market may not require an increase in the number of plants serving that market.

But the above assertion holds only if the plants are re-vamped, so as to assimilate improvements. Imagine that the demand for the industry's output (measured in terms of the rate at which raw material is consumed) increases by six times over a half-century, and assume that none of the industry's plants is re-vamped. At first, it might seem that in order to satisfy market demand, five new plants (each of the same capacity as the original plant) would have to be constructed for each plant existing at the beginning of the period. But this greatly exaggerates the need for new plant construction, because a later plant would have the capacity appropriate to the technology at the date of construction. Thus, based on the data in Tables 6.1 and 6.3, a new plant built in 1952 would not have a capacity of 15,100 bpsd, but a capacity of 48,418 bpsd or 38,700 bpsd, depending upon which gravity feed stock it was planned to charge. Two plants in 1952, one an unre-vamped plant of 1943 vintage, at 15,100 bpsd, and the other a new plant of, say 38,700 bpsd, would have a total capacity of 53,800 bpsd. Only a third plant, built at the time of the next re-vamp – say 1955 – and contributing an increment of capacity of 40,200 bpsd, would be needed to meet the ultimate demand of 94,000 bpsd in 1992. Of course, in the case of three plants, the third of which was built in 1955, there would be excess capacity in the industry in all those years from 1955 to 1992, when demand finally caught up with the ability of the three plants to process raw material; and this possibility brings me to the subject of China's experience with fluid catalytic cracking.

FLUID CATALYTIC CRACKING IN CHINA

Of the two polar cases described previously – regularly carrying out re-vamps to a single FCC unit or adding a sequence of units each of fixed capacity – China has tended towards the second. The oil company which has been granted a monopoly on the refining of crude petroleum, Sinopec, has ensured that all its major refineries have at least one FCC unit. Since the company operates some thirty integrated oil refineries, this means that there are more than that substantial number of FCC units in the country: Sinopec probably operates the largest number of FCC units in the world.

On the basis of my inquiries it would seem that the majority of these FCC units are of similar size and configuration, designed to a standard pattern. Design capacity is 24,000 bpsd (equivalent to 1.2 million tonnes per year). Most of these units are currently operating at, or below, design. To my knowledge, none is being operated at more than its original design rate.

Almost all these FCC units were designed by an affiliate of Sinopec, the Beijing Design Institute. The Institute has also carried out the engineering and procurement for the units, and, in those cases where the refining company did not have its own construction firm, the construction as well. All told, the Beijing Design Institute has designed fifty-nine units, commencing with the unit at the Fushun refinery in 1965 and continuing to the present. Although the majority of its FCC units have been of the standard size and configuration, the Institute has also experimented with smaller units and has in recent years designed a larger one of 40,000 bpsd (2.0 million tonnes per year) for the Luoyang refinery (Sinopec Beijing Design Institute, 1994).

Rarely are these FCC units re-vamped, but when they are, it is usually at more or less the same time and for the same purpose: to introduce an improvement that was assimilated in the refineries of the USA a decade or more earlier. The major example is the improvement of 'riser' cracking, which was fully developed in the USA by 1971 but not adopted in China until the middle of the 1980s (and then, in one case, in an FCC unit built only two years previously). Moreover, re-vamps have not resulted in the stretching of capacity. Rather, when additional FCC capacity was needed, a new unit was built alongside the existing one.

This pattern of repetition has continued in the last few years, although Sinopec has, since 1986, been forced to seek the assistance of foreign design and engineering firms in order to acquire the technology for processing very heavy oils (the so-called 'resid' FCC technology; see the *Oil and Gas Journal*, annual refining issues, 1986–present). These very heavy oils are residues left after the distillation of the Indonesian and Middle Eastern crude oils upon which the refineries of the central and south coastal regions of China are becoming increasingly dependent.

TECHNOLOGICAL CAPABILITIES

Considering the three-plant alternative discussed earlier (p. 128), I should like to make one further point about the capability of the industry to master an advancing technology. Assume that the three plants are in different locations, an assumption not unrealistic in an industry whose plants, in the absence of an extensive pipeline network, tend to be market-orientated. Assume also that the plants are administratively independent, so that the personnel in each plant would need to master just one state of the art: the personnel in the plant constructed at the beginning would have had to master the technology of 1943; the personnel in the second plant constructed in 1952 the technology of 1952; and those in the third plant that of 1955. Since it is usually the case that the more advanced is the technology, the more difficult it is to master, the personnel in the first plant would need be less capable technologically, and those in the third plant more capable, than the average (approximated, if not equalled, by those in the second plant).

In the three-plant alternative none of the personnel – scientists, engineers, managers – in any of the plants need master more than the technology as of the date of their plant's construction. It would be enough, for efficient production, that the personnel in the first plant learn how to operate successfully a plant of vintage 1943; their knowledge need not extend to improvements made subsequently. And so on, for the later plants' personnel.

Think how much more demanding are the tasks set the personnel in a continuously re-vamped plant. If I simplify matters by assuming that all the planning, design, procurement and construction of subsequent re-vamps are undertaken by outside suppliers, the only parts of the entire technology that must be mastered by the plant's personnel are those relating to operation. Yet the personnel of the frequently re-vamped plant must master the productive aspects of the original technology, of the improved technology assimilated in the first re-vamp, of the still further improved technology assimilated in the second re-vamp, and so on, through all re-vamps up to the last. These tasks are never ending: no sooner have they mastered one state of the art than the scientists, engineers and managers must begin to master its successor. Improvements come so fast that they can never relax in the knowledge that they have absorbed the current set, for the next set of improvements is already upon them. Sometimes, the improvements are extrapolations of existing phenomena, and so their mastery requires only an extension beyond the present boundaries; but at other times the improvements involve the opening up of new areas of knowledge, and so their mastery confronts the operating personnel with novel phenomena.

Such opening up of a new area of knowledge, requiring the acquisition of new skills, has happened at least five times in the course of improvements to fluid catalytic cracking: the first after the end of the Second World War with the shift from production of aviation gasoline to that of motor gasoline; the second in the early 1960s with the introduction of crystalline catalysts ('zeolites'); the third in the decades of the 1960s and 1970s, with the much-reduced contact time between raw material and catalyst (via 'riser' cracking); the fourth in the 1970s and 1980s with the tendency to charge heavier and heavier feed stocks, giving rise to concomitant problems of high carbon deposition on the catalyst, difficulty in maintaining heat balance and contamination (chiefly of the catalyst by such trace elements as nickel and vanadium); and the fifth, currently, with the changes needed to meet environmental regulations.

To be sure, the major advances in technology, requiring acquisition of new areas of knowledge, have happened rarely enough so that one person, in the course of his career, would encounter two or three at the most; but production in the realm of an advanced technology does not proceed on the basis of one man's knowledge. It proceeds on the basis of the collective knowledge of an entire team; in fluid catalytic cracking the team may amount to forty or more persons, including operating labour, engineers, scientists and technicians in quality control and R&D laboratories, supervisors, programmers, planners and managers. Within the team, not only must the relevant specialized knowledge be acquired by the individual but also a sufficient portion of it must be communicated to the other members, so that their activities will mesh in and be synchronized with each other. Shortcomings on the part of an operator or a supervisor or a manager or anyone else will prevent the complete assimilation of a single improvement. Imagine how often this will occur when improvements follow one another in rapid succession.

IMPLICATIONS FOR DEVELOPING COUNTRIES

Thus the final thesis in this chapter is that keeping abreast of improvements in technology – assimilating them in a sequence of plant modernizations – is a much more daunting task than mastering the single technology embedded in a plant of given vintage. An organization must be far more competent technically to advance with the times (meaning to advance with the state of the art) than to stay still. Difficult it may be to master the state of the art; far, far more difficult is it to master progressive states of the art (Bell and Pavitt, 1993).

The implication of this thesis governing the demands for, and acquisition of, technological capability in developing countries is that keeping abreast of *every* technical improvement, and incorporating the improvement via revamps of equipment, may be beyond their capability. In attempting to assimilate every improvement at the first opportunity, the developing country may stretch its limited technical resources too far, failing to master one improvement before attempting to adopt the next.

This is a general warning, of course, and does not make allowance for any massing of talents in one activity. It may be, and does happen, that a country will decide to devote a particularly large share of its scarce resources, particularly its technical, managerial and financial resources, to furthering a single industry. In many countries, developing and developed, armaments industries appropriate the lions' share of scarce resources, so that *they* are able to keep up with improvements in military technology. They concentrate within one set of institutions all the necessary talents, as does the petroleum refining industry in developed countries; they allocate to the assimilation of improvements all easily transferable resources, chiefly financial capital and political support, as does the petroleum refining industry in developed countries; they re-vamp their plants at every opportunity, as does the petroleum refining industry in developed countries. The difference between the developed and the developing countries in these respects is that the developed countries have 'scarce' resources in relative abundance and the developing countries do not. That the petroleum refining industry in the United States of America, from which country our examples of technical change have been drawn, has appropriated enough 'scarce' resources to re-vamp its refineries frequently has not denuded other industries of the same 'scarce' resources: there are enough to go around.

In most developing countries, there are not enough 'scarce' resources to go around. Appropriating a sufficient volume of 'scarce' resources for, say, the petroleum refining industry so as to keep *it* abreast of improvements will deprive some other industry, perhaps several other industries, of what they require to keep them abreast. An economist would argue that the answer to this problem of allocation among competing users would be to focus on the marginal unit of resource (say, the last engineer), calculate his contribution in all the different activities (in petroleum refining, in armaments, and so on), and then assign him to the activity where his contribution is the greatest.

The outcome of such assignments would be likely to leave all industries, petroleum refining included, with insufficient resources to match the frequency of re-vamping in the developed countries; they would have to be content with infrequent modernizations, but infrequent modernizations across all their technically sophisticated industries. Such a policy would place their industries in a position similar to petroleum refining in China: somewhere between the two polar cases imagined earlier, neither re-vamping at every opportunity nor failing to re-vamp at all. The outcome would fall between the outcomes in the two cases: over the long run productivity would rise, but at less frequent intervals and at a lower average over the years; plant capacities would adhere to the same pattern (here China differs); and their industries would be at a competitive disadvantage, *vis-à-vis* those in the developed countries, in all years except those immediately after re-vamps.

But this dismal prognosis neglects certain advantages accruing to the developing countries. Theory suggests that the greater the capital, managerial and political costs relative to the savings attributable to being at the technological frontier, the longer would be the spacing between successive re-vamps. If the cost of capital is very high, re-vamps would be undertaken infrequently; if management is inflexible or overtaxed or motivated chiefly by factors other than productive efficiency, re-vamps would be infrequent; or if political leaders are seeking strict adherence to fixed physical targets, re-vamps would be rare. Under all these conditions, and others it is easy to conjure up, the optimum course for a developing country would be to space re-vamps a greater time apart than would the refiners in the developed world.

There are other advantages to sparse spacing. For infrequent, costly re-vamps, firms in the developing countries may be able to borrow money and acquire technical assistance very cheaply indeed. Political alignment with one of the major powers among the developed countries may bring subsidies and preferential treatment; for example, suppliers of new catalytic cracking plants and modernizers of existing plants can be found in Italy, the Netherlands, the UK and the USA. Finally, developing countries and their developing industries can profit from the experience of those who have gone earlier. Not all the developed countries' petroleum refiners are as alert to technical change as the company cited in this chapter; some of them have not taken to heart the merits of frequent re-vamps – the merits of frequent increases in plant capacity, frequent gains in productivity and frequent reductions in average costs. The refiners in developing countries can steal a march on them.

SUMMARY

In the area of technology transfer, most of the attention focuses on the acquisition of modern techniques – their nature, availability and costs; the terms on which they can be acquired; and the negotiations between the acquiring firms or countries and the suppliers of the technology (Enos, 1989). Much less attention is devoted to improvements that are subsequently made by the suppliers, and by other firms in the developed countries, and the extent to which these subsequent improvements are accessible to, and exploited by, the organizations in the developing countries. In this chapter, I attempt to redress the balance. Because they are so diverse, and because they arise so sporadically, improvements to innovations are seldom studied systematically;

nevertheless, their cumulative significance is well recognized: in one case I am studying, they have resulted in an increase in the productivity of the factors of production by approximately 4.5 times. Even though an adopter may master the technology incorporated in the initial project, if he fails to keep up with improvements he may find himself at an ever-increasing competitive disadvantage. Firms in developing counties face this difficulty, a difficulty that is aggravated particularly by their lack of technological and managerial capabilities.

NOTE

1. I should like to thank all the participants of the Joint BA/CASS Seminar on Technology Transfer for their comments, particularly Paul David, whose alert response enabled me to eliminate a shortcoming in my estimate of the average rate of productivity increase in fluid catalytic cracking (FCC). Any remaining errors that an equally alert reader may find are to be attributed to me.

    I am also grateful to the Beijing Yanshan Petrochemical Corporation and the Tianjin Petroleum and Chemical Company for permitting me to inspect their refineries; to the Beijing Design Institute for providing me with data on their construction of FCC units; to the Chinese Academy of Social Sciences (CASS) for establishing the contacts with these three firms; and to Yi Ding for making the arrangements and accompanying me on the visits.

REFERENCES

Antonelli, C., Petit, P. and Tahar, G. (1992), *The Economics of Industrial Modernization*, New York: Academic Press.
Bell, M. and Pavitt, K. (1993), 'Technological accumulation and industrial growth: contrasts between developed and developing countries', *Industrial and Corporate Change*, 2, 157–210.
Enos, J.L. (1962), *Petroleum Progress and Profits: A History of Process Innovation*, Cambridge, Mass.: MIT Press.
—— (1989), 'Transfer of technology', *Asian-Pacific Economic Literature*, 3, 3–38.
—— (forthcoming), *Petroleum Progress and Profits II: A History of Process Improvement*.
Frankel, P.H. and Newton, W.L. (1969), *Comparative Evaluation of Crude Oils*, London: Institute of Petroleum.
Gary, J.H. and Hardwerk, G.E. (1984), *Petroleum Refining: Technology and Economics*, 2nd edn, New York: Marcel Dekker.
Maples, R.E. (1993), *Petroleum Refinery Process Economics*, Tulsa, Okla.: PennWell.
Nelson, W.L. (1949), *Petroleum Refinery Engineering*, New York: McGraw-Hill.
Reichle, A.D., Murcia, A.A., Avidan, A.A. and Murphy, J.R. (1992), 'A half century of fluid catalytic cracking', *Oil and Gas Journal*, Special Issue, 41–71.
Shankland, R.V. (1954), 'Industrial catalytic cracking', *Advances in Catalysis*, VI, 272–434.

Sinopec Beijing Design Institute (1994), *Company Brochure*, Liupukang, Xicheng District, Beijing.

Venuto, P.B. and Habib, E.T. Jr (1979), *Fluid Catalytic Cracking with Zeolite Catalysts*, New York: Marcel Dekker.

7. Chinese government policy towards science and technology and its influence on the technical development of industrial enterprises

Jiang Xiaojuan

INTRODUCTION

Since the end of the 1970s, with the implementation of the policy of economic reform and opening up to the outside world, marked changes have taken place in Chinese scientific and technological systems and policies. These changes have had a profound influence on enterprises' technological behaviour. This chapter attempts to provides a general survey of this topic and is divided into four parts.

First, I outline the major characteristics of China's scientific and technological systems and policies. Generally speaking, it remains the case that the government retains its important role in scientific research and technical development, but the role of the market in guiding scientific research and technical development has, at the same time, been greatly strengthened. Second, I analyse government plans and policies for technical development in enterprises, as well as their influence on the behaviour of enterprises. Third, I analyse the characteristics of enterprise behaviour in respect of technical development, with emphasis on the way government policies influence enterprises of different sizes and types of ownership structure. Finally, I conclude with an appraisal of the present state of Chinese technology policy and underlying issues.

AN OVERVIEW OF THE POST-1978 SCIENTIFIC AND TECHNOLOGICAL SYSTEM AND POLICIES

Prior to the adoption of the policy of reform and opening up to the outside world, projects for scientific research and technological development were determined according to compulsory government plans, and were undertaken by designated institutes with government funds. During the period from 1949 to the eve of reform in the late 1970s, China adopted two overall plans for scientific and technological development: *The Long-Term General Programme for Science and Technology 1956–1967* and *The 1963–1972 Outline Programme for Scientific and Technical Development.*

The first programme set out fifty-seven major tasks, while the second listed 374 tasks. The emphasis of both documents was on the major issues facing China's economic development and national defence, as well as a number of basic theoretical issues. The first programme was carried out smoothly, with fifty of the fifty-seven tasks meeting the requirements. The second, which clearly stated that the modernization of science and technology is the key to the modernization of agriculture, industry and national defence, failed to meet its objectives because of the Cultural Revolution.

A major orientation towards the market has taken place in China's scientific and technological system and policies since the adoption of the policies of reform. First, scientific research and technical development are no longer subject to compulsory government plans alone; instead, they are under a combination of compulsory and guidance government plans and are managed in many cases by non-governmental undertakings.

Second, prior to reform, China's scientific research and technical development was conducted mainly in free-standing research institutes, but since the reform, industrial enterprises and non-governmental organizations have become the mainstay of technical development. Third, the results of scientific research and technical development can now be transferred through a technology market as commodities. Fourth, policies have been put in place to provide much more encouragement to individual scientists and engineers.

Let me now turn to a general introduction to China's scientific and technological system and policies towards science and technology.[1] The following are the four main features of the reformed system.

The Government and New Technology

The government now chooses and finances fundamental research projects and major projects for technological development. This involves four types of activity.

First, the government defines the major topics and orientation of scientific research. Since adopting the policy of reform and opening up to the outside world, the central government has worked out two programmes for long-term development. These are *The 1978–1985 National Programme for Scientific and Technical Development*, drafted in 1978, and the *1986–2000 Programme for Scientific and Technical Development*, adopted in 1984. In addition, the government has drafted a series of medium-term plans such as the *Plan for Scientific and Technological Development during the Seventh Five-Year Plan* and the *General Plan for the Eighth Five-Year Plan* and the *Ten-Year Outline Programme for Scientific and Technological Development*. Each of these programmes has identified key areas for development and key research topics.

Second, it drafts specific plans for basic scientific research topics and technical development. In 1982, the central government began drafting and implementing a number of such plans. Most were associated with important basic research projects. These included the *State Plan for Solving Key Scientific and Technological Problems during the Sixth Five-Year Plan Period* (1983); the *State Plan for Key Laboratories* (1984); the *State Plan for Key Industrial Experiments* (1984); the *General Outline 863* (1986); the *National Plan for Major Basic Projects* (1991); and *Key State Projects for Technical Development* (1992).

Third, it now drafts specific plans for the commercialization and industrialization of scientific and technical research results. In order to speed up the process whereby scientific and technical results can be quickly popularized and put to practical use, the government has drafted a number of specific plans. These include the *'Sparks' Plan* (1985) for promoting advanced and practical technology in the rural areas, the *'Torch' Plan* (1985) for promoting the commercialization and industrialization of high and new technology, and the *Plan for the Trial Production of New Products* (1988) to facilitate the prompt trial production and screening of newly developed products.

In the early 1990s, in order to solve the problem of unsatisfactory application of scientific and technical results to production, China worked out a *State Plan for the Popularization of Scientific and Technical Results* (1990) and the *State Plan for the Popularization of Key Technology* (1991).

Finally, the government is responsible for planning the incorporation of foreign technology. This topic is dealt with elsewhere in this book, and so will not be discussed further in the present chapter.

Table 7.1 and Figure 7.1 provide a general summary of China's plans and programmes for scientific and technological development. Plans for scientific research now fall into two categories: those that are mandatory and those that are indicative or guidance plans. A crucial difference between them is their source of finance. Compulsory plans are financed mainly from government allocations. In the case of guidance plans, the government supplies few or no funds but does grant them preferential treatment by way of loan priority, low-interest loans and special priority to import. At the same time, localities and enterprises are encouraged to raise their own funds; for further details, see Table 7.1.

Table 7.1   *Major compulsory and guiding plans for scientific and*
technological development

Compulsory plans[a]	Guidance plans[b]
Plan for solving difficult scientific and technological problems	'Sparks' Plan
	'Torch' Plan
State plan for key industrial experiments	State plan for the trial production of key new products
State plan for key projects for technological development	State plan for the popularization of key scientific and technological results
Plan '863'	
Plan for scaling new scientific and technological heights	State plan for the popularization of key new technology
Plan for projects financed by the National Science Foundation	

Notes:
[a] Mainly financed through government allocations.
[b] Mainly financed through small government funds, preferential funds or self-finance.

Rewarding Scientists and Engineers

The reform introduced new systems for rewarding outstanding scientists and engineers. In 1979 the government promulgated new *Regulations of the People's Republic of China Concerning Natural Science Awards* designed to reward those scientists and technical workers who make outstanding professional contributions. The state has also formulated, and continues to formulate, policies for rewarding those who have invented new technology or achieved outstanding technological results. In addition, the government has stipulated that enterprises may set aside a proportion of the revenue earned by selling new technical developments and use it to reward those who have made the contributions.

The government also encourages local governments and organizations and individuals at home and abroad to establish new scientific and technological awards and foundations for such awards. During the last few years, some local governments and enterprises have rewarded scientists and technicians who have made outstanding achievements in technical development with cars, houses and large bonuses, thereby giving great motivation to those who work in the scientific and technological fields.

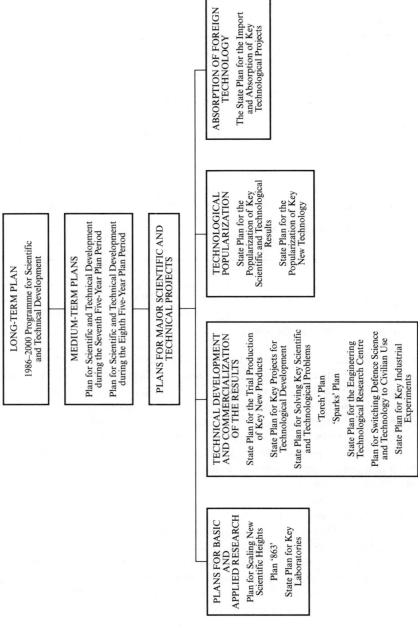

LONG-TERM PLAN

1986–2000 Programme for Scientific and Technical Development

MEDIUM-TERM PLANS

Plan for Scientific and Technical Development during the Seventh Five-Year Plan Period

Plan for Scientific and Technical Development during the Eighth Five-Year Plan Period

PLANS FOR MAJOR SCIENTIFIC AND TECHNICAL PROJECTS

PLANS FOR BASIC AND APPLIED RESEARCH

Plan for Scaling New Scientific Heights

Plan '863'

State Plan for Key Laboratories

TECHNICAL DEVELOPMENT AND COMMERCIALIZATION OF THE RESULTS

State Plan for the Trial Production of Key New Products

State Plan for Key Projects for Technological Development

State Plan for Solving Key Scientific and Technological Problems

'Torch' Plan

'Sparks' Plan

State Plan for the Engineering Technological Research Centre

Plan for Switching Defence Science and Technology to Civilian Use

State Plan for Key Industrial Experiments

TECHNOLOGICAL POPULARIZATION

State Plan for the Popularization of Key Scientific and Technological Results

State Plan for the Popularization of Key New Technology

ABSORPTION OF FOREIGN TECHNOLOGY

The State Plan for the Import and Absorption of Key Technological Projects

Source: Gao Xiaosu *et al.* (1993, p. 24).

Figure 7.1 The structure of China's plans for scientific and technical development

Opening Up the Market for Scientific and Technological Results

In the period before economic restructuring, China's major projects for scientific research and technological development were conducted in government-run institutes. Results belonged to the state and could not be bought and sold as commodities. This system failed to provide incentives for research institutes and researchers.

In 1987, China enacted the Technical Contract Law, which provided a legal guarantee that scientific and technical results could be put on the market. Since the mid-1980s, a number of technical exchange markets have been set up; the volume of transactions on these markets increased from 7.2 billion yuan in 1988 to 20.7 billion yuan in 1993.[2] However, the actual number of scientific and technical results traded and the volume of transactions have far outstripped the reported figures because most of the transactions are not conducted on the established markets.

The chief beneficiaries of the newly founded scientific and technological markets are research institutes and their staff members on the one hand, and medium-sized and small enterprises on the other. These markets have provided an effective source of applicable technology for medium and small enterprises that lack the ability to develop their own.

Encouraging Enterprises to Develop Their Own Technological Plans

In addition to central government activities, local governments also map out their own plans for scientific and technological development, and special funds are allocated by local financial authorities for scientific research and technological development. The policies adopted by local governments for encouraging scientific research institutes and enterprises to engage in technological development involve the same kind of preferential treatment as the policies adopted by the central government. Likewise, local research projects fall into the mandatory or compulsory categories.

GOVERNMENT TECHNOLOGY POLICY AND ENTERPRISE BEHAVIOUR

Prior to reform and opening up to the outside world, as we have seen, technology projects in China were mainly conducted in specialized scientific research institutes. Enterprises themselves were seldom engaged in technological development, and as a result their products and technology could remain unchanged for as long as several decades. A major change in China's policy towards science and technology since the adoption of the policy of reform is that the government, while continuing to support professional institutes in research and development, has started to pay attention to technological development projects and has encouraged enterprises to conduct their own projects.

As a major form of such government encouragement, enterprises are asked to engage in what is called 'technical renovation' aimed at developing new products, raising product quality, saving energy and raw materials and increasing exports.

In January 1982, the State Council promulgated the *Decision for Carrying Out Technical Renovation of Existing Enterprises in a Selected and Systematic Way*. Thus technical renovation has been put high on the government agenda, with the State Economic Commission in charge. Since then the central government has adopted the following policies and measures for technical renovation.

Defining Key Projects for Technical Renovation

Key projects for technical renovation during a given period are designated by the State Economic Commission in co-ordination with various localities and departments. During the Sixth and Seventh Five-Year Plan Periods, the emphasis of the government was on the import of 3,000 items of technology for technical renovation – 1,150 (in two batches) for the machine-building industry; 296 (in two batches) for transferring the defence industry to civilian uses; 400 for the nation's machine-building industrial export centres; 1,200 for light and textile industries, export and coastal facilities; and twelve for the import and incorporation of major technological projects.

During the Eighth Five-Year Plan Period, sixty-two key projects have been arranged for energy and raw-material conservation, developing new products, raising product quality and promoting exports. In 1992, the state added a number of major projects for technical renovation and importation.

Choosing Key Enterprises, Industries and Areas for Technical Renovation

The government selects key enterprises, industries and areas for technical renovation. During a given period of time, the selection may be concentrated on a given industry or group of enterprises which meets the requirements for renovation. For instance, during the Sixth and Seventh Five-Year Plan periods, the emphasis was laid on enterprises in coastal areas and the light, textile and machine-building industries. At the Sixth National Conference on Technical Renovation convened in 1992, the focus of attention was on those first or second state-class enterprises which played the leading role and were the leading profit-makers in their respective industries.

Preferential Policies to Encourage Enterprises to Develop Technology Independently

Since the beginning of economic restructuring, the central government has adopted a series of measures to encourage enterprises to be self-reliant in technical development:

1. Other things being equal, priority is given to the technical renovation of old enterprises instead of building new enterprises. Special funds are allocated for this purpose, and more loans are granted for key technical renovation projects. In the mid-1980s, when the government still substantially controlled materials distribution, priority was given to the deployment of materials needed for the technical renovation of enterprises.
2. Priority is still given by arranging the foreign exchange necessary for the import of equipment and raw materials needed for technical renovation.
3. Enterprises are allowed to draw 1–2 per cent of their total profits to finance the trial development of new products.
4. For key enterprises undergoing technical renovation the depreciation rate has been increased from 5 to 8 per cent. In addition, some large and medium-sized state enterprises are exempt from the payments normally made from their depreciation funds for energy, transportation, construction and other designated budgetary purposes.
5. Enterprises and research institutes are encouraged to integrate their efforts so that research activities can be made to serve the enterprises directly.
6. Technological development centres are established in a number of large and medium-sized enterprises and enterprise groups, which are also exempt from income tax on products during the intermediate experimental stage.

Appraising Enterprises' Technical Renovation and Technological Capability

When formulating preferential (discretionary) policies for industrial enterprises, the Chinese government often uses indicators of technical renovation and technical development capability as major factors for grading the enterprises, selecting priority enterprises for renovation and establishing new enterprise groups. Apart from central government, local governments at various levels have also made plans for technical renovation.

During the 1979–93 period, 1,046 billion yuan were invested in the technical renovation of various enterprises. This included 37 billion yuan of financial allocations (26.7 billion yuan from the central authorities, the rest from local authorities) and 372 billion yuan of loans. The remainder was raised by localities and enterprises or drawn from foreign investment. During this fifteen-year period a total of $US70 billion was spent on the import of technology for technical renovation.[3]

Encouraged by these policies and measures, and under pressure from market competition, large and medium-sized state enterprises have conducted more technical development projects than ever before. During the early years of reform and opening up to the outside world, very few industrial enterprises in China had their own organizations for technical development. In 1985, only 1,913 large and medium-sized enterprises, or 24 per cent of the total, had their own institutes for technical development; by 1993 the figure had increased to 9,503 (50.7 per cent). China's large and medium-sized enterprises are also increasing their expenditure on technical development year by year. In 1985, they spent a total of 5.3 billion yuan for this purpose; in 1993, the amount reached 24.86 billion yuan.[4]

AN APPRAISAL OF THE ROLE OF GOVERNMENT POLICY ON SCIENCE AND TECHNOLOGY

During the years of reform and opening up, China's scientific and technological system and policies have been marked by several new features, of which the following are most important.

Diminished Government Influence on Scientific Research and Technical Development

Although the government is aware of the major role that science and technology play in economic development, with the progress of economic restructuring the proportion of expenditure in this field and the total volume of government investment have both noticeably declined. It is also the case that government control both of enterprises and of the general orientation of industrial and technical development has been weakened. Direct government financial support for scientific research and technical development has also diminished considerably.

Before reform, government-run research institutes depended on the government entirely for financial support. In 1985, the government share of institutes' financial resources dropped to 67 per cent of the total; by 1993 it had dropped to 37 per cent, the balance coming from bank loans or money raised by research institutes themselves.[5] Government allocations have also dwindled for technical renovation. In 1982 only 11.4 per cent of the money for technical renovation came from central and local government funding; in

1993 the figure was reduced to 1.4 per cent, the rest of the money again being bank loans or money raised by the enterprises themselves.[6]

Nevertheless, it would be a serious mistake to equate the level of government influence with the changes indicated by these figures. Indeed, government influence far surpasses what is suggested by these data. First, virtually all the key research topics in basic sciences are chosen and conducted by government departments even though the funds may come from many other channels. Second, although direct government funding has become negligible in non-basic research projects and in programmes of technical renovation of enterprises, the government has retained its strong ability to intervene by influencing the direction of bank loans. Only with the approval of the government can an enterprise obtain a bank loan for its own technical development projects. Moreover, only with government approval can an enterprise raise funds from its leading department or the local government.

Large and Medium-Sized State Enterprises as Major Beneficiaries

The policies formulated by central and local governments for promoting technical renovation in various enterprises are directed mainly towards large and medium-sized state enterprises, whose numbers are very limited. Since the mid-1980s nearly all the 20,000 such enterprises in China have conducted technical renovation with government support. Most of the government's funds, as well as technical renovation loans which are largely government-controlled, are spent on these enterprises.

Of the total of 149 billion yuan spent in 1993 for technical renovation in industrial enterprises, 122 billion yuan, or 81.2 per cent, were used by large and medium-sized state enterprises, they are also the major beneficiaries of the various research and development projects conducted by government-funded research institutes. The various plans arranged by central government for technical development and promotion are mainly designed for large and medium-sized state enterprises. The technical development of these enterprises is associated in one way or another with certain plans mapped out by the central or local government. One study of this topic indicates that all the country's large state enterprises have participated in the government's scientific and technical plans.[7]

However, despite the fact that the government has kept the emphasis of its work on large and medium-sized state enterprises, the dependence of these enterprises on government intervention has markedly diminished in the field of technical renovation. This is illustrated in two ways. First, the proportion of government funding in the total amount of money for the technical development in these enterprises has shrunk noticeably, while the amount of money they have raised themselves has considerably increased. In the early 1980s, government funding and the money enterprises have raised for themselves for technical development were approximately equal, but by 1993 government funding had dropped to a mere 6.3 per cent of the total.

Second, of the total number of projects for technical development in all kinds of enterprises, the percentage of those under direct government plans had dropped considerably. In pre-reform years, virtually all technical development projects to be conducted in large and medium-sized state enterprises were decided by government plans, but by 1993 the number of projects chosen by the enterprises themselves accounted for 64.2 per cent of the total.[8] It is expected that, with the intensification of market competition and with further transformation of the managerial mechanisms of large and medium-sized state enterprises, the impact on them of government planning and policy will be continuously eroded.

Less-affected Small Enterprises

The influence of government policies on science and technology is hardly felt by small and medium-sized enterprises, particularly those not in the government sector. There are three reasons for this. First, the number of technical development projects in which the government can directly intervene is very limited. It can only concentrate its attention on a small number of large projects and large enterprises; it lacks the resources to intervene directly in the technical development of hundreds of thousands of non-governmental medium-sized and small enterprises.

Second, within the framework of government plans and policies, the emphasis of technical development is laid on the renovation of existing enterprises, mainly state enterprises which have been in existence for many years. Those enterprises which were established in the last decade or so, which account for the majority of existing non-governmental enterprises, can hardly be included in government policy for technically transforming *existing* enterprises.

Third, owing to their inadequate ability to obtain information, most non-governmental enterprises know little about preferential government policies for technical development; even if they know about them, they would not know how to obtain the benefits of preferential government programmes.[9]

However, the fact that medium-sized and small enterprises are little influenced by state policies on science and technology does not mean that the technical level of these enterprises is low. The pressure of market competition has given these enterprises, especially the non-governmental ones, a strong motivation for technical improvement and, because of this, they compare favourably with large and medium-sized state enterprises in terms of ability to engage in technical development. Despite the fact that due to technical

Table 7.2 *Technical development and types of industrial enterprises, Yichuang City, 1985–89 (%)*

Indicator (1989)	Scale of enterprise			Ownership system		Administrative level			
	Large	Medium	Small	Public	Collective	Central	Municipality	County	Township
Creation rate of new products	58	64	59	62	60	61	60	63	83
Creation rate of new products using imported technology	11	12	12	11	15	7	13	2	0
New product marketing success rate	74	80	83	81	82	78	81	97	75
Share of new products in total output	37	26	29	25	35	35	25	25	65

Source: Jia Wenwei and others (1994, Tables 3 and 18)

147

limitations the new products and new technology developed by non-government enterprises cannot match the country's top level – most of their technology and products are at the middle level – their technical development and product quality are more closely associated with market demand.

Quarterly product quality surveys conducted by the State Technical Supervision Administration since the early 1990s have indicated that non-government enterprises have a higher rate of up-to-standard products than large and medium-sized state enterprises. A sample survey of product quality conducted in the fourth quarter of 1994 by the administration put the average up-to-standard rate of industrial products at 69 per cent, but the rate of those from rural enterprises stood much higher, at 75 per cent.

Other surveys have shown that small enterprises have outdone their larger counterparts, non-government enterprises have done better than state enterprises, and local enterprises have done better than centrally owned enterprises in terms of four important indicators: the creation rate for new products, the creation rate of products based on imported technology, the success rate of new products in marketing, and the proportion of new products in total sales (see Table 7.2).

Projects for Technical Renovation that Fail to Achieve Satisfactory Results

To date, there are few adequate analyses of the overall results achieved in China by enterprises that have undertaken new technical development, but partial studies have indicated that some have failed to yield satisfactory results. Figures from different sources show that one-quarter to one-fifth of technical renovation projects have failed to boost production capacity or have actually caused deterioration in these factories' conditions. Even more projects have failed to measure up to their basic design standards for capacity, product quality and financial returns.[10]

There are three main reasons for these failures. First, the new production capacity cannot yield good results because the newly developed product is unsuitable for the market or is uncompetitive in some respect. Second, some projects cannot be completed or have to be given up midway due to financial difficulties; in some cases market opportunities are missed because of failure to obtain the necessary funds in good time. Third, because of management problems the project cannot be completed on schedule; or there are money shortages caused by fund abuse. Sometimes projects are completed after large sums of money have been added, but then the subsequent debt burden has worsened the enterprise's financial situation.

Among newly developed technology and products, those by research institutes not associated with any enterprises stand a smaller chance of finding their way to the market. A survey of the transfer of scientific and technological results in Shanghai found that none of the eighty-five optical-fibre telecommunications research results registered financial success. Only 40 per cent of the 164 research results obtained by the Second Municipal Light Industrial Bureau, 38 per cent of the 122 results achieved by the Municipal Pharmaceutical Bureau, and 48 per cent of the 38 results obtained by the Municipal United Electricity Company, were successful on the market.[11]

CONCLUSIONS

Since the adoption of the policy of reform and opening up to the outside world, the government has attached more importance to scientific research and technical development. Using measures of direct intervention such as financial allocation, the government has exerted obvious influence on scientific research and technical development. The research and development projects conducted by government research institutes and by large and medium-sized state enterprises are still subject to the influence of government plans for scientific and technical development and technical renovation. However, the influence of the government is diminishing in such fields as the selection of research topics and the sources of research funding.

Market demand now provides the main indicator for technical development in non-state enterprises. Although most new products developed by non-state enterprises are not at the most advanced technical level, these enterprises are able to adapt their technical development to market demand, and they are more motivated than state enterprises in their pursuit of technical progress. As a result, non-state enterprises enjoy a rather high technological success rate, and this explains why non-state enterprises often enjoy a competitive edge in the market over their state-run counterparts.

As things stand now in China, the role of the government is indispensable to scientific research and technical development. However, with the establishment of the market economy and the increasing ability of enterprises to develop their own technology, it is essential gradually to turn the market into the steering force for technical development. Only thus can the limited funds available be put to effective use and technical development better serve market demand. China has now reached a point of development where the limited government-controlled funds still available should be used mainly to promote research in basic sciences and to assist the development of applied technologies that involve exceptionally high risks and costs.

NOTES

1. For a more detailed description, see Wu Heng and Yang Jun (1992) and the work by Gao Xiaosu *et al.* (1993).
2. State Statistical Bureau (1994, p. 604).
3. Yan Xiuzhen and Chen Huashan (1994).
4. State Statistical Bureau (1994); Tang Shiguo (1994).
5. See data in Tang Shiguo (1994) and State Statistical Bureau (1994).
6. See data in State Statistical Bureau (1994).
7. Jia Wenwei *et al.* (1994).
8. See note 4.
9. The existence of this kind of problem is indicated by the research programme of Wei Jiang and Xu Qingrui (1994) and Jia Wenwei *et al.* (1994).
10. Chen Hua (1994); Wang Suliang *et al.* (1994); Research Group of the State Scientific and Technological Commission (1994). In his report, Chen provides information about nineteen counties and cities in the province of Shandong; Wang provides data for Fushun city; and the Research Group of the State Scientific and Technological Commission deals with Shanghai.
11. Research Group of the State Scientific and Technological Commission (1994).

BIBLIOGRAPHY

Chen Hua (1994), 'Technical reform projects: why the rough sailing?', *Gong shang shibao* [Industrial and Commercial Times], 28 October.
Gao Xiaosu and Yuan Guangzhen *et al.* (eds.) (1993), *Fazhan, keji, zhengfu. Zhongguo keji jihua de zhiding he shishi* [Development, Science and Government: The Making and Implementation of Science and Technology Plans in China], Beijing: Defence Industry Press.
Hua Peng (1993), 'Pool funds, sharpen priorities, and speed up implementation', *Zhongguo qiye bao* [China Enterprise News], 26 January.
Jia Wenwei, Ma Chi and Tang Shiguo (1994), *Jishu chungxin: keji yu jingji yitihua fazhan de daolu* [Technical Innovation: The Road to the Integration of Science and Technology and the Economy], Beijing: China Economics Publishing House.
Li Chang (1994), 'Technical progress in Chinese enterprises: the basic situation and prospects', *Keji jinbu yu duice* [Progress and Policies for Science and Technology], 1.
Research Group of the State Scientific and Technological Commission (1994), *Keji chengguo zhuanhua de wenti yu duice* [The Transfer of Technological Results: Problems and Countermeasures], Beijing: China Economics Publishing House.
State Statistical Bureau (1994), *Zhongguo tongji nianjian* [China Statistical Yearbook], Beijing: China Statistical Publishing House.
Tang Shiguo (1994), *Jishu chuangxin – jingji huoli zhi yuan* [Technical Innovation – the Source of Economic Vitality], Beijing: Science and Technology Literature Press.
Wang Suliang, Li Yingfan and Wen Chenquan (1994), 'The technical renovation of industrial enterprises in Fushun: achievements, problems and counter measures', *Fushun jingji* [Fushun Economics], no. 1.
Wei Jiang and Xu Qingrui (1994), 'A study of the technical capacity of small and medium size enterprises', *Kexue guanli yanjiu* [Science Management Research], no. 4.

Wu Heng and Yang Jun (eds) (1992), *Dangdai Zhongguo keji jishu shujie* [Science and Technology Undertakings in Contemporary China], Beijing: Chinese Academy of Social Sciences Press.

Yan Xiuzhen and Chen Huashan (1994), *Shiwunian ji-gai chengji feiran* [Remarkable Achievements in Technical Renovation Over the Past Fifteen Years] *Qiye jishu jinbu* [Progress in Enterprise Technology], 6.

Zhao Yulin (1994), 'Understanding and implementing [the policy] of integrating science, technology and the economy in China since the adoption of the policies of reform and opening up to the outside world', *Keji jinbu yu duice* [Progress and Policies for Science and Technology], 5.

Zhongguo jingji nianjian, [China Economic Yearbook] (various years), Beijing: China Economic Yearbook Publishing House.

8. Sino-Japanese technology transfer and its effects

Tang Shiguo

INTRODUCTION

Modern economic growth can be regarded as a process in which new knowledge is continually accumulated and applied to production.[1] Technology transfer and the accumulation and assimilation of science and technology are particularly important for economic growth in developing countries where science and technology and economic strength are generally weak.

Between the 1950s and the 1970s, technology transfer in China was very inadequate under the 'closed-door' policy. Therefore a big technology gap opened up between most Chinese enterprises and those in the advanced countries. Since the policies of opening up and reform were implemented in 1978, the pace of technology transfer has accelerated. Statistics from the Ministry of Foreign Economic Relations and Trade show that for the period from 1979 to the first half of 1994, the number of contracts for technology transfer totalled 5,621, with a contract value of US$422.7 billion. These figures were, respectively, 6.65 times and 3.66 times the total recorded in the thirty years before 1979. During this period, foreign direct investment has had a contract value of US$244 billion, and the actual investment amounted to US$74.7 billion.[2] The introduction of new technologies has had a great influence on the development of Chinese technology and economy.

Compared to other countries, Japan plays a very important role in technology transfer to China. For the period 1973–93, Japan was the leading country in technology transfer to China with 1,284 projects and a contract value of US$11.818 billion (see Table 8.1). During this period, Japan also directly invested in 7,180 projects in China, with a contract investment value of US$8.9 billion (see Table 8.1). Japan has been a major direct investor in China, second only to the United States if overseas Chinese investors are excluded (from Hong Kong, Macao and Taiwan). Therefore, it is essential to analyse the efficiency of Japanese technology transfer to China in order to understand the impact of international technology transfer generally on the development of the Chinese economy.

Table 8.1   Technology transfer from Japan, 1973–93

Year	Number of contracts	Value (US$ million)
1973–82	203	5,275
1983	44	233
1984	73	344
1985	175	511
1986	175	787
1987	138	710
1988	81	272
1989	52	203
1990	43	92
1991	63	269
1992	136	1,376
1993	101	1,746
Totals	1,284	11,818

Source: Annual Statistics of China's Ministry of Foreign Economy and Trade, various years

THE DEVELOPMENT OF SINO-JAPANESE TECHNOLOGY TRANSFER

Technology transfer from Japan to China has been undertaken in three main ways: first, by technology imports; second, by direct investment from Japanese enterprises; third, by scientific and technological co-operation agreements. This chapter will concentrate on the first two of these.

Technology Imports

Small-scale technology imports from Japan can be traced back to the 1960s. The trade grew with the normalization of the relationship between the two countries, and has been rapid since 1979. Contracts for the importation of fifty complete sets of equipment were made during 1978 and 1979. According to the statistics from the Ministry of Foreign Economic Relations and Trade, during the years from 1979 to 1987 Japan was the largest trading partner in technology transfer in terms of the number of contracts and trade volume.[3] Despite the impact of the 'Toshiba Incident', which caused a decrease of trade volume, Japan has remained one of the major suppliers of technology since 1987. Table 8.1 shows the number and value of technology contracts from Japan to China.

The import of complete sets of equipment takes a considerable share in the technology transfer from Japan to China. In the 1970s, the import of such equipment accounted for more than 90 per cent of total imports of technology in terms of contracts and trade volume. These imports were mainly related to fertilizers, petrochemicals, metallurgy, consumer electronics – all areas which China urgently needed to develop. The import of licences did not often occur in the early period, and were limited to the machinery industry. In the 1980s, the import of licences was more frequent. In 1985, eighty-six projects were imported through licences, almost the same number as the imports of technological equipment.

Although at first the import of licences was fewer than 10 per cent of total projects, they grew rapidly. According to the Japanese statistics, the figures were: 1.7 billion yen by 1977, the tenth largest destination for Japanese technology exports; 4.8 billion yen in 1981, the eighth largest destination; and 19.7 billion yen by 1986, with China behind only the USA and Korea as an export destination for this kind of transaction.[4] In 1993, the number of import of licences was sixty, exceeding the number of imported equipment, among which one-third of the import total was in electronics technology.

Direct Investment by Japanese Enterprises

In recent years, foreign direct investment (FDI) has become an important route for the transfer of foreign technology to China. There has been a lot of discussion about the impact of FDI on technology transfer to developing countries other than China, and in his discussion of the subject, Svennilson has argued that the most successful cases are those made through the investment of the western businessmen in the developing countries.[5]

According to the Japanese Ministry of Finance, the first Japanese investment in China started in 1974, but only came into operation in 1979 with an investment of only US$14 million in that year. Between 1979 and 1990, Japan invested in 859 projects in China, with a value of US$2.8 billion.[6] Statistics from the Chinese Ministry of Foreign Economy and Trade, however, show that from 1979 to 1990, Japan directly invested in 1,290 projects, with a contract value of US$3.1 billion and an actual investment of US$2.493 billion. New progress has been made in the 1990s. In 1993, Japan invested in 3,488 projects, 2.7 times the total recorded for 1979–90, with a contract value of almost US$3.0 billion, and an actual investment of US$1.324 billion (see Table 8.2).

At first, investment was concentrated in service and 'non-production' activities, then in the labour-intensive areas of textiles, foodstuffs and light industry. In the 1990s it moved into infrastructure and high technology, including the energy, transportation, communication and raw materials sectors. According to Japan's Ministry of Finance, manufacturing accounted for

Table 8.2   Japanese direct investment in China, 1979–93

Year	Number of projects	Value of investment (US$ million)
1979–86	306	1,010
1987	110	297
1988	239	296
1989	294	356
1990	341	534
1991	599	533
1992	1,805	710
1993	3,488	1,324
Totals	7,182	5,060

Source: As for Table 8.1

56 per cent of its direct investment in China, of which 16 per cent was in the electrical and electronics industry, 10.6 per cent in textiles and 6.5 per cent in machinery. All non-manufacturing accounting for 38.9 per cent of the total, and of this 27.3 per cent was in services and 4.5 per cent in real estate.

Japanese investment at one time was concentrated in Dalian, Beijing, Shanghai and Guangdong, but has recently begun to move to the hinterland.

MAJOR FACTORS AFFECTING SINO-JAPANESE TECHNOLOGY TRANSFER

Many problems exist and need to be solved in spite of the rapid development of Sino-Japanese technology transfer. The process is basically a one-way transfer from Japan to China, which is understandable since China is a developing country. From the Chinese point of view, however, technology transferred from Japan has been less advanced and more expensive than was wished and has often had harsh terms, including restrictions on exports and diffusion or on the supply of raw materials and parts.

Japanese direct investment in China started rather late and on a small scale. In spite of the rapid increase of the number of projects in recent years, investments were typically small. In 1993, the average investment in each project was only US$380,000. Moreover, these investments were often in the non-manufacturing industries, or in labour-intensive manufacturing industries, while investment in technology-intensive industries has been rare. However, from the Japanese point of view, China has expected too much from the technology transfer, and expectations have exceeded realities in both countries. The investment environment and the management of enterprises also need to be improved.[7]

Based on the development of the transfer process, we find that the following factors have exercised great influence on the transfer of Japanese technology to China.

Economic Relations Between Japan and China

The sound development of Sino-Japanese economic relations is an important basis for the transfer. Technology transfer booms when economic relations are smooth and is hindered when the relationship is poor. Since the normalization of their relationship in the early 1970s, the promotion of their relationship has been an important target of the two governments, despite the restrictions placed on economic relations by various factors, among which the US–Japanese relationship is an important element. Postwar development of Sino-Japanese relations proves that Japan has been following the US stance towards China, and its exchanges with China have been subordinate to US policies towards China.

The US–Japanese relationship has remained the basis of Japan's foreign strategy, despite the fact that Japan has been increasingly independent in its foreign policy. Japan remains dependent on the US relationship to a considerable extent, and this influences its economic and technological exchanges and other co-operative relationships with China, which are designed to keep intact the global US–Japanese partnership.

The 'Toshiba Incident' in which China was not directly involved illustrates this point. As a result, the export of many advanced technologies to China was restricted using the cover of the Co-ordinating Committee for Export Control (COCOM), which obviously reflected pressure from the USA. Moreover, with the development of economic relations between China and Japan, trade frictions and conflicts are bound to happen, and their trade relations have more direct influence on the development of the technology transfer.

The Environment of Economic Development

The environment of economic development in both countries also has an important influence on technology transfer. When the Chinese economy grows at a high speed, technology transfer from Japan grows rapidly; whereas when China adjusts its economy, the scale of transfer declines. The rapid growth of the Chinese economy and the improvement of the investment environment has built confidence in the Japanese investment in China and promoted the scale of Japanese direct investment in China.

On the Japanese side, the increase in economic strength and technological capabilities has accelerated the pace of technological improvements. Japan is active in transferring its mature technologies to foreign countries as well as in developing new technologies, in an attempt to obtain more profits or explore new markets. In recent years, however, because of the slowing pace of economic growth and the appreciation of the Japanese yen, Japanese enterprises have been increasingly active in transferring capital abroad and exploring new markets. Therefore, there has been an obvious growth in Japanese direct investment in China. Technology transfer is also greatly influenced by state macroeconomic policies and planning. For instance, at the end of 1970s, the Chinese government planned to import 3,000 projects from abroad within a few years, and technology transfer increased accordingly afterwards.

The Attitude of Japanese Enterprises

The attitude and behaviour of an enterprise plays an important role in technology transfer and market behaviour. This is particularly true in Japan where as much as 70 per cent of R&D expenditures are met by companies. This therefore gives the private companies a high degree of autonomy in using or selling the results of R&D.

However, Japanese enterprises as a rule are not active in offering technology because of their conservative attitude. Transfer usually occurs only as a result of partner pressure. According to one Japanese survey made in 1984, only 30 per cent of companies were willing to transfer their technology, and more than half of the companies were not willing to do so. In recent years, Japan has been more active in offering its technology to China in response to the changing international economic situation.

Japanese enterprises are more conservative in terms of their offers of technology transfer, i.e. they are usually reluctant to transfer their advanced technology. In a recent exhibition of China's achievements of technology transfer in the last fifteen years, we interviewed thirty-five Chinese enterprises which had imported technology from Japan as well as from the USA and Germany: 60 per cent of the Chinese enterprises found that Japanese technology was easy to apply but less advanced; 40 per cent believed that it was relatively expensive; and 30 per cent believed that the terms for the transfer were harsh.

Most of the products made by using transferred Japanese technology are restricted to sales in the Chinese market and are unlikely to be exported. Some Japanese scholars also agree that Japanese companies only wish to offer technology which is no threat to their overseas markets. They take risk-proofed and cautious attitudes towards their investment in China.

The Behaviour of Chinese Enterprises

With the development of a socialist market economy in China, Chinese enterprises have been increasingly required to increase their technology and improve their competitiveness. Since importing is an effective path to obtain technology and expand production quickly, and since they are not completely in a market situation but usually face low risks and high profits, almost every enterprise is willing to introduce technology.

When we interviewed thirty-five enterprises and asked whether the technology they imported could be developed in China, the answer was unanimously no. When we asked whether, if the technology *could* be developed in China, they would import it or develop it themselves, the answer was again that they would import it. The reasoning was that it would take more time to develop the technology on their own, that the quality would be less reliable, and the probability of success would be lower.

Thus while the great demand for foreign technology on one hand has promoted the technology transfer, on the other hand it has led to problems. Technologies have been imported in haste with an absence of necessary information, with incomplete investigations and by unskilful negotiation, all of which has led to high levels of duplication and other problems. Some Japanese companies take advantage of the urgent needs of the Chinese enterprises by exporting less-advanced technology or raising prices.

A PRELIMINARY EVALUATION OF SINO-JAPANESE TECHNOLOGY TRANSFER

There is no doubt that Sino-Japanese technology transfer is playing an important role in the development of the Chinese economy. However, it is still difficult to judge the results because, on one hand, little has been done to evaluate the effectiveness of technology transfer in China, and on the other hand, it is not easy to distinguish the impact of Japanese technology from the whole process of technology transfer from abroad. Here I shall attempt a preliminary evaluation of Sino-Japanese transfer in terms of production capacity, innovative capability and impact on exports.

The Expansion of Productive Capacity

The most obvious result of technology transfer is the rapid expansion of productive capacity in industries which have applied the transferred technology. For example, let us look at the colour TV industry, which imported more technology from Japan than any other industry. In the early 1980s there was no domestic production of colour TVs in China. During the 1980s more than a hundred production lines were imported, 60 per cent from Japan, among which thirteen were from the Victory Company and eight from the Panasonic Corporation. The introduction of technology rapidly increased the production capacity of colour TVs in China. There were only 56,000 sets produced from 1970 to 1980, but in 1984 alone the capacity was 1,294 million sets, 45 per cent of the total output value of the domestic electronics industry.[8]

By the end of 1994, China had become a major world producer of colour TVs, with an annual capacity of 14 million sets, almost 440 times the output of 1980.[9] Such a rapid increase in production capacity could never have been achieved without technology transfer. Some of the news media commented when reporting the development of the domestic colour TV industry that it took only fifteen years to cover the path which had taken the developed countries forty years.[10] Table 8.3 illustrates the development of China's colour TV industry before and after the introduction of foreign technology.

However, despite the great profits brought about by the expansion of production capacity and the increase of output value, people often criticize the import of complete sets of equipment and the attempts to expand production capacity quickly. The successful introduction of 100 production lines of colour TV, which has made great contributions to the development of the industry, is often cited as a typical example of poor management and duplication of technology transfer. The critics argue, first, that the rapid expansion of production capacity could not be matched by the Chinese firms providing components or by actual demand – thereby leading to surplus production. As estimated in the mid-1980s, the full capacity of the 100 lines was 15 million sets, but demand was less than half this level. The actual output was 4.13 million sets, using only 25 per cent of the capacity.

Second, the domestic industry is not able to match the rapid increase in productive capacity, and consequently a lot of foreign currency is needed to import components. During 1979 and 1983, in particular, China was not able to match the imported foreign technology.

Third, we have to ask whether it is worthwhile to use such large funds to expand capacity. Would it not be better to import only a few lines, and expand capacity by assimilation and innovation at a gradual pace; or, along the lines suggested by sequential economic theories, to import a few production lines and colour kinescopes to integrate technology imports with the expansion of domestic capacities?

In 1985, a national sampling was done by the National Research Centre for Science and Technology (NRCSTD) into 220 projects to import foreign technology during the period from 1973 to 1984. Only 39 per cent of the

Table 8.3   Growth of colour TV output in China, 1971–93 (thousand units)

Year	Before technical imports	After technical imports
1971	0.2	
1972	0.1	
1973	0.6	
1974	2.4	
1975	2.9	
1976	2.8	
1977	2.5	
1978	3.7	
1979	9.4	
1980		32
1981		152
1982		288
1983		531
1984		1,244
1985		4,100
1986		4,146
1987		6,727
1988		10,377
1989		9,502
1990		10,330
1991		12,051
1992		13,333
1993		14,358

Sources: Taiwan Economic Research Institute (1989); *Zhongguo tongji nianjian*, various years.

sample projects realized 80 per cent of their original design capacity and only 21 per cent had 80 per cent of the necessary domestic matching equipment (components, etc.).[11] Ten years later, in spite of significant progress, there was still a considerable number of projects which were not able to realize their planned capacity. The actual operation of even the successful enterprises was not as inspiring as it appeared.

Almost all of the thirty enterprises in the exhibition which had successfully introduced foreign technology had reached or surpassed their design capacity, and their production and output value grew substantially. However, a number of them had had a hard time or were in debt, despite the output increase, due to such factors as the pressure of debt caused by the reform of the foreign currency policy and price increases of raw materials caused by inflation.

The Impact on Domestic Innovative Capability

The ultimate goal of introducing technology is to raise technological capability, and innovative capability in particular. Only in this way can sustainable and stable economic growth be achieved. Japan and Korea are regarded as successful examples in this sense. In the process of technology transfer, China has been trying to follow their examples and has made some progress. Most significantly, the technical transformation in Chinese enterprises has accelerated and the technical level has improved through technology transfer.

By the end of the 1970s, because of the long duration of the closed-door policy and neglect of market competition, technology in many Chinese enterprises remained at the level of the 1960s or even the 1950s, by international standards. The import of technology has enabled many enterprises to make a leap forward of ten, twenty or even thirty years in just a few years, and to obtain the technical level of the late 1970s or early 1980s by international standards.

Let me return to the example of colour TVs. By the mid-1980s, China had developed forty-eight models of colour TV, including models using dual circuit boards, dual screens, dual language systems. The technological level of Chinese colour TVs generally had reached international standards in the early 1980s, with reliability and consistency indicators raised significantly and an average of safe operation for 15,000 hours. By the 1990s, the modelling, quality and technology levels of Chinese colour TVs are among the most advanced in the international market. The average safe operating performance time is now more than 20,000 hours, some even reaching 30–40,000 hours, thereby surpassing the international criterion of 15,000 hours.

Another indicator of the rising technology level is the recent growth of licence imports. For a long time, complete sets of equipment dominated the import of technology in China, and is widely believed to be a problem reflecting administrative behaviour and faulty policy-making. In fact, the government has recently encouraged the import of licences as part of its strategy for importing foreign technology. In the early 1980s, the import of licences increased greatly for a short period of time but thereafter declined because direct import of complete sets made production easier and showed a more immediate result than could be obtained by importing licences. This reflected the low technological capacity of some Chinese enterprises.

By 1993, although consumer electronics remained an important area in the import of Japanese technology, none the less some 80 per cent of imports took the form of licence purchase. This demonstrates that the introduction of production lines has improved technological capability in China to such an extent that Chinese enterprises are now able to assimilate technology by importing licences.

Improvement in the efficiency of technology transfer should lay the basis for improvements in domestic innovative capability. This has happened in China to a certain extent. However, real improvement depends on the assimilation of the imported technology and the strengthening of in-house R&D. In the development of the colour TV industry, China followed a strategy of combining assimilation and innovation in order to assimilate the overall technology as well as to promote the localization of component parts manufacture and raw materials.

At the present time, 95 per cent of the parts in small and medium-sized screen colour TV sets can be made domestically. Independent development of colour TV sets is being strengthened; advanced technology such as CAD/CAM is applied to the production; and new models and new functions which are at the forefront of international trends are being developed. Some enterprises are now able to create their own new technology. All this shows that the introduction of technology has made contributions to the development of innovative capacity in the colour TV industry.

In 1993, we conducted a survey to try to understand the role of the technology institutions in the technology development of six industries including machinery, automobiles, casting, petrochemicals and software. The survey showed that technology transfer from abroad has been an important factor in promoting technology innovation. Of the 108 firms interviewed, 28.7 per cent (31 firms) reported that their major product changes were mainly due to technology import; 31.5 per cent (34 firms) reported that major process changes were mainly the result of technology import. Table 8.4 shows the

Table 8.4   The contribution of technology transfer to domestic technical progress in six industries (cases reported in survey)

Industry	Major product change	Major process change	Minor product change	Minor process change
Textiles	11	8	4	1
Autoparts	8	8	5	3
Polymers	5	6	7	3
Machine tools	4	10	2	6
Metal castings	2	2	2	2
Software	1	0	0	0
Total	31	34	20	15

Source: Wang *et al.* (1996).

differences among the six sectors in the contribution of technology transfer to technology development.[12]

However, there exist differences of opinion about the effect of technology transfer on innovative activities. As noted by many scholars, assimilation and innovation are the weakest points in the technology transfer process in China. The problems of assimilation are neglected by the economic bureaucrats and by enterprises; and the funds allocated for future assimilation when technology transfers are planned are too small. In addition, investment in R&D is not increased to the level needed to ensure the assimilation, absorption and ultimate innovation based on imported technology.

Even in our interviews with thirty-five successful enterprises, we found that only 80 per cent of them had assimilated and innovated on the basis of transferred technology, and only a few enterprises had increased substantially their input of R&D. Substantive assimilation had never occurred in 10 per cent of the enterprises, and these had no plans to change the situation. If we look at the overall national position, assimilation and innovation based on imported technology is even less impressive. Our sampling of the problem in the mid-1980s showed that partial improvements and imitations were done with the imported technology in only 13 per cent of the 220 imported projects looked at.

In Chinese academic circles, some scientists take the view that technology transfer from abroad is a barrier to, rather than a catalyst for, technology innovation. This is because technology imports make Chinese firms less interested in domestic R&D activities and their results, and it thus hampers domestic technology transfer from R&D laboratories to industrial firms.[13]

Contributions to Exports

Technology imports have made an important contribution to the promotion of exports. For example, there was no export of colour TVs in the early 1980s, but exports approached 1 million sets in 1987 and 4.6 million sets in 1994 (see Table 8.5). TVs have thus became a major export component in the machine and electrical appliance sectors. However, in terms of all imported projects, technology transfer has made very little contribution to exports. For example, in the 220 enterprises investigated by NRCSTD, only 7 per cent have entered the international market.

More obvious contributions to exports have been made by foreign direct investment. In 1993, total exports by China were US$91.77 billion, and 27.5 per cent (US$25.24 billion) of these were achieved by foreign-invested enterprises. By comparison, in 1981 the exports of this group were only US$32 million, 0.35 per cent of the total. China's recent stable export growth can be attributed to a great extent to the rapid export growth achieved by foreign-

Table 8.5   Exports of colour TV sets by China, 1985–94

Year	Number (Thousands)	Value (US$ million)
1985	236	33.8
1986	424	86.1
1987	906	131.2
1988	1,511	220.2
1989	1,790	252.0
1990	2,620	405.1
1991	3,403	632.6
1992	3,174	499.4
1993	3,108	423.3
1994	4,600	—

Source: *Yearbook of China's Machinery and Electrical Appliances Industry,* various years

invested enterprises (see Table 8.6). If we try to measure the contribution of foreign invested enterprises to the increase of exports we find that in the early 1990s this was 40 per cent and in 1993, 115 per cent. Within these data it is difficult to identify the contribution of Japanese investment, but the role of Japanese-invested enterprises is obvious in the case of China's exports to Japan.

Table 8.7 illustrates the development of the trade between the two countries. It shows that China's exports to Japan have enjoyed fast growth and, especially in recent years, the growth rate is faster than the overall growth. Therefore, we may conclude that the contributions made by Japanese-invested enterprise have been relatively great. However, export growth usually coincides with a corresponding growth of imports. In 1993, foreign-invested enterprises imported goods to the value of US$67 billion, which was 34.3 per cent of total imports.

Another important effect of foreign direct investment has been on the formation of Chinese capital. In 1993, foreign direct investment in fixed assets was US$25.76 billion, 12.3 per cent of a total of US$209 billion. From 1983 to 1993, the average growth of investment in fixed assets in China was 11.3 per cent, but the average growth of direct overseas investment was 44.8 per cent. The Japanese direct investment was only 4 per cent of total FDI, so we may conclude that Japan's contribution was relatively limited in this respect.

Table 8.6   *Contribution to China's exports of goods produced by foreign capital, 1981–93*

Year	Total exports		Exports of goods produced by foreign capital		
	Value (US$ billion)	Growth rate (%)	Value (US$ billion)	Share of total (%)	Growth rate (%)
1981	22.01	20.5	0.03	0.1	—
1982	22.32	1.4	0.05	0.2	67.0
1983	22.23	–0.4	0.33	1.5	560.0
1984	26.14	17.6	0.07	0.3	–78.8
1985	27.35	4.6	0.30	1.1	328.6
1986	30.94	13.1	0.58	1.9	93.3
1987	39.44	24.5	1.21	3.1	108.6
1988	47.52	20.5	2.46	5.2	103.3
1989	52.54	10.6	4.91	9.4	99.2
1990	62.09	18.2	7.81	12.6	58.8
1991	71.91	15.8	12.06	16.8	54.8
1992	85.00	18.2	17.36	20.4	44.2
1993	91.77	8.0	25.24	27.5	45.4

Source: *Annual Statistics of China's Foreign Economy and Trade,* various years; *Zhongguo tongji nianjian*, various years

Table 8.7   *Growth of Sino-Japanese trade, 1979–93 (US$ thousand million)*

Year	China's imports from Japan	China's exports to Japan
1979	36.99	29.55
1980	50.78	43.80
1981	50.97	52.91
1982	35.11	53.52
1983	49.12	50.87
1984	72.17	64.83
1986	98.56	56.52
1988	94.76	98.59
1989	85.16	111.46
1990	61.30	120.54
1991	85.93	142.16
1992	119.49	169.53
1993	172.81	205.63

Source: Li (1994), based on Japanese trade statistics

CONCLUSIONS

Technology transfer is an important path to the accumulation and application of science and technology and to the stimulation of rapid economic growth. The pace of foreign technology imports has been accelerating since the adoption of policies of reform and opening up at the end of the 1970s in China. The following is a summary analysis of technology transfer between Japan and China.

Imports of Technology

1. From 1973 to 1993, technology imports from Japan were larger than from any other source in terms of the number of contracts and trade value, with a contract value of US$11.818 billion in 1,284 projects (Table 8.1). There have been three 'high tides' of technology importing from Japan: 1979–81, 1985–87 and 1992–93. The import of complete sets of equipment and of key equipment have dominated recent technology transfer and the import of licences is also a growing trend.
2. The general state of Sino-Japanese economic relations has a particularly strong impact on trends in technology transfer; and the development of economic relations is closely related to the economic and foreign polices of the two governments. Thus technology transfer is particularly influenced by US–Japanese and US–Chinese relations.
3. The attitude and behaviour of Chinese and Japanese enterprises are the most direct factors which influence technology transfer between the two countries. Chinese enterprises are enthusiastic about technology transfer and have great expectations of it because they see their needs and are aware of the Japanese role as a model for economic development in this respect. However, many problems have surfaced in Chinese enterprises due to poor management and inexperience in introducing foreign technology. Further, Japanese enterprises are conservative about transferring advanced technology.
4. The technology transfer between Japan and China has been of great importance to the economic development of China, particularly in the expansion of production in some industries. The production capacity of colour TVs has been increased by several hundred times in a decade as a result of imports of production lines.
5. Technology transfer has promoted technological improvements in the enterprises which imported Japanese technology, increased their level of technology and improved their innovative capability to a certain extent. However, fundamental improvement in the ability to innovate has not

taken place in most Chinese enterprises, because they have not yet made enough effort to assimilate the imported technology.

6. Japanese technology transfer has made a limited contribution to China's export performance because the transfered technology tends to be of a less advanced kind and is usually accompanied by restrictions on exports.

Japanese Direct Investment in China

1. From 1979 to 1993, the contract volume of Japanese direct investment was 7,182 projects, with realized investment of US$5.060 billion (Table 8.2).
2. Data are insufficient to evaluate the influence of Japanese direct investment on the development of technology in China. However, FDI has definitely played an important role in technology transfer to China, and this is reflected by the active attitude of Chinese enterprises in attracting foreign investment and the obvious success of the foreign-invested enterprises.
3. Obvious contributions have been made by Japanese direct investment to the rapid growth of China's exports, particularly in recent years.

NOTES

1. Kuznets (1966).
2. Data from the *Exhibition of Forty Five Years of Achievement in Technology Introduction in China*.
3. *Riben wenti yanjiu* (1989).
4. Statistical Bureau, General Affairs Administration (1988).
5. Svennilson (1967).
6. Japan Society for Commerce and Legal Affairs (1991).
7. *Ni-Chu keizai gijutsu gosaku daisanji kenkyu tokei shiryo* (1986).
8. Institute of Electronics (1987).
9. *Jinrong shibao* (1995).
10. *Jingji cankao* (1994).
11. National Research Centre for Science and Technology Development (NRCSTD) (1987).
12. An investigation done jointly by NRCSTD and the Development Research Centre under the State Council, sponsored by the World Bank.
13. Kong Derong and Tang Shiguo (1993).

REFERENCES

Exhibition of Forty Five Years of Achievement in Technology Introduction in China (organized by the State Economic and Trade Commission, May 1995).

Institute of Electronics (1987), *Case Study on the Technology Introduction in Color TV and Integrated Circuits*, Beijing: Ministry of Electronics Industry.

Japan Society for Commerce and Legal Affairs (ed.) (1991), *Saikin Ni-Chu goshi kigyo* [The Most Recent Developments in Sino-Japanese Joint Enterprises], October.

Jingji cankao [Economic Reference] (1994), 4 December.

Jinrong shibao [Financial Times] (1995), 20 January.

Kong Derong and Tang Shiguo (1993), *Jishu shangyehua* [The Commercialization of Technology], Beijing: China Economics Publishing House.

Kuznets, S. (1966), *Modern Economic Growth, Rate, Structure and Spread*, New Haven, Conn.: Yale University Press.

Li Xiao (1994), 'Sino-Japanese economic relations towards the 21st century', *Jindai riben jingji* [The Modern Japanese Economy], 4.

National Research Centre for Science and Technology Development (NRCSTD) (1987), *Zhongguo jishu yinjin zhanliu yu zhengxe yanjiu* [The Strategy and Policy of Technology Introduction in China], Beijing.

Ni-Chu keizai gijutsu gosaku daisanji kenkyu tokei shiryo [Materials from the third seminar on Sino-Japanese economic cooperation] (1986), Tokyo.

Riben wenti yanjiu [Research on Japanese Problems] (1989), 4.

Statistical Bureau, General Affairs Administration (1988), *Kagaku gijutsu kenkyu hokoku* [Report on Scientific and Technological Research], Tokyo.

Svennilson, I. (1967), 'The strategy of transfer', in D.L. Spencer and A. Woroniak (eds), *The Transfer of Technology to Developing Countries*, New York: Praeger.

Taiwan Economic Research Institute (1989), *Riben jishu yinchu fuwu taixi yanjiu baogao* [A Report on the Service Network of Japanese Technology Trade], Taipei.

Wang Huijun, Hu Zhaoxiang, Tang Shigo and Lu Wei (1996), *Zhongguo gongyeh qiyeh jisha fazhan* (Technology Development in Chinese enterprises), Beijing: China Development Press.

Yearbook of China's Machinery and Electrical Appliances Industry, various years.

Zhongguo tongji nianjian [China Statistical Yearbook] (various years), Beijing: Statistical Publishing House.

9. Technology development and export performance: is China a frog or a goose?

David Wall and Yin Xiangshuo

INTRODUCTION

A major part of the logic of the 'open door' policy introduced by the Government of China in the late 1970s was the need to import technology in order to strengthen the development of Chinese industry, in both the import-substitution and export sectors.[1] The leaders believed that an important reason for the backward condition of the industrial sector was the obsolescent technology on which it was based. There was a widespread conviction that by importing technology and using it to develop its science and technology capability China could and should 'leapfrog' over several generations of technology and move itself into the modern phase of high-tech industry.[2] Fear of becoming indebted to the west meant that the importance of establishing a strong export sector to pay for the technology imports was stressed from the outset. However, it was also strongly felt that China should not be satisfied with the role of a hewer of wood and drawer of water for developed countries, exporting low value-added labour-intensive products to them, but that it should develop a high value-added hi-tech export sector as soon as possible. This in turn meant that it was important to develop and assimilate modern technological capability as soon as possible.

The 'leapfrog' strategy for science and technology was in contrast to the 'feel for the stones as you cross the river' approach successfully adopted in most other areas of economic reform. The trade-oriented science and technology strategy adopted by the 'newly industrialized countries' (NICs) of east and south-east Asia has been described, for example by Yamazawa *et al.* (1991), as the 'flying geese' strategy. The allusion is to the V-shaped pattern geese make when flying in formation, the argument being that Asian development is characterized by one economy (Japan) having a comparative advantage in exports based on the most modern technologies, while the other countries in the region follow behind in neat formation as they work their way through the various stages of technological development in sequence. The implication is that countries can be ranked according to their technological capability and that their ranking will determine in which industries they have a comparative advantage. The conclusion is that if countries set up industries in advance of their technology ranking then those industries will be inefficient and uncompetitive on world markets.

The significance of exports in the technological development equation is not only that they help generate the income required to finance increased imports of technology but also that they improve the efficiency and therefore the competitiveness of the economy. Extensive research (for example, by Little *et al.*, 1970; Bhagwati, 1978; Krueger, 1978; and Shepherd and Langoni, 1991) has demonstrated that the more open an economy, the more likely it is to be able to sustain higher levels of economic growth, and that increased access to and adaptation of new technology is an important element in that process.[3] The frequent emphasis which the Government of China has placed on the need to open up the Chinese economy indicates that it is aware of the importance of improving technological capability and through that the economy's international competitiveness.[4] There are indications, however, that its ability to turn this awareness into action has had only a limited effect.

As early as 1987, western economists were questioning the wisdom of China's adoption of the 'leapfrog' strategy of trade-oriented technological development; for example Hughes (1987, p. 163) concluded that the strategy's reliance on subsidies on the use of capital and new technology meant that 'High capital intensity in the [Chinese] economy generally, suggests that while labour is overpriced in relation to its productivity, capital is under priced, making for excessive capital and technological intensity and hence for unnecessarily high operating costs.' Other western economists have raised more general doubts about the efficiency and effectiveness of China's science and technology policy (most notably Conroy, 1992) and its effect on export performance (for example, World Bank, 1994). This chapter examines, briefly, the measures that China has taken to enhance its technological capability and the extent to which its export performance reflects that technological change.

THE TECHNOLOGY ENHANCEMENT PROGRAMMES

Since the economic reform programme was introduced in 1978, China's economy has experienced a period of rapid development. But economic growth has not been a steady process. By the late 1980s the problem of low efficiency in industry became especially conspicuous: much of industry was seen to have low capacity utilization, poor quality control and high cost techniques. The central government, in order to increase the efficiency of manufacturing industry and to promote steady and sustained long-run growth in the 1990s and into the next century, began to put more emphasis on the development of technology. In March 1985, Deng Xiaoping, then the chairman of the Central Advisory Commission of the Chinese Communist Party, said in an address to a national science conference that reforms were urgently needed to help link scientific research with economic development.[5] Later, the Central Committee of the Communist Party issued a decision on reforming the management of science and technology as part of the overall reforms.

In 1987, in his report to the Thirteenth Party Congress, Zhao Ziyang pointed out that the most serious problem faced in the attempt to realize the target of doubling GNP by the end of the century was the low efficiency of economic activities. In order to solve this problem he argued that it was of primary importance to develop science and technology and education in order to enhance technological progress and achieve an improvement in the quality of labour.[6] The crucial, strategic importance of developing a coherent science and technology policy was stressed at the Congress and was enshrined in its report. It was reiterated later in the report of the Fourteenth Congress.

The government also has the intention of upgrading the level and technological sophistication of exports. Since the reforms began, China has rapidly increased its exports and changed its export structure. The share of total exports in GNP and of manufactured exports in total exports have risen rapidly. However, its manufactured exports are still largely labour-intensive with low added value. According to the statistics from the Ministry of Foreign Trade and Economic Co-operation (MOFTEC),[7] the index of total volume of China's exports was 315.5 in 1990 (1980=100), but the corresponding index for total value was only 284.9.[8] Thus, increasing the share of capital- and technology-intensive exports became an important task. As the then Minister of Foreign Economic Relations and Trade put it:

> China will strive to raise the quality and grades of export commodities, increase the export ratio of electrical and electronic products and complete sets of equipment, i.e. instead of the current export structure of light industrial products, stress will be placed on the export of high-tech items and more value-added products.[9]

Since the late 1980s, the Chinese government has adopted several technology enhancement programmes under the direction of the State Commission of Science and Technology. These programmes include the '863' Programme, the Key Task Programme and the 'Torch' Programme. The '863' Programme, approved by the State Council in March 1986, is aimed at tracing the most advanced science and technology in the world and enhancing China's basic research in these newest areas. The Key Task Programme is designed to address the important technological problems in both scientific research and

key economic construction programmes. The 'Torch' Programme, introduced in August 1988, is the most widespread programme and involves a
great many technological personnel. Its purpose is mainly to integrate research achievements, especially those from the above-mentioned programmes, into economic practice so as to raise the productivity of the
national economic activities. In order to better carry out this programme,
many hi-tech industrial development zones (i.e. hi-tech parks) have been
established throughout China.

Although all the hi-tech programmes are aimed at raising the national level
of technology, each of them has different functions. The '863' and Key Task
Programmes are mandatory plans, with the former aiming at following the
latest scientific and technological developments in the world and the latter
focusing on big key technological problems in the national Five-Year Plans.
The 'Torch' Programme, being a guidance plan, was designed to bridge the
divide between the scientific and technological achievements from the above-
mentioned programmes and business activities. So the aims of these programmes, especially of the 'Torch' Programme, can be summarized as being
intended to commercialize, industrialize and internationalize technological
achievements.

Commercialization and industrialization are literally understandable by
themselves, the intention being to direct most of the research into applied
fields so that new hi-tech industries can be established and hi-tech products
produced competitively. Internationalization, to a certain extent, is also a part
of commercialization. It means to import technology by various commercial
means, to co-operate with foreigners in research and development, and, more
importantly, relying on its own technological strength, to produce and increase the share of capital- and technology-intensive exports, especially hi-
tech products, so as to raise the added value of the exports and upgrade
China's export structure. As Song Jian, Director of the State Commission of
Science and Technology, said at the Third National Working Conference on
the 'Torch' Programme: 'the "Torch" Programme is a banner and a great
policy which, market-oriented, guides the science and technology sector into
the world economy'.[10] So internationalization, broadly speaking, is to help
the Chinese economy better integrate with the world economy and narrow the
gap between it and the advanced countries. More specifically, the aims can be
simplified into two figures: the share of hi-tech industries in GNP should
increase to 10 per cent, and in exports to 8 per cent by the end of the
century.[11]

The Implementation of the Hi-tech Programmes

The measures introduced to promote the implementation of hi-tech programmes are two-fold. One is institutional: a special office for the 'Torch' Programme was set up under the State Commission of Science and Technology to co-ordinate and guide the programme; and some hi-tech industrial development zones were established to be the bases of hi-tech industries.[12] The other is policy treatment: certain preferential measures were taken to promote the development of hi-tech industries.

Since the late 1980s, hi-tech industrial development zones (HTIDZs) have been established throughout the country to serve as the production base of hi-tech industries. In 1991, the State Council approved the first twenty-seven state HTIDZs. By 1993, there were fifty-two HTIDZs at the national level which were approved by the State Council. There are many more at provincial and local levels. The HTIDZs are designed to be different from special economic zones (SEZs) and economic and technology development zones (ETDZs) in the following ways: first, SEZs and ETDZs are set up to absorb foreign investment in coastal areas so as to stimulate the economic development of the whole country, while the HTIDZs are designed to promote the commercialization, industrialization and internationalization of technology achievements, depending mainly on China's own scientific and technological personnel; second, although HTIDZs also take an open-door stance, the policy treatment is quite different from SEZs and ETDZs. In HTIDZs, preferential treatment is only given to hi-tech industrial enterprises, whether they are domestic or foreign-owned, and no preferential treatment will be granted to general and traditional technology and products.[13]

In order to promote the development of hi-tech industries and hi-tech industrial development zones, preferential policy measures were also adopted. On 6 March 1991, the State Council approved the *Provisional Stipulations about Some Policy Measures on State Hi-tech Industrial Development Zones* and the *Stipulations about Tax Policies on State Hi-tech Industrial Development Zones*.[14] According to these two documents, the hi-tech enterprises in the zones can enjoy several preferential treatments, including:

1. Import and export policy
   - imported raw materials and parts for production of exports are exempted from import licences;
   - certain instruments and equipment that cannot be produced domestically are exempted from import tariffs;
   - exports from hi-tech enterprises, except for those restricted by the state or otherwise stipulated, are exempted from export taxes;

- hi-tech enterprises can establish bonded warehouses and plants in the zones;
- better-performing hi-tech enterprises can be granted foreign trade rights and even establish overseas branches; and
- the hi-tech products developed by hi-tech enterprises, when they reach the same standards as imports, can be put on the list of restricted imports.

2. Finance
- banks are encouraged to provide the necessary funds for hi-tech enterprises to develop;
- hi-tech industrial development zones can issue long-term bonds with the arrangement of banks, and risk-investment funds can be established in the zones to help the development of high-risk hi-tech products; and
- instruments and equipment for hi-tech development enjoy accelerated depreciation.

3. Taxation
- using 1990 as the base year, incremental taxation due from hi-tech enterprises over the following five years should be rebated;
- the income tax rate for hi-tech enterprises (from the day they are recognized as hi-tech enterprises) in the zone is reduced by 15 per cent;
- if the share of exports in total output exceeds 70 per cent, the income tax rate for enterprises in the zones can be reduced by 10 per cent; and
- newly established hi-tech enterprises in the zones enjoy a tax holiday for two years.

Besides these state policies, different provinces and regions also provide certain preferential measures to encourage the development of technology-intensive and hi-tech industries, which are not necessarily restricted to enterprises in the hi-tech industrial development zones. Shenzhen and Shanghai are the two examples. Both these regions, aware of the importance of technological progress, introduced preferential measures to promote the development of hi-tech industries. These include reductions in and exemptions from local taxes, preferential loans, easy access to land, and so on (see appendices A and B for details).

This section has outlined briefly the nature of the hi-tech programme in China and the measures which have been introduced to implement that programme. The following section examines China's export performance and analyses the technological aspects of shifts in the composition of those exports.

EXPORT PERFORMANCE

Since 1979, China has not only increased its exports but has also substantially changed the composition of those exports. From Table 9.1 we can see that total exports in 1991 reached US$71.91 billion, nearly four times the level in 1980. These data are in current prices as price-adjusted trade data are not available for China; over the period covered, producer prices for manufactured goods rose by only 6 per cent in total so the bias in the data is likely to be small. Manufactured exports had a more rapid increase. Their share in total exports rose from 49.7 per cent in 1980 to 77.5 per cent in 1991. Some heavy industrial goods also had a rapid increase. For example, exports of chemical and related products increased 3.4 times and machinery and transport equipment increased 8.5 times.

The rapid increase of machinery and electrical exports can be seen more clearly in Table 9.2. It shows that the export of mechanical and electrical products, which are mostly heavy industrial products, increased ten times during the eleven years. There are three points to be made here. The first is that the increase in mechanical and electrical exports was much more rapid than the increase of general exports. The second is that the increase was much faster in the second half of the 1980s, about 43.3 per cent annually, than it was in the first half, when it was only about 9.9 per cent. The third is that the increase of processing and assembling was especially marked: it reached US$3,897 million in 1991, 10.5 times that in 1985; it accounted for 27.6 per cent of total mechanical and electrical products – the largest category.

Comparatively speaking, the increase of light industrial exports was not so fast as that of heavy industrial goods, though its share in the total exports also rose, from 19.6 per cent in 1980 to 26.7 per cent in 1991. Table 9.3 gives a brief summary of the export of light industrial products.[15] Light industrial products include processing exports, which increased by 5.3 times between 1985 and 1991, becoming the largest component, and accounting for 22.5 per cent of total light industrial exports. Light industrial and textile products increased their share of total exports from 35.5 per cent to 41.3 per cent between 1979 and 1990. Heavy industrial exports also rapidly increased their share of total exports, rising from 10.9 per cent in 1979 to 26.4 per cent in 1990.[16]

The rapid increase of manufactured exports, especially the increase of the share of heavy products in total exports, does not necessarily mean that the export structure has moved toward a more capital- and technology-intensive one. China's exports have in fact become more labour-intensive in the past few years. Table 9.4 shows that the share of labour-intensive manufactures in total exports actually increased from 39 per cent in 1980 to 74 per cent in

Table 9.1 Value of China's exports, 1980–91 (US$ hundred million)[a]

Items	1980	1981	1982	1983	1984	1985	1986	1987	1988	1989	1990	1991
Total exports	181.19	220.07	223.21	222.26	261.39	273.50	309.42	394.37	475.40	525.38	620.91	719.10
1. Primary goods	91.14	102.48	100.51	96.20	119.34	138.28	112.72	132.31	144.30	150.78	158.86	162.12
2. Manufactured goods	90.05	117.59	122.70	126.06	142.05	135.22	196.70	262.06	331.10	374.60	462.05	556.98
(a) Chemicals and related products, n.e.s.	11.19	13.42	11.96	12.51	13.64	13.58	17.33	22.35	28.97	32.01	37.30	38.18
(b) Manufactured goods classified chiefly by material	39.99	47.06	43.02	43.65	50.54	44.93	58.86	85.70	104.91	108.97	125.76	144.56
(c) Machinery and transport equipment	8.43	10.87	12.62	12.21	14.93	7.72	10.94	17.41	27.69	38.74	55.88	71.49
(d) Miscellaneous manufactured articles	28.36	37.25	37.05	38.04	46.97	34.86	49.48	62.73	82.68	107.55	126.86	166.20
(e) Products not classified elsewhere	2.08	8.99	18.05	19.65	15.97	34.13	60.09	73.87	86.85	87.33	116.25	136.55

Note: [a] Imports and exports are classified according to commodity classification for China's Customs Statistics, which is based on the UN's SITC, Rev. 2, with some modifications to meet China's special needs.

Source: China Statistical Information and Consultancy Service Center (1992, pp. 30–5).

Table 9.2   China's exports of mechanical and electrical products, 1980–91 (US$ ten thousand)

Item	1980	1981	1982	1983	1984	1985	1986	1987	1988	1989	1990	1991
Total Value	141,004	181,996	196,083	195,394	221,761	166,899	248,154	379,540	615,881	831,771	1,108,820	1,412,204
1. Manufactures of metals	42,445	54,464	52,377	51,638	47,667	42,564	55,289	79,670	100,563	120,964	143,733	170,368
2. Power generating machinery and equipment	8,859	6,884	10,641	9,405	11,808	4,920	7,289	9,992	18,802	25,006	27,135	36,512
3. Machinery specialized for particular industries	25,072	34,020	36,102	21,880	19,980	15,315	16,408	17,049	23,830	36,453	53,615	59,658
4. Metalworking machinery	7,075	6,556	4,148	3,187	2,977	2,847	5,893	9,926	16,468	21,845	26,146	26,291
5. General industrial machinery and equipment	4,961	8,377	7,634	6,080	6,001	5,109	7,571	14,509	30,049	42,214	53,584	58,430
6. Office machines and automatic data processing machines	794	586	605	1,356	1,963	1,043	4,207	7,632	12,026	18,225	30,588	44,710
7. Telecommunications, sound recording and reproducing apparatus and equipment	6,129	8,723	11,573	20,438	33,743	9,292	24,389	50,254	78,936	114,017	173,788	202,183

Table 9.2 continued

Item	1980	1981	1982	1983	1984	1985	1986	1987	1988	1989	1990	1991
8. Electrical machinery, apparatus and appliances and parts thereof	15,185	19,457	16,428	16,414	18,401	11,815	18,653	33,584	57,060	81,947	121,924	167,942
9. Road vehicles	6,347	10,493	8,859	6,764	8,387	5,776	10,356	11,568	19,454	29,518	46,837	84,400
10. Other transport equipment	9,868	13,541	30,260	36,437	45,997	21,049	14,662	19,563	26,470	27,823	40,487	61,206
11. Professional, scientific and controlling instruments and apparatus	2,065	3,840	3,665	3,138	3,386	3,344	3,834	5,936	8,828	14,715	19,342	22,132
12. Photographic and cinematographic supplies, optical goods, watches and clocks	10,072	12,497	11,881	16,802	18,933	5,518	10,252	15,267	21,620	30,138	54,433	58,801
13. Miscellaneous manufactured articles	2,132	2,558	1,910	1,810	2,518	1,508	3,004	3,959	5,351	11,275	18,664	29,918
14. Export of processing and assembling						36,799	66,347	100,631	196,424	257,631	298,544	389,653

Source: China Statistical Information and Consultancy Service Center (1992, pp. 150–155)

Table 9.3 China's exports of light industrial products, 1980–91 (US$ ten thousand)

Classificaton	1980	1981	1982	1983	1984	1985	1986	1987	1988	1989	1990	1991
Total	354,309	409,916	381,461	383,265	427,960	418,368	534,665	760,652	997,388	1,260,095	1,556,338	1,921,281
1. Paper, paperboard and articles of pulp, paper or paperboard	11,671	13,642	12,505	13,781	15,591	13,361	17,641	22,984	24,409	25,574	25,613	26,962
2. Food and beverages	60,332	54,116	53,853	53,785	59,298	59,602	65,014	77,814	98,172	113,832	110,655	125,528
3. Products of Portland, glassware and ceramics	21,670	24,795	18,354	18,125	17,333	16,196	21,639	28,056	34,292	41,287	55,870	69,383
4. Chemical manufactured goods for daily use	14,712	15,955	14,643	14,848	16,337	15,661	13,675	19,716	24,716	29,203	37,710	27,982
5. Leather and fur manufactures	28,143	31,820	26,099	26,432	33,677	24,627	36,700	55,421	68,889	95,348	137,677	187,410
6. Wood manufactures	1,131	1,883	1,960	2,083	2,170	2,076	2,983	4,801	7,150	10,750	16,233	20,713
7. Furniture	11,505	6,912	6,397	5,526	5,985	4,001	5,588	9,736	14,573	18,849	24,956	39,823
8. Articles for cultural life, sports and recreation	21,257	23,007	22,498	22,393	32,703	19,420	29,564	49,125	64,063	86,755	105,451	144,624
9. Arts and crafts	85,611	120,061	104,638	104,653	116,606	90,164	102,828	154,053	193,660	226,282	234,779	246,349
10. Plastic articles	7,156	9,447	10,058	10,687	12,487	10,480	13,904	22,415	41,320	58,247	86,542	120,995
11. Miscellaneous commodities	28,119	34,825	35,913	35,635	41,246	28,127	39,821	56,383	62,814	88,978	98,484	132,407
12. Manufactures of mechanical and electrical appliances	63,002	73,453	74,543	75,317	74,527	52,404	70,392	102,247	143,592	172,669	272,686	345,351
13. Export of processing materials						82,246	114,916	157,901	219,738	272,321	349,682	433,664

Source: China Statistical Information and Consultancy Service Center (1992, pp. 162–4)

179

Table 9.4 The value and share of various types of products in China's manufactured exports: selected years, 1965–90[a]

Product category	1965	1975	1980	1985	1990	Growth rate (%) 1965–90	Growth rate (%) 1980–90
A. Value of China's exports (US$ million)							
Total exports	1,718	6,303	18,237	27,764	80,541	16.6	16.0
Labour-intensive manufactures	570	2,253	7,168	12,319	59,787	20.5	23.6
Unskilled labour-intensive manufactures	454	1,557	5,254	9,742	41,222	19.8	22.9
Capital-intensive manufactures	1,113	3,128	6,353	7,984	14,987	10.9	8.9
Human capital-intensive goods	148	473	1,292	1,708	12,325	19.3	25.3
Natural resource-based products	961	3,665	9,116	13,339	16,585	12.1	6.2
Coal, petroleum and gas	32	897	3,974	7,157	5,290	22.7	2.9
B. As a share of total exports (%)							
Total exports	100	100	100	100	100		
Labour-intensive manufactures	33	36	39	44	74		
Unskilled labour-intensive manufactures	26	25	29	35	51		
Capital-intensive manufactures	65	50	35	29	19		
Human capital-intensive goods	9	8	7	6	15		
Natural resource-based products	56	58	50	48	21		
Coal, petroleum and gas	2	14	22	26	7		

Note: [a] Since this is from a World Bank report, the figures of total exports here are not the same as those from the Chinese official data. The procedures used for identifying labour-intensive and capital-intensive goods are shown in Annex 1.1 of the report.

Source: World Bank (1993, p. 9)

1990, while capital-intensive goods declined from 35 per cent to 19 per cent.[17]

It is also worthwhile pointing out that within the category of labour-intensive manufactured exports, the share of products using unskilled labour has been declining since 1985. That China has begun to turn to products apparently requiring higher skill levels for its exports is suggested by the rapid rise in its exports of relatively simple telecommunications equipment and domestic electric goods since 1985 (World Bank, 1993). This is also shown in Table 9.2. We can, then, say that to a certain extent China's export structure since 1985 has become relatively more technology- or skill-intensive, but there is still very little that can be counted as hi-tech exports. The production of hi-tech exports does not necessarily involve the application of hi-tech technology in China, the processes used to produce them may well be intensive in the use of low-skilled workers, the technology being embodied in the imports of the intermediate goods being processed and assembled.

A second point to note is that, although heavy industrial exports grew more quickly than exports of light industrial and textile products, the latter, especially clothing, are still the major exports. Certain categories such as clothing and footwear are among the fastest growing export categories. According to World Bank statistics, clothing more than doubled its share in ten years, accounting for 19.6 per cent of China's total exports in 1990. Toys and sporting goods were the second most important export item for China in 1990, followed by footwear, accounting for 7.5 per cent and 3.7 per cent, respectively, of China's exports in that year (World Bank, 1993, p. 10*)*.

The rapid increase of manufactured exports, especially the export of machinery and electrical products since 1985, is largely due to the assembly operations under the schemes of 'processing with supplied materials' and 'processing with imported materials'. From Table 9.2 we see that this kind of activity accounted for 27.6 per cent of total machinery and electrical exports. Table 9.5 shows that in 1991 processed exports accounted for over 45 per cent of total exports. The large share of processed exports indicates that, although China's exports have been moving toward relatively technology- or skill-intensive products, since the technology contents of the products might be high-tech, the assembling process carried out in China might not be technology- or skill-intensive at all.

Another important point to note is that the share of township and village enterprises and foreign-invested enterprises in total exports has increased rapidly. The share of township and village enterprises in total exports increased fivefold between 1985 and 1990. Their share was estimated to have exceeded 25 per cent by 1992.[18] According to MOFTEC, the share of foreign-invested enterprises in total exports in 1993 reached 27.5 per cent and their share in total imports and exports exceeded one-third.[19] Thus, the share

Table 9.5   China's exports from assembly operations, 1988 and 1991 (US$ billion)

	1988	1991
1. Exports processed with supplied materials	6.5	12.9
2. Exports processed with imported materials	6.4	19.5
3. Total value of processed exports	12.9	32.4
of which, from SEZs	2.6	6.2
4. Imports of materials for export processing	13.7	25.0
of which, into SEZs	2.6	5.1
Memo item		
Total merchandise exports	47.5	71.8
Total merchandise imports	55.3	63.8

Source: World Bank (1993, p. 12)

of both township and village enterprises and foreign-invested enterprises in total exports was more than 50 per cent of the total. Though we have no exact data, it is generally acknowledged that the exports of township and village enterprises (TVEs) are mostly unskilled labour-intensive products. Most TVEs take the form of 'informal' investment and processing businesses. In comparison, although the foreign-invested enterprises tend to be more technology- or skill-intensive and involve more 'formal' investment vehicles, they mostly sell in the domestic market.[20]

By any standards, there has been a large increase of trade in technology in China. According to MOFTEC, in 1990 China concluded 232 contracts of imported technology with a total value of US$1.274 million, about 3.9 per cent of total imports in MOFTEC's statistics. China also exported technology in the form of technical licences, technical service and complete plants, totalling US$989 million, or about 1.9 per cent of its total exports in 1990 (Liu, 1993). The rapid increase can also been seen from the trading records of China National Technology Import and Export Corporation, the largest specialized technology trading company in China. The company started to export technology in 1986. The technology exports of this single company in 1987 were US$2.29 million but by 1990 they had increased by 31.4 times to US$71.91 million (Tong, 1992). However, this is still a small figure, and even if all the US$989 million exports in 1990 are counted as hi-tech exports, there is still a long way to go to reach the target of 8 per cent of total exports.

This section has shown that all sectors, hi-tech and low-tech, of China's exports have seen remarkable growth since the commencement of the reforms. The emphasis has, however, been on the growth of exports of products which are produced in China in enterprises using relatively low-tech labour-intensive processes. In the next section we examine how far the internationalization of the Chinese economy, through the growth in hi-tech exports, can be attributed to the hi-tech programmes introduced by the Government of China.

THE INTERNATIONALIZING EFFECTS OF HI-TECH PROGRAMMES

It is claimed that the hi-tech programmes, especially the 'Torch' Programme, have had quite positive results. As Song Jian, Director of the State Commission of Science and Technology, pointed out, the 'Torch' Programme has achieved unexpected results: a large number of hi-tech enterprises were established, which promoted the development of China's hi-tech industries, and these enterprises became a new force in China's economic development. As already mentioned, many hi-tech industrial development zones were established, including fifty-two which were approved by the State Council. These hi-tech industrial zones have played an important role in raising China's economic and technological strength and in the construction of the socialist market economy. Another result was that many scientific personnel were diverted to the business sector, and some new entrepreneurs, who not only had technical knowledge but were also good at business and marketing, were trained and became established (Song, 1993).

To take the 'Torch' Programme as an example: according to Li Xuer, the Deputy Director of the State Commission of Science and Technology, 2,895 projects had been set up by the end of 1991. The State had cumulatively invested 4.4 billion yuan in these projects and, after they had come on stream, an increment of annual output of 19.4 billion yuan, profits and taxes of 5.4 billion yuan, and foreign exchange earnings of US$900 million was expected. On this basis the input–output ratio would be 1:4.4. The Programme also promoted the reform of research institutions and diversion of personnel. Among the state projects, 43 per cent were undertaken by research institutions and universities. As for industrialization, a few hi-tech enterprise groups with strong competitiveness and output over 100 million yuan have emerged. With respect to internationalization, some bonded warehouses and plants have been established in HTIDZs, a certain amount of foreign investment has been attracted into the zones, some hi-tech enterprises have established overseas branches, and some (hi-tech) products have edged into international markets.[21]

According to the State Council, by the end of 1991, in the then twenty-seven HTIDZs, there were over 3,400 new technology enterprises with 138,000 employees, among which were 67,000 scientific and technological personnel. They had developed over 3,900 new-technology products. The total technological, industrial and trade income in 1991 was 8.73 billion yuan, total output 7.12 billion yuan with profits and taxes 1.61 billion yuan. Their total exports stood at 0.71 billion yuan,[22] approximately 0.17 per cent of China's total exports. By 1993 export from the fifty-two state-level HTIDZs reached US$730, or roughly 0.8 per cent of total exports.[23]

One of the most important objectives of the internationalization of hi-tech industries is to promote hi-tech exports. Data presented above showed that the technology content of China's exports has increased since 1985. This is consistent with the government's efforts to promote technology development in the second half of the 1980s. However, it is not clear what role the hi-tech programmes have played in promoting these exports. Are they the results of the hi-tech programmes, or are they affected by other factors, such as the growth of assembly operations and the emergence of township and village enterprises? Since no systematic data are available, we take one of the earliest hi-tech industrial development zones, the Caohejing New Technology Development Zone (CNTDZ) in Shanghai to throw some light on the issues. Table 9.6 compares CNTDZ, a state HTIDZ, with Minhang Economic and Technology Development Zone. Table 9.6 shows that, by the end of 1992, the enterprises in Caohejing exported a total value of US$36.04 million and

Table 9.6   Basic statistics of Caohejing New Technology Development Zone and Minhang Economic and Technology Development Zone

	Unit	Minhang	Caohejing
Total output of industries (current price)	RMB10,000	326,621	319,110
of which, foreign-invested enterprises	RMB10,000	326,621	77,119
Business income	RMB10,000	349,167	374,955
of which, foreign-invested enterprises	RMB10,000	349,167	110,164
Total profits	RMB10,000	54,823	26,166
of which, foreign-invested enterprises	RMB10,000	54,823	16,760
Total taxes	RMB10,000	15,091	16,202
of which, foreign-invested enterprises	RMB10,000	15,091	5,636
Total exports	US$10,000	21,191	3,604
of which, foreign-invested enterprises	US$10,000	21,191	1,638
Total imports	US$10,000	18,016	15,883
of which, foreign-invested enterprises	US$10,000	18,016	11,089
Business foreign exchange income	US$10,000	23,017	11,083
of which, foreign-invested enterprises	US$10,000	23,017	9,404
Business foreign exchange expenses	US$10,000	22,578	18,230
of which, foreign-invested enterprises	US$10,000	22,578	12,758

Source: *Shanghai duiwai jingji tongji nianjian* (1993, p. 89)

imported a total value of US$158.83 million, which is 4.4 times that of exports. Business foreign exchange earnings were US$110.83 million, US$71.47 million less than business foreign exchange expenses of US$182.30 million. By contrast, Minhang had a much higher export value, and both its total exports and business foreign exchange income exceeded total imports and business foreign exchange expenditure.

This suggests, if Caohejing is typical, that HTIDZs, perhaps with more domestic technology, are more domestically oriented. They are also foreign exchange consuming rather than foreign exchange creating. If the technological level in Caohejing is higher than in Minhang (since it is a HTIDZ, it should be), this also indicates that the higher the technological level of a zone, the more domestically oriented it is, no matter whether the technology is imported or domestically created. This coincides with the finding (Gang, 1993) that 'formal' foreign direct investment is mostly domestic-market-oriented while 'informal' foreign direct investment is more outward-looking.

Perhaps it is still too early to evaluate the HTIDZs and hi-tech programmes, but some problems can already be identified. According to one report, there are two major problems affecting the further development of HTIDZs.[24] The first is that market economic structure and market mechanisms have not been established in HTIDZs. On the one hand, enterprises in HTIDZs, even if they are state-owned, 'are basically excluded from the state budget and development plans. They can hardly get the necessary means of production and capital through the usual planning channel.'[25] On the other hand, some HTIDZs are still administratively managed by governments of different levels. They are sometimes poorly managed and their development is not integrated into state and local development programmes. Some products manufactured in the zones have to compete with the output of enterprises outside the zones. As for new and hi-tech products, few have reached efficient scales of production.

The second problem is that big research institutions, universities and large enterprises have not played their role fully in the development of hi-tech industries. Although 43 per cent of the research projects in the 'Torch' Programme were carried out by research institutions and universities, these institutions and universities have not been much involved in the development of hi-tech industries. For example, in Xian, a city with a high concentration of universities and research institutes, the hi-tech enterprises in HTIDZs run by the universities and research institutions accounted for only 11.48 per cent and 10.61 per cent of the total, respectively. The number of research projects that applied to enter HTIDZs accounted for only 1.65 per cent and 25.62 per cent, respectively, of total research projects.[26] As for those large and medium-sized enterprises, they simply have not taken the initiative to enter HTIDZs to develop hi-tech products.

The reasons these problems arise can perhaps be attributed to the following factors. One is that the programmes and the HTIDZs are not well integrated with the rest of the economy both institutionally and operationally. The hi-tech programmes and the HTIDZs are under the direction and management of the State Commission of Science and Technology and its local branches. The programmes are not formally incorporated into the state and local development plans (annual plan or five-year plan); the HTIDZs, though designed to be different from other economic and technological development zones, are not much advanced and their development seems to be separate from other development zones.

The other, and probably more important, factor is the lack of risk-taking entrepreneurs to commercialize the hi-tech products. Very few of the researchers in institutions and universities understand business operations, so the commercial prospects of many products cannot be evaluated and put into business operation.

In sum, China's economy has become much more internationalized over the years since the reforms began. Its hi-tech programmes have, however, played only a small part in that process.

CONCLUSIONS

Is China a frog or a goose? It has certainly attempted to 'leapfrog' over some stages in technological development and to move to the forefront of technology in some areas. This chapter has argued that, as far as exports go, this policy has had little impact. While some exports of high-tech products have emerged, for the most part the hi-tech industries established with the encouragement of the technology-enhancement programmes have been high-cost and uncompetitive. They have only survived by having their domestic market protected from international competition and with state subsidies in one form or another.

The hi-tech programmes' failure to stimulate the establishment of internationally competitive industry is not, however, to be regretted, except to the extent that the resources it absorbed could have been better employed. As the World Bank comments, 'Revealed comparative advantage calculations suggest that China's exports have been moving in line with its comparative advantage, which lies in labor-intensive (and especially in skilled labor-intensive) exports as well as in higher technology exports that can be assembled locally.' The report also argues that 'China does not yet have a broad-based comparative advantage in machinery and electronics, despite all the programs of support to this sector, and it is unlikely to develop, for a few years yet, any significant advantage in ... high technology exports'. The World Bank's conclusion was, therefore, that there is no need for China 'to reorient its export structure rapidly towards higher technology or knowledge based products'.[27] In other words, China should be content to play the role of a goose for the foreseeable future.

APPENDIX A: PREFERENTIAL POLICIES FOR HI-TECH ENTERPRISES IN SHENZHEN

The city administration of Shenzhen Special Economic Zone has formulated and implemented preferential policies for high-tech enterprises with the following main aspects.[28]

Taxation

1. Enterprises with more than ten years' operational experience are exempted from income tax for the first and second years after becoming profitable and are then exempted from half of their income tax liabilities from the third to the eighth years.
2. In the year after income tax exemptions and reductions have expired, enterprises that generate an export and output value amounting to 70 per cent of their plan are to receive a 10 per cent income tax exemption.
3. High-tech products approved on state, ministry, commission and province levels are exempted from product tax and added value tax from one to three years beginning from the day of trial selling.
4. The net income earned from the transfer of a high-tech enterprise's own inventions, special technology or technical achievement, which have passed the appraisal of municipal or higher-level institutions, amounting to less than RMB300,000, can be exempted from income tax 'for the time being'. Amounts exceeding RMB300,000 should be taxed accordingly. The transfer of technical achievement is exempted from business tax for the time being.
5. Ten percent of the income earned from the above-mentioned technical transfer can be used as new-tech development funds to be included as costs in the accounts. This money is to be used exclusively for the development of science and research.
6. Money used as awards to scientific and technical staff for their outstanding contributions in developing high-tech products is exempted from wage regulated tax, subject to tax department approval.
7. Following the need of technical renewal, high-tech enterprises can accelerate the years of depreciation.
8. All the money in relation to the reduction and exemption of tax in accordance with this regulation should be subject to independent business accounting.

Loans

1. The bank each year will allocate a certain amount of money from the total sum of loans to be used as loans for the development of science and technology and offer preferential interest rate treatment.
2. The city investment administration corporation each year allocates a certain amount of money from total investment to support high-tech projects of state-owned enterprises in the form of preferential loans, long-term low-interest loans and investment through shares.
3. The bank each year allocates 20 per cent of all bonds to high-tech enterprises eligible to issue bonds.
4. The city administration will give preferential approval to the marketing of shares in high-tech enterprises that are eligible for such treatment.

Land for Construction and the Purchase of Residential Property

1. Related departments should lease land for high-tech projects in the area and carry out construction on it with a concerted effort.
2. The city administration will give priority to the approval of land to be used for high-tech enterprises, reduce land prices by 10–20 per cent or collect only half land use fees for a period of five years.
3. In bonded areas, part of the land sold at a preferential price should be allocated to high-tech enterprises.
4. Relevant departments should give precedence when high-tech enterprises apply to purchase low-interest commercial housing or land to build residential buildings for their own use.

Other Aspects

1. The city administration will give priority to approving the transfer of technical staff working for high-tech enterprises, personnel who have made important inventions for the state, and technical staff with expert skills. It will relax the limits approving the transfer of technical staff from inland cities and give priority to gaining approval for their stay.
2. It will introduce scientific and technical staff from abroad in an organized manner.
3. The administration will give priority to the examination and approval of the applications of high-tech enterprises to set up offices outside China.
4. Within the state brief, the city administration will give priority to the importing of raw materials, spare parts, equipment and technical data for registered high-tech study and development. Customs should make things easy for them.

5. The city administration will give priority to high-tech enterprises in the supply of water, power and telecommunications facilities.
6. The city administration will give liberal treatment to the proportion of domestic sales of high-tech products to be included in projects.
7. High-tech enterprises set up with important new technology, provided by domestic or foreign businessmen, can raise the proportion of their technical investment to 25 per cent of their registered capital, subject to approval.

APPENDIX B: HI-TECH INDUSTRIES TO BE GRANTED PREFERENTIAL TREATMENT IN PUDONG NEW AREA

As early as 3 April 1988, Shanghai drew up a 'measure' to give foreign-invested technology- and knowledge-intensive projects 15 per cent income tax reduction.[29] When Pudong New Area was formally established, the municipal government again provided preferential measures similar to those available in Shenzhen in order to attract investment in technology-intensive industries. The following is a list of hi-tech industries that can be granted various types of preferential treatment in Pudong New Area, Shanghai, as set out in the document *Industrial Policy and Investment Guide for Pudong New Area, Shanghai*.[30]

I. Energy and transportation [details omitted here].
II. Urban infrastructure [details omitted here].
III. Industries for export expansion and import substitution (including both industrial and agricultural):
    1. telecommunications equipment;
    2. electronic computers;
    3. electronic components;
    4. semiconductor components;
    5. other electronics parts;
    6. precision instruments and meters;
    7. precision machine tools and efficient forging equipment;
    8. precision medical and clinical equipment;
    9. automatic office devices;
    10. basic parts for precision machinery;
    11. precision mouldings;
    12. electrical machinery;
    13. automobile parts;
    14. large type special whole-set equipment;
    15. other machinery and electric equipment;
    16. semi-synthetic antibiotics and other new medicines;
    17. medium- to high-grade dyestuffs and agents;
    18. high-efficiency and low-toxicity pesticides;

19. food and feed additives;
20. chemical and biochemical agents;
21. other refined chemical products of high added value and low pollution;
22. new-generation electrical household appliances;
23. high-efficiency lamps and equipment;
24. high-quality serial cosmetics;
25. medium- to high-grade name brand garments, fashion and design;
26. high-grade decorative textiles;
27. other light and textile products for export;
28. engineering plastics, special resins and products;
29. special chemical fibres;
30. new-type building materials;
31. other new-type materials;
32. bio-tech engineering;
33. laser engineering;
34. other new technologies;
35. farm and sideline products for export.

NOTES

1. For a discussion of China's technology import policy, see Zhao (1995) and chs 5 and 6 of the important study of technological change in China by Conroy (1992).
2. The original work on the concept of 'technological leapfrogging' was Soete (1985). A recent example of its application can be found in Hobday (1994).
3. See Yung *et al.* (1984) for an excellent account of the importance of technology in developing competitiveness in the case of Korea.
4. See Fukasaku and Wall (1994) for an account of China's opening up process.
5. 'Scientific system due for reform', *Beijing Review*, vol. 28, no. 11, 18 March 1985.
6. Zhao Ziyang, 'Report to the Thirteenth Party Congress', *Renmin Ribao* [The People's Daily], 5 November 1987.
7. Previously known as the Ministry of Foreign Economic Relations and Trade (MOFERT). The new name is used in this chapter, except where publications are referred to, when the name at the time of publication is used.
8. Editorial Board of the Almanac of China's Foreign Economic Relations and Trade (1993, p. 397).
9. 'Minister of MOFERT on China's ambition to become a major trading nation', *China's Foreign Trade*, no. 10, 1993.
10. Song (1993).
11. The Research Office of the State Council, 'Quickening the reform and construction of our hi-tech industrial development zones: research report on the perfection of hi-tech industrial development zone policies', *Renmin Ribao* [The People's Daily], 25 November 1992.
12. There are different names for the zones, but they are generally called hi-tech industrial development zones, which are similar to hi-tech parks in other countries.
13. 'The head of the State Commission of Science and Technology answering questions by journalists on state hi-tech industrial development zones', *Renmin Ribao* [The People's Daily], 1 April 1991.
14. The two documents are in *Yanhai yanjiang yanbian kaifang falu fahui guifanxing wenjian huibian* (1992).
15. Note that there is some overlapping between mechanical and electrical exports and light industrial exports, as we can see from Table 9.3.
16. Editorial Board of the Almanac of China's Foreign Economic Relations and Trade (1993, p. 403).

17. Table 9.4 is from a World Bank report (1993), whose figures are different from the Chinese official figures, so they are not totally comparable.
18. Ibid., p. 14.
19. *Renmin Ribao* [The People's Daily], overseas edition, 18 May 1994.
20. See Gang (1993). In his thesis, he defined informal foreign direct investment as compensation trade, processing, assembling and leasing of equipment, and formal foreign direct investment as equity joint ventures, contractual joint ventures, co-operative development and wholly foreign-owned enterprises.
21. Song (1993).
22. See note 10.
23. As reported in the *Shanghai Star*, 26 April 1994, p. 9.
24. Ibid.
25. Ibid.
26. Song (1993).
27. World Bank (1993, pp. xxii–xxiii).
28. 'Preferential policies on high-tech enterprises in Shenzhen', *Zhongguo maoyi* [China's Foreign Trade], no. 1, 1992.
29. Approved by the People's Municipal Government of Shanghai, 6 September 1990. For this measure, see the *Collection of Laws, Regulations and Standard Documents on Opening Along Coastal, Riverside and Bordering Areas*, p. 1715.
30. Ibid., p. 1740.

REFERENCES

Bhagwati, J. (1978), *Anatomy and Consequences of Exchange Control Regimes*, Cambridge, Mass.: Ballinger.
China Statistical Information and Consultancy Service Center (1992), *China Foreign Economic Statistics 1979–1991*, Beijing: The Center.
Conroy, R. (1992), *Technological Change in China*, Paris: OECD.
Editorial Board of the Almanac of China's Foreign Economic Relations and Trade (1993), *Zhongguo duiwai jingji maoyi nianjian* [Almanac of China's Foreign Economic Relations and Trade 1991/92], Beijing: China Prospect Publishing House.
Fukasaku, K. and Wall, D. (1994), *China's Long March to an Open Economy,* Paris: OECD.
Gang Yang (1993), *The Impact of Direct Foreign Investment on Manufactured Exports from China, 1979–1990*, PhD dissertation, Canberra: Australian National University.
Hobday, M. (1994), 'Technological learning in Singapore: a test case of leapfrogging', *Journal of Development Studies*, 30.
Hughes, Helen (1987), 'The costs and benefits of free port and export processing zone concepts with particular application to Xiamen', in B. Brogan (ed.), *Xiamen Special Economic Zone: A Report of a Workshop*, National Centre for Development Studies, Canberra: Australian National University.
Krueger, Anne O. (1978), *Liberalisation Attempts and Consequences*, Cambridge, Mass.: Ballinger.
Lardy, N. (1992), *Foreign Trade and Economic Reform in China*, 1978–1990, Cambridge: Cambridge University Press.
Little, I.M.D., Scitovsky, T. and Scott, M.F. (1970), *Industry and Trade in Some Developing Countries: A Comparative Study*, Oxford: Oxford University Press.
Liu Hu (1993), 'A summary of technical trade of China in 1900', *Almanac of China's*

Foreign Economic Relations and Trade 1991/92: China Resources Advertising Co. Ltd.

Shanghai duiwai jingji tongji nianjian [Foreign Economic Statistical Yearbook of Shanghai] (1993), Shanghai: Statistical Bureau of Shanghai.

Shepherd, G. and Langoni, C.G. (eds) (1991), *Trade Reform: Lessons from Eight Countries,* San Francisco: International Center for Economic Growth.

Soete, L. (1985), 'International diffusion of technology, industrial development and technological leapfrogging', *World Development*, Special Issue on Microelectronics, 13.

Song Jian (1988), 'Speech at the First National Working Conference on Torch Programme', *Renminjibao*, 26 October (People's Daily).

—— (1993): 'Speech at the Third National Working Conference of the Torch Programme', *Science and Technology Daily*, 18 January; quoted in *Xinghua Journal*, no. 1 (in Chinese).

Tong Changyin (1992), 'China's technology import and export trade', *Zhongguo maoyi* [China's Foreign Trade], 1.

World Bank (1993), *China Foreign Trade Reform: Meeting the Challenge of the 1990s*, Report no. 11568-CHA, Washington, D.C.: Country Operation Division, China and Mongolia Department, East Asia and Pacific Regional Office.

—— (1994): *China: Foreign Trade Reform*, Washington, D.C.: World Bank.

Yamazawa, I., Hirata, A. and Yokata, K. (1991), 'Evolving patterns of comparative advantage in the Pacific economies', in M. Ariff (ed.), *The Pacific Economy: Growth and External Stability*, London: Allen & Unwin.

Yanhai yanjiang yanbian kaifang falu fahui gui fanxing wenjian huibian [Collection of Laws, Regulations and Standard Documents on Opening along Coastal, Riverside and Bordering Areas] (1992), Beijing: Law Press.

Yung Whee Rhee, Ross-Larson, B. and Pursell, G. (1984), *Korea's Competitive Edge*, Baltimore, Md: Johns Hopkins University Press, for World Bank.

Zhao Hongxin (1995), 'Technology imports and their impact on the enhancement of China's indigenous technological capability', *Journal of Development Studies*, 31(4).

10. Economic growth and technology transfer in China

Zheng Youjing

INTRODUCTION

China's First Five-Year Plan started in 1953, immediately after the three-year recovery period (1949–52). In the thirty-eight years since 1953, the growth rate of real GDP has been 6.8 per cent and total GDP has multiplied twelve times. However, because population growth has also been brisk, per capita GDP has multiplied only sixfold. In relation to the increased input of resources to the economy, however, this growth has not been satisfactory. The 'left' thinking prevalent in the 1950s and 1960s and the disasters of the Cultural Revolution were partly responsible for the low quality of Chinese growth and the consequent failure to raise living standards.

In the course of implementing the policies of reform and the open door, China has made an evaluation of past experience and drawn lessons that have helped the economy to grow and to import advanced technology and management methods from abroad. In this chapter, I shall make a quantitative analysis of China's economic growth and discuss the changing sources of growth. I shall also discuss the role of technology transfer in shifting growth from a quantitative to a qualitative type, and from a labour-intensive, 'extensive' pattern to a technology-intensive one.

GROWTH OF OUTPUT AND PRODUCTIVITY

Before the implementation of the open and reform policies that started in 1978, economic growth in China was highly unstable. During the twenty-six years from 1953 to 1978, the record of real GDP shows that there were six negative growth years (1960, 1961, 1962, 1967, 1968, 1976). Especially serious were the three negative years 1960–62, after which the 1959 level of output was not regained until 1965 (see Table 10.1 and Figure 10.1). Further years of negative growth in 1967 and 1968 caused the national economy to

Table 10.1 Growth of China's GDP, 1953–94 (US$ thousand million)

Year	At 1978 prices	At 1990 prices	At current prices
1953	86.94	157.10	81.46
1954	91.96	166.18	85.91
1955	97.88	176.88	90.58
1956	111.70	201.84	101.36
1957	116.72	210.92	104.36
1958	142.52	257.54	128.54
1959	154.00	278.28	140.34
1960	151.81	274.33	140.12
1961	108.65	196.33	116.40
1962	101.58	183.56	108.01
1963	112.45	203.20	116.89
1964	131.04	236.79	136.33
1965	153.25	276.92	162.17
1966	179.33	324.06	185.44
1967	166.34	300.59	173.87
1968	155.47	280.94	165.43
1969	185.58	335.34	190.99
1970	228.67	413.21	225.19
1971	249.55	450.95	247.62
1972	256.66	463.79	254.62
1973	277.97	502.30	276.35
1974	281.16	508.97	279.95
1975	304.56	550.34	298.36
1976	296.48	535.76	289.39
1977	319.59	577.51	315.27
1978	358.81	648.38	358.81
1979	386.08	697.66	399.81
1980	419.77	758.54	447.00
1981	434.84	785.77	477.51
1982	472.84	854.43	518.23
1983	521.60	942.55	578.70
1984	597.67	1,080.00	692.82
1985	673.67	1,217.33	852.74
1986	729.60	1,318.41	968.76
1987	809.94	1,463.59	1,130.71
1988	898.21	1,623.09	1,407.42
1989	930.11	1,680.73	1,599.76
1990	978.47	1,768.13	1,768.13
1991	1,060.64	1,916.61	2,018.83
1992	1,200.22	2,168.83	2,402.02
1993	1,358.81	2,455.41	3,134.20
1994	1,519.15	2,745.07	4,100.00

Source: *Zhongguo tongji nianjian*, various years

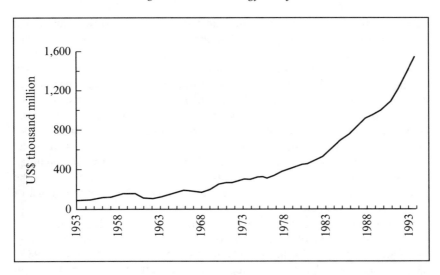

Figure 10.1   *Growth of China's real GDP, 1953–94 (US$ thousand million at 1978 prices)*

Figure 10.2   *Fluctuations in the rate of growth of China's GDP at constant prices, 1954–94 (per cent)*

suffer another heavy blow. In a statistical sense, these two downturns cost
China nine years of economic development. In the post-reform period, economic growth has been far more stable (see Figure 10.2).

According to our analytical study of China's sources of economic growth
during the years 1953–90, there was a significant change in the character of
economic growth in the period after 1978.[1] First, the average growth rate of
GDP at constant prices in the first twenty-six years of this period was 5.9 per
cent, while in the latter twelve years it was 8.4 per cent. Second, in the earlier
period, growth was based entirely on capital and labour inputs, and the
contribution of productivity to the growth rate was negative. By contrast,
during the last twelve years, the contribution of capital investment to the
growth rate was 51 per cent; that of the labour input 19 per cent; and that of
productivity 30 per cent.

If we divide our analysis into seven sub-periods according to the usual
Chinese classification of the First to the Seventh Five-Year Plans, the following features emerge. During the period of the Sixth Five-Year Plan (1981–
85), although the 'adjustment' of economic policy affected the growth rate to
a certain degree, the development in this period was stable and fast.[2] This
period is known as 'The First Golden Age' of the open and reform policies. In
this period, average annual growth was 9.6 per cent. Even more remarkable is
the fact that the productivity contribution to growth reached 41 per cent, and
for the first time it surpassed the contribution of capital. This shows that the
strategic policy of relying on a combination of China's internal technical
progress and of advanced foreign technology and equipment is correct, and
that technology transfer has an important role to play in China's growth.

During the period of the Seventh Five-Year Plan (1986–90), China's growth
rate was affected by inflation and political events, but the average annual
growth rate reached 7.4 per cent and the productivity contribution to growth
was 20 per cent. This period is considered to be the second good period of
economic growth since the founding of the People's Republic in 1949. Apart
from these two periods, and except for the Fifth Five-Year Plan (1976–80)
when productivity growth was also positive (9 per cent), the other periods all
recorded negative productivity growth.

The above analysis reveals two important points. First, although the speed
of China's economic growth before 1979 was not slow (5.92 per cent) (in
fact, higher than many developed countries), growth depended entirely on
inputs of capital and labour. This input was the *only* source of growth. Thus,
the foundation of growth was unstable and growth tended to follow severe
cyclical patterns. Since the open and reform policies began, great changes
have taken place. Not only has growth been more rapid, but there has been an
improvement in its quality. One important factor has been that, since 1978,
China has emphasized reliance on technical progress in the development of

the economy. It has strengthened its co-operation and economic exchanges with foreign countries, and improved the technical and material foundations of its development. Second, China's modern growth is closely linked to technological transfer and the speed of its implementation. Without this vigorous transfer and development of new technology, China's performance would not have been as good as it has been.

THE HUANAN ECONOMIC SPHERE

Of particular interest in China's growth since 1978 has been the performance of the Huanan (South China) Economic Sphere, i.e. the provinces of Guangdong and Fujian and Hainan Island. This sphere has provided China with the results of many valuable institutional experiences, especially those that have explored the use of market mechanisms. The sphere has also pioneered new forms of technical exchange and opening up to the world.

Let us first take the question of the sphere's rate of development. In the twenty-six years (1953–78) before implementation of the open and reform policies, the rate of economic development of the three elements of the sphere was below the national average. As can be seen in Table 10.2, the national average growth rate was 6 per cent, whereas that for Guangdong (Hainan included) was only 5.3 per cent, and that for Fujian 5.4 per cent. In the twelve years since 1979, however, Guangdong's growth rate has leapt

Table 10.2   The changing position and rate of growth of the Huanan Economic Sphere, 1953–90

	1953–78		1978–90	
	Growth of national income (% p.a.)	National growth rank	Growth of national income (% p.a.)	National growth rank
China	6.0		8.4	
Huanan Sphere[a]				
Guangdong	5.3	22	—	—
Fujian	5.4	19	11.5	2
Hainan	—	—	11.0	3

Note: [a] Hainan became an independent province in 1988; prior to that it was part of Guangdong province.

Source: As for Table 10.1

forward to become the second highest in China, while Fujian has achieved
the third highest rate. (The national rate was 8.4 per cent, that for Guangdong
11.5 per cent and for Fujian 11.0 per cent).

Since 1990, the Huanan Economic Sphere has become the fastest-growing
part of China in several respects. As can be seen in the final column of Table
10.3, the growth rate of real GDP in the region exceeded that for the country
as a whole by a very large margin: for Guangdong the difference was as much
as 9 percentage points. The sphere similarly outpaced the rest of the country
in respect of the expansion of national income and of retail sales.

*Table 10.3   Comparison of the Huanan Economic Sphere and China: GDP,
national income and retail sales, 1990–92 (RMB thousand
million and growth rates)*

	Value at current prices			Percentage increase on previous year at constant prices	
	1990	1991	1992	1991	1992
GDP					
Guangdong	147.18	178.06	229.35	17.3	22.0
Fujian	46.58	55.78	70.52	15.4	20.4
Hainan	9.50	ˌ10.79	14.17	12.4	23.3
China	1,769.50	2,023.60	2,403.60	7.7	13.0
National income[a]					
Guangdong	113.22	138.03	179.36	18.5	23.2
Fujian	38.89	45.98	59.00	14.6	22.3
Hainan	7.70	8.77	11.11	10.9	21.9
China	1,438.40	1,655.70	1,984.50	11.4	14.4
Retail sales					
Guangdong	309.39	389.01	534.04	22.3	30.7
Fujian	92.00	111.85	150.46	18.1	28.9
Hainan	15.56	18.43	25.03	16.8	28.6
China	3,803.50	4,414.20	5,584.20	11.9	21.8

Note: [a] National income is the value of the five material production branches and is similar
to the UN's 'net material product'.

Source: As for Table 10.1

Let us now turn to foreign economic relations. The Huanan Sphere has developed extremely rapidly in this respect. In 1979, Guangdong's external orientation measured by the ratio of exports to GDP was only 12.3 per cent – below Tianjin (19.7 per cent), Shanghai (19.3 per cent) and Liaoning (16.3 per cent). Fujian was even lower in this respect. However, by 1990, Guangdong's export ratio reached 34.2 per cent, the highest for any part of China. In 1992, the ratio climbed to 45.8 per cent, far ahead of any other part of China. In 1992, Hainan's ratio was 35.7 per cent, the third highest in China, while that of Fujian was 33.1 per cent, standing in fifth place in the country (see row 1 of Table 10.4).

If we use as our indicator the ratio given by the sum of exports and imports (see row 3 of Table 10.4), the three elements of the Huanan Sphere accounted for the top three places in the national rankings in 1992, with Guangdong alone accounting for 24.1 per cent of national total exports (row 3).

Finally, if we look at the utilization of foreign capital, the Huanan Economic Sphere is also top of the national rankings. From Table 10.4 (row 4)

Table 10.4   Foreign orientation of the Huanan Economic Sphere, 1992

	Guangdong	Fujian	Hainan
1. Degree of foreign orientation[a]			
Per cent	45.8	33.1	35.7
National rank	1	5	3
2. Gross imports and exports			
US$ thousand million	29.6	6.6	1.7
Per cent of total for China	17.9	7.7	2.0
3. Gross exports			
US$ thousand million	18.4	4.3	0.9
Per cent of total for China	24.1	5.6	1.1
4. Use of foreign capital			
US$ million	4,746.4	1,465.6	514.8
Per cent of total for China	24.2	7.6	2.7
5. Registration of enterprises based on foreign investment			
Annual number	26,365.0	7,423.0	2,829.0
Per cent of total for China	31.2	8.8	3.4
Total capital (US$ thousand)	31,720.2	6,027.7	3,841.2
Per cent of total for China	30.9	5.9	3.7
Registered capital (US$ thousand)	20,469.3	3,708.1	2,837.5
Per cent of total for China	30.2	5.5	4.2

Note: [a] Gross export value as a per cent of GDP.

Sources: As for Table 10.1, and *Zhongguo duiwai jingji maoyi nianjian,* various years

we see that 24 per cent of the country's total foreign capital was used by Guangdong. If to this figure we add those of Fujian and Hainan, the sum would be over one-third of the national total. The annual registration data for enterprises based on foreign investment (row 5) show that the number of enterprises in these three provinces reached 43.4 per cent of the total for the whole country. The Guangdong figure alone was 31 per cent of the national total. The capital data show that the three provinces accounted for 40 per cent of the national total.

The key reasons why Huanan Economic Sphere is able to keep developing its economy at a high speed are as follows: the three provinces have Hong Kong, Macao and Taiwan as their neighbours; they possess advantageous conditions in terms of people and resources; and many overseas Chinese have their roots in these three provinces. Hence the most advanced technology, equipment, management and market information can be obtained much more easily than in most of the other provinces of China and, generally, technology transfer to the sphere is exceptionally fast.

CONCLUSIONS

From the above analysis and my examination of the Huanan Sphere, we may draw the following conclusions. First, in order to achieve steady and stable economic growth, China has to accelerate the tempo of technology transfer from other countries and regions, and generally enlarge the scale of its international technical and economic contacts. We must both introduce new technology and transform our existing technology; increase the exports of Chinese manufactures; fill the gaps in China's present technology, and thereby improve our material and technical foundation. This line of argument is supported by the finding that the productivity contribution to growth has risen to 41 per cent.

Second, in order to improve the quality of growth, China has to learn to compete in both home and foreign markets, complete and perfect its internal market mechanisms, improve the flow of information, and make the market the means to drive technical progress forward. In these respects, the experience of the Huanan Economic Sphere provides much valuable guidance.

Third, in order to lessen the technology gaps between our economy and technology and those of the advanced countries, China has to improve its creative abilities while accelerating technology transfer. We must adopt the strategy of combining imitation and creation. Though we must keep on introducing foreign technology and equipment, we have to digest and absorb what we take from abroad, make improvements, and so eventually create new products.

Fourth, since the founding of the People's Republic, and especially after the country's implementation of open and reform policies, we have achieved great results in the field of technology transfer. However, from the general point of view, we still have the following problems: the slow speed of technical development; the weak foundation of our present industrial technology; and the small share of technical progress in accounting for growth. There are many reasons for these problems, but the most important factor is that China still lacks the systemic means to produce dynamic growth.

For the future, therefore, we need to improve the technological level of the enterprises, the formation and transmission of national technology policies, and the general functioning of the economic system. The substance of technology transfer should be undertaken by enterprises using their independent authority and acting according to market principles. The enterprises must select the country, method and time to introduce the technology they need based on their capabilities, information, finance, engineering development, production situation, marketing, and so on. As a result of the implementation of technology imports, enterprises will develop a large number of engineers and technicians, senior management members and market development and sales personnel and this will enable them to achieve their medium and long-term development plans.

China will in future need to rely on the strength (and correctness) of policy to achieve its key targets. Policies should ensure that we perfect and standardize technical transfer behaviour. The state should direct and control the overall process of technical transfer, including its different stages of research, evaluation, implementation, absorption and creative production. The state must also ensure a good macroeconomic environment by means of banking, financial and fiscal measures.

Finally, the present system should be one that integrates the various elements of the economy (i.e. the state, local government, foreign-invested enterprises, etc.), taking account of the experience of the Huanan Sphere. This means increasing the orientation towards marketization, opening up the economy still further and encouraging technology transfer and other mechanisms that favour productivity growth.

NOTES

1. See Li Jingwen *et al.* (1993).
2. *Editors' note*: The adjustment referred to here was a sharp macroeconomic contraction in 1980–81.

REFERENCES

Li Jingwen and Zheng Youjing (1992), 'An analysis of Chinese economic growth', *Zhongguo shehui kexue* [China's Social Sciences], 1.

Li Jingwen, Jorgenson, Dale W., Zheng Youjing, Masahiro Kuroda *et al.* (1993), *Shengchanliu yu Zhong, Mei, Ri jingji tsengchang yanjiu* [Research into Productivity and Economic Growth in China, the United States and Japan], Beijing: China Social Science Publishing House.

Zheng Youjing (1995), 'The current situation of China's regional economic development and prospects for the future', *Shuliang jingji jishu jingji yanjiu* [Research on Quantitative and Technical Economics], 1.

Zhongguo duiwai jingji maoyi nianjian [China Yearbook of External Economic Relations), (various years], Beijing: Statistical Publishing House.

Zhongguo tongji nianjian [China Statistical Yearbook], (various years), Beijing: Statistical Publishing House.

11. The transfer of process technologies in comparative perspective

Nick von Tunzelmann

Many formal economic models, and much of comparative history, when they come to analyse the transfer of technology, concentrate intentionally or unintentionally upon the transfer of product innovations. In some of the 'new growth theory', for example, it is supposed that new products are developed in the leading industrial countries (the 'north') and these products are subsequently imitated in the catching-up countries (the 'south'), which puts pressure back on the north to come up with further products. Paul Krugman, one of the founders of such work, simply 'assumed away' the issue of process innovation in his focus on product innovation and imitation.[1]

Economic historians and historians of technology have tended in the same direction. An obvious reason for this emphasis has been the relatively straightforward nature of the data on product innovation and imitation and its much greater abundance for the pre-industrial era. We can chart reasonably well when China or Germany obtained the silk-reeling machine or the rocket, but it is usually considerably more difficult to obtain information on the ways in which these products were constructed and used. This is not to deny that a massive amount of material has been accumulated on comparative process technologies, but until recent years and the rise of 'innovation studies', I believe it is fair to say that much of this material lay uncollated, and was treated as something of a by-product of the transfer of product innovations. The result has been, if anything, to exaggerate the amount of transfer that has taken place. For instance, in steel-making at about the end of the eighteenth century, there were a number of leading producers of steel spread across Asia and Europe, but each main area used processes that the other areas were unable to replicate.[2]

The above examples hint at the distinction being drawn between product and process innovation. Since this distinction is important for the present analysis, some further clarification is warranted. It is probably often supposed that in discussing innovations or imitations of machinery, for example, or of steel, one is dealing in process innovations. But for the machine-making industry, a new type of machine is a product innovation; similarly for the steel industry, a new type of steel is a product innovation. Either of these may of course require the development of new processes in order to produce them efficiently, in which case there is interrelatedness between the product and the process innovation. Thus the Gilchrist-Thomas process for making steel (1878) permitted the large-scale production of basic rather than acid steel. Hence, fairly obviously, product innovation concerns what things are done, while process innovation concerns how they are done. Another difficulty is that the same innovation may be viewed as either product innovation or process innovation, depending on the relationship to the industry concerned. A new machine as a product innovation for the machinery industry becomes a potential process innovation for the industry acquiring those machines – think, for instance, of the power-loom, which was a product innovation for the textile machinery (upstream) but a process innovation for the textile weaving industry (downstream).

THE ORGANIZATION AND ADMINISTRATION FUNCTIONS

The basic argument of the present chapter is that the transfer of process technologies involves a more complicated set of requirements and perspectives than product technologies do, although the interrelatedness issue means that both will normally be required in any given circumstance. Process technologies can be imported in 'turnkey' projects without adaptation to the conditions in the country importing the technologies, but *successful* transfer of process technologies is likely to involve indigenization. That is, the country importing a type of blast furnace (say) does not wish to be dependent on more advanced countries for every additional furnace, but aims to build up its own capability: first to operate the successive plants, then to construct them, and ultimately to improve them.[3] These each represent levels of indigenous technological capability (ITC).

In order to understand the accumulation of ITC in a catching-up country, it is first necessary to understand what the existing process technologies are aiming to achieve in the more advanced countries. They can then be adjusted to the needs of the later industrializers. In my forthcoming book, I have argued that the functions of the firm or enterprise can be expressed in four categories, which I refer to as (a) technology, (b) organization, (c) administration, (d) products.[4] In this chapter I shall give only secondary consideration to the first and fourth categories, since these are somewhat specific in focus and in any event are better understood. My emphasis here will fall on the less well understood functions of organization (processes) and administration (management/finance). As with the other two functions, these can each be analysed by charting them in a two-dimensional array.

In the literature on business history, the administration function is characteristically described as the outcome of 'scale and scope'.[5] Equivalently, the literature on industrial organization talks in terms of 'barriers to entry' and barriers to mobility',[6] which are the same as scale and scope except that they stress the obstacles to enlarging scale (barriers to entry) or scope (barriers to mobility). Both have tended to presume that greater scale and greater scope are desirable. Scale and scope are usually assessed by the levels of operation of the enterprise. Thus scale is often equated with size of firm; though it is in fact possible to increase scale without increasing size, when scale is more accurately defined as the number of *processes* that the firm uses.[7] Similarly, scope is often taken to refer to the number of *products* the firm produces. Thus we can think of scale as reflecting the degree of 'integration' of the firm and scope as reflecting the degree of 'diversification', and since scale is related to process while scope is related to product, it is quite possible for the firm to expand in both scale and scope.

In the top panel of Figure 11.1, I have made a rough attempt to classify the firms of different countries during their major industrialization era according to these criteria. In this diagram, scope (or diversification) is graphed on the horizontal axis, from low to high degrees of diversification. Scale is graphed downwards on the vertical axis, proceeding from low degrees of integration to high degrees. Thus a point near the top left-hand corner, like 'UK 19C' indicates that, in the Industrial Revolution period, UK firms typically had very limited degrees of both diversification (narrow range of products produced) and integration (narrow range of processes utilized). Practically all countries will have some big and some small firms, some concentrated and some diversified. The country labels in the figure are intended in the first place to identify those firms that are usually regarded as having been the main source of the industrialization effort in the respective countries. Thus South Korea has many small firms, but its recent industrialization has been led by the large *chaebol*. Some countries have a pronounced 'dualistic' structure of their industrial sectors, notably Japan over the past century or more, with significant roles for both larger and smaller firms. Ideally, each country should be represented by a distribution of patterns of integration and diversification rather than by a single point; so in the cases of 'dualistic' structures, the labels in the diagram constitute a compromise. It hardly needs to be emphasized that the data on which these diagrams are based are highly impressionistic and drawn from secondary interpretations rather than primary sources.

Even after allowing for the errors that may have been induced by these approximations, it is evident that there is no detectable relationship between the scale-and-scope choice made by different countries and their overall success in industrialization. Countries with firms or enterprises of low scale

1.   Administration

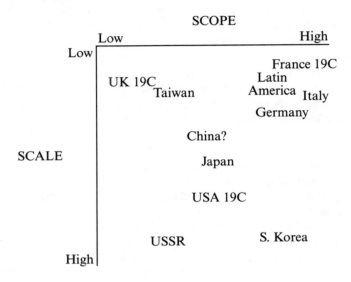

2.   Organization

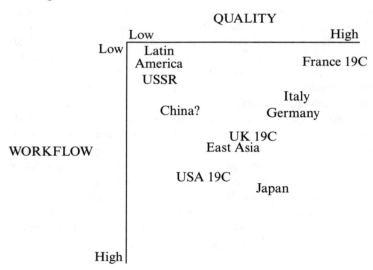

*Figure 11.1   Administrative and organizational patterns of industrializing
             countries*

and low scope have succeeded (e.g. Britain in the Industrial Revolution and Taiwan today), as have countries whose dynamic firms have large scale and scope (e.g. South Korea). No doubt both of those extreme sets of cases would also include other countries whose industrializations have been less success-ful. Certainly we see that the other quadrants, of either large scale and low scope or small scale and high scope, include cases of both relative failure (USSR, Latin America) and relative success (USA, Japan, Germany, etc.). While there may be some dispute over the exact location of individual coun-tries – which in principle better data could resolve – it seems scarcely possi-ble to challenge the conclusion that success has been compatible with many different levels and combinations of scale and scope.

China shares the characteristic of Japan in its dualistic industrial structure (see Jiang, Chapter 7 in this volume). The lack of a legacy of *zaibatsu*, etc., together with casual observation, however, suggests it should be located somewhere between Japan and Taiwan in this figure. To provide a classification more satisfactory in terms of its ability to rate differences in performances across countries, we need to examine the organization function, as in the second panel of Figure 11.1. Like the administration sphere, this relates process to product, but in a rather different way. The horizontal axis now represents the quality of products rather than their degree of diversification (in practice, of course, the two are quite often linked, as comparison between the two panels of Figure 11.1 suggests). The vertical axis again is related to processes, and here I have used workflow as an index of quality of process. The reason for this will become more obvious as the chapter unfolds.

It will be noted that industrialization success, at least as it can be gauged by the extent of development of ITCs, is roughly in proportion to the distance of the country label from the origin. The USSR in this sense was a case of relative failure, as Feinstein (Chapter 3 in this volume) demonstrates. Simi-larly, most larger Latin American countries have been regarded, even (or especially) by their own scholars, as rather unsuccessful industrializers. Both of these ended up producing low-quality goods using low-quality processes (with low rates of throughflow from inputs to outputs). China in recent years has probably been more successful than either in its technological accumula-tion, but from casual evidence appears to lie well below the now advanced countries. This suggests that China may need to give much greater attention to the organization function in the years ahead. Most of the currently ad-vanced countries lie along the 45° line, representing different balances struck between quality of products and quality of processes. This arises because, while ideally one would like to get high quality in both dimensions, in practice this is very difficult to do. We can see this if we crudely equate high product quality with high unit price, and high process quality with low unit costs – it is then evident that, whatever the desirability of the combination of high price and low cost may be to the producer, few are likely to achieve both of these in a competitive world.

The different possible trade-offs between product and process quality have been roughly equal in their impact on rates of technological accumulation (development of ITCs), but have not been equal in terms of rates of overall industrial or economic growth attained. Some of the differences in the rates of economic growth reflect global rather than national trends, such as the catching-up possibilities stressed by the 'new growth theory'. But even if we try to correct for this by applying a relative rather than an absolute measure of economic growth, differences remain between, say, France in the late nineteenth century (near the top right-hand end) and the USA in the same era (bottom left-hand end). The variety of reasonably effective combinations of scale and scope, process quality and product quality is superficially some- what like that which emerges from the 'strategic management' literature.[8] Aside from the greater ability to dimension these alternatives by using the approach adopted here, there are two more fundamental differences between the latter and the strategic management perspective. The first is that we do not assume that different countries, or more precisely the firms of different coun- tries, are equally 'free to choose' their 'strategy'.[9] Second, we do not regard all the 'choices' as having equal potential for growth, as just pointed out.

Most counties have in fact sought fast growth by aiming to improve process rather than product quality. The East Asian countries in the figure (i.e. the 'Four Tigers') are cases in point. Reasons exist on both the supply side and the demand side why the opportunities seem greater for enhancing process rather than product quality.

On the demand side, the *market potential* for expansion of high-quality products is rather limited. The world is of course getting richer, and there are more high-income consumers emerging. But demands here depend on main- taining niche markets among the seriously wealthy, and almost by definition these are difficult to sustain. Once large quantities of the products become available, they lose their prestige value and become commoditized. At this stage, they are amenable to production by automated as well as craft meth- ods, and the latter are likely to be out-competed by the former. Moreover, income distributions in general are probably becoming more equal, which is tending to bunch demand nearer to the middle groups of the income range.[10]

On the supply side, the *productivity potential* for development of process quality has been considerably greater since the British Industrial Revolution. Elsewhere I have explained this as the result of the emergence of powerful technological 'paradigms', beginning with mechanization, which have en- sured *sustained* technological development.[11] Within these paradigms, pro- duction knowhow gave rise to particular 'heuristics' which guided and encouraged innovation of specific kinds.

To be more explicit, innovation was aimed especially – though not exclusively – at intensifying the workflow, i.e. by a downward movement in the second panel of Figure 11.1. This was achieved through what I describe as 'time-saving' technological change. Time-saving change can be thought of as producing greater output from a fixed supply of inputs. In mathematical terms, this is no different from the usual case examined by economists, of producing the same output from a smaller supply of inputs, apart from a multiplicative factor. However, my view is that in practice it was very different, not least in the determinants which gave rise to such patterns of innovation in the first place.

TIME-SAVING INNOVATION

In everyday language, innovations are spoken of as 'saving time' or 'saving labour', sometimes interchangeably. Orthodox economic analysis, however, only considers the latter. A number of reasons can be given for ignoring the saving of time, but for present purposes it is sufficient to mention two: (a) the static ('timeless') nature of neoclassical economic analysis; (b) the presumption that time, unlike labour, is not a factor of production. In classical political economy, I have shown elsewhere that time-saving, labour-saving and capital-saving were treated more or less interchangeably in analysing process improvement, with all three considered but with only modest efforts to disentangle them.[12]

The quintessential classical analysis of processes, which in many respects has never been superseded, is that of Adam Smith in the opening pages of *The Wealth of Nations*. Here Smith gave the arguments in favour of the division of labour, which he listed as: (a) specialization and concentration, (b) reducing time losses from moving between tasks, (c) increasing technical progress through a focus on processes, especially mechanization.[13] The time-saving gain from (b) has been frequently slighted as once-for-all,[14] but if seen in conjunction with (c) as innovation, it raises wider issues.

Adam Smith referred to innovations as 'facilitating and abridging labour',[15] which gave the appearance of saving labour rather than saving time. But Smith's context lay in his argument that the division of labour is limited by the 'extent of the market'.[16] According to the definition of time-saving I have just given, larger markets can therefore be served from an existing supply of inputs such as labour. In the language of the economics of innovation, the inputs will be 'augmented' (labour-augmenting, capital-augmenting, etc.) as their productivity rises. In this way, labour may indeed be 'facilitated and abridged', without necessarily saving labour in the stricter economic sense.

In similar vein, Marx's well-known thesis about the historical inevitability of labour-saving technological change under industrial capitalism has been misrepresented: Marx specifically argued for savings in *necessary labour-time*. As he was well aware, these could come about variously through labour-saving proper (employing fewer workers for the same length of time) or time-saving (employing the same number for a shorter period), and usually both.[17] Naturally Marx chose to stress the labour-saving rather than the time-saving. Part of the reason was that he linked time-saving proper, i.e. declines in time required per unit of output, to declines in time worked; for example, the number of hours needed to produce a certain type of machine fell with the number of hours worked per day. The latter, he presumed, directly helped to cause the former, as exemplified by the speed-up following the passage of the Ten Hours Act in Britain.[18] Moreover, it was not just labour-time that was saved, because under modern capitalism the emphasis had switched from 'labour process' to 'capital process';[19] hence capital-saving could also be associated with time-saving.

Where Marx explicitly parted company with Adam Smith was in denying that demand (or extent of the market) was the major cause of technological advance in *production* in capitalist societies – instead Marx regarded this as being driven by the imperatives of industrial capitalism.[20] In this debate, my view accords with that of Smith rather than of Marx. However, Marx himself went on to develop the point that the capitalist is interested in the total turnover time for his capital, and this comprises a 'circulation period' as well as a production period. For the speeding up of 'circulation', Marx did allow that demand forces may be important.[21]

The cause of time-saving is thus traced here primarily to expansion of demand, whereas in the factor-saving perspectives of conventional economics it is customarily supposed that the main cause derives from efforts to cut costs. With time-saving innovation, cost bills per unit of time may not actually fall and could possibly rise a little, but costs per unit of output will of course fall through the production of greater output per unit of time. In practice, both cost conditions, i.e. the supply side, and demand conditions are likely to matter.

A key reason why time-saving change has proved so popular is that it permits greater output without necessarily leading to technological unemployment or the like along Ricardian lines. In a loose sense, some labour is 'saved' through its greater unit efficiency, but this comes about *as a result* of the expansion of output through time-saving innovation. In the stricter formal sense, labour may not be saved any more than other factor inputs such as capital, in which case the innovation may be 'neutral' rather than truly labour-saving. An extension of the argument allows us to see why there may have been stronger motivation at certain times and places to save materials or other inputs, whose supply was genuinely scarce. The main point is that causes of innovation need to be distinguished from effects – with time-saving as a cause, labour-saving may come about as an effect, in the manner described above. Our enquiries at the R&D institute of a major Chinese steel firm, visited during our stay in Beijing, elicited a similar response: that the outcome of innovation had not been any decline in employment, which had in fact risen somewhat, while output had grown more rapidly. It is apparent that this strategy is more acceptable politically and socially than is one of reducing labour inputs.

Expansion of demand is not the only cause of time-saving change. In agriculture, seasonality has been a noteworthy factor in promoting the use of faster techniques, for instance, to cope with short harvesting seasons. In manufacturing perishable products such as processed food, again speed may be of the essence.

The general case, however, has been the conjuncture of market potential with productivity potential. The market potential arose through expansion of demand, perhaps through the opening up of foreign trade possibilities in the way Adam Smith described in his discussion of the 'extent of the market'. The productivity potential arose through developing technological heuristics which made speed-up an especially fruitful way to progress. Evidence for such change dates back as far as we have records; for instance, the early medieval period in north Europe witnessed a shift from ploughing by oxen to ploughing by horses, where 'the horse moves so much more rapidly that he produces 50 per cent. more foot-pounds per second'.[22] I have elsewhere examined the machinery of the cotton industry in the 'First Industrial Revolution' in this light,[23] and there is no need to repeat here the extensive findings that relate to speed-up, which came both from the adoption of machinery (especially the substitution of rotary motion for the natural to-and-fro motion of the human arm or leg) and from the use of chemical compounds for purposes such as bleaching or dyeing. It is worth briefly recounting the forms that such time-saving took:

- reduced *downtime*, as the improvement of machines made them more reliable: for example, improved power-looms were less liable to tear the fabric and adopted mechanisms to stop the weaving quickly if breakages did occur;
- more obviously, increased *throughput*, i.e. faster processing during the actual production phase, most often by this adoption of rotary motion for mounting the key items of equipment (and subsequently rotating them faster);
- increased *machine co-ordination*, as different parts of the machines were better able to synchronize with one another, for example through

relating the feeding-in and taking-out phases more closely to the principal processes;

- increased *system co-ordination*, as different processes were each speeded up in turn: for example, the faster spinning of cotton induced a speed-up of weaving and also finishing processes (bleaching, printing, etc.); and similarly in iron, with speed-up of the blast furnaces (smelting) inducing matching changes in the forge (for wrought iron), in rolling the products, etc.

In similar fashion, the materials associated with the British Industrial Revolution could be seen as time-saving, both in their usage and in their production. In terms of production, the development and steady improvement of the puddling and rolling processes for making iron are estimated to have raised the speed of throughput eventually by some twenty-five times.[24] In terms of use, the English economist Alfred Marshall pointed out that

> iron, the material of all these industries, was largely used in England because she had large uses for it; though she had not a plentiful supply of it. Iron is the great saver of time, and the chief engine of thorough solid work; as well as the chief material of those subtle and powerful engines and instruments, in which modern invention has found its scope.[25]

The time-saving nature of innovation linked to new forms of organization, most notably the factory system. The pre-industrial 'putting-out system' had established a production structure based on the division of labour *according to product*.[26] This permitted dynamic learning effects, arising out of the large degree of responsibility entrusted to the individual worker in his or her own home. The basic problems of the system had to do with the speed and quality of production. Workflow was lethargically slow, as the materials went the rounds of the many processes conducted in homes which might be scattered over considerable distances. Quality of product could not be guaranteed because of the absence of direct supervision, and there was much (sometimes apparently valid) suspicion that workers were often secretly embezzling the materials.[27]

Thus the factory emerged in such sectors as a mode of organization intended to remedy these two defects: to control workplace by Smith's strategy of reducing the gaps between each process, and to control the quality of work through direct supervision (overseers, etc.). These are of course the dimensions in which the organization function is charted in the second panel of Figure 11.1. Division of labour by product in sectors such as textiles was replaced by division of labour *according to process*, which squared with the shift in innovational patterns. Both the technologies and the organizational structures had to progress for success.[28]

Some of the best data I have seen that bears out the pattern of time-saving in more recent times is in Enos (Chapter 6 in this volume), relating to petroleum refining in Louisiana. Enos's data show the feed rate of the materials rising from 15,100 bpsd in 1943 to 94,000 in 1992, by 're-vamping' the existing plant, in this case without much sacrifice of capital.

The significance of such time-saving changes is threefold. First, they represented the heuristic principle for guiding innovation: to provide a 'rule of thumb' whereby machines were initially introduced, and subsequently improved, in accordance with their ability to save time (as in the four ways noted above). Second, the principle was a technological rather than an economic one: this meant that the more narrowly economic concerns such as saving labour or capital came about *in response to* the technology changes rather than truly causing them. This does not signify that the economic aspects were unimportant – on the contrary, they helped to shape the precise 'trajectories' which technologies pursued, within the general ambit of the paradigm of mechanization and the (engineering) rule of thumb about saving time. Third, these time-savings constituted a direct link between demand determinants (growth of markets, etc.) and the evolution of technology, by dint of their permitting the production of greater output per unit of time.

PATTERNS OF INNOVATION IN DIFFERENT COUNTRIES

In turning to the transfer of these technologies to the other early industrializing countries of the west, we have to allow that there were trade-offs associated with the pursuit of time-saving. Some of these have already been implied above: in particular it has been observed in the lower panel of Figure 11.1 that in general a rise in workflow may require some sacrifice in product quality (some important exceptions will be noted below). The basic argument in this section is that different countries encountered different demand and supply contexts into which these technologies were imported. As a result, they came to different decisions about whether to place the major emphasis on improving product quality or process quality. Countries generally began by copying the *type* of product produced in the leader countries they were trying to catch up, of which cotton textiles and iron – the 'leading sectors' of the British Industrial Revolution[29] – were the most common in the early nineteenth century. The type of *process* might also be copied at first, but processes were altered more drastically than were products over the next phase of industrialization.

France

First of the countries given in Figure 11.1 to try to emulate Britain was France. Two main considerations influenced the choice of product quality in the French case. On the supply side, France had established a powerful commercial position in high-quality fabrics, especially fine silks. It thus provided a tradition of craft skills for manufacturing high-quality textiles, on the one side, and an infrastructure of trading and financial networks for dealing in such products, on the other. However, the early cotton mills were set up in regions like Alsace that were some distance away from the nucleus of the silk industry in Lyon. Hence demand was at least as important as supply in determining the levels of product quality that characterized French textiles.

French industry during the era of industrialization was characterized by a continuing insistence on product innovation and on design-intensive activity. French culture was long regarded as setting the standards for dress in the rest of Europe.[30] The French lead in retailing was at the up-market end in Paris, in contrast to British leadership in selling to the working classes.[31] The economist Alfred Marshall also stressed the role of schools of design and of copyright on designs in France, and indeed the whole emphasis placed on the design function: 'In France a single manufacturer would have several designers at work on his premises, while in England a single designer would work for several manufacturers'.[32] What struck him particularly was that French governments had poured money into certain industries, to little productive effect, while virtually ignoring the funding of design, which had been so successful.[33]

The price paid for this high-quality, design-intensive activity was seen in the sphere of processes employed, with low rates of throughput and a reliance on craft methods of production with only limited amounts of standardization. Production remained centred in many small and medium-sized firms (SMFs). Spindle speeds in cotton spinning remained consistently below those attained in the UK. As late as the 1890s, spindle speeds for good-quality yarn in the Alsace spinning industry were 25 per cent below those in Lancashire, and downtime was 20 per cent as compared with 5 per cent in Lancashire.[34] Similarly in power-loom weaving: average picks per minute on plain cotton goods around 1890 were 240 in Lancashire, 190–200 in Switzerland, and only 150–160 in Alsace.[35] Cost considerations, i.e. the supply side, partly accounted for this slower workflow rate, especially the high cost of coal in Alsace.[36] The demand side and the desire to maintain product quality, however, entered into the French calculations. Consequently, France was led to the point at the top right of the second panel of Figure 11.1.

Germany

The German pattern of industrialization differed from that in France, though Germany too – like France – began industrializing in activities which had characterized Britain during the Industrial Revolution, such as cotton. But demand and supply conditions for textile products differed from those in France. On the supply side, the existing industry was based on producing linens of low to medium quality for poorer consumers. Moreover, the commercial infrastructure was highly fragmented because of a lack of economic and political integration. On the demand side, incomes were very unequally distributed in eastern Germany, but high incomes were generally to be found among the rural landowners (*Junkers*) rather than an urban *haute bourgeoisie* as in France. In general, product quality was therefore a less important consideration for German producers.

Instead, German industry came to be driven by process quality in a peculiarly distinctive way. Technology, and technical efficiency, came to set the standards for desirability. Levels of technical efficiency in turn flowed from the nature of the German educational system, which concentrated on disseminating technical information well down the ladder of opportunity, through polytechnics, mechanics' institutes, schools of apprenticeship, and so on. By contrast, the French and British systems of education were much more elitist, and arguably remain so today. This predominance of technology gave Germany after 1870, newly unified under Bismarck, a head start in all the major technological fields associated with the so-called 'Second Industrial Revolution' of this time: steel, electrical equipment, motor vehicles and above all chemicals. Germany led in establishing in-house R&D departments in large firms, borrowing the organizational patterns of university laboratories as developed by scientists such as Liebig. However, this high level of technical efficiency did not necessarily mean success in the competitive market place. Despite the German technological lead in motor vehicles and their engines, the French automobile industry grew considerably faster in the late years of the nineteenth century, and eclipsed the German until the Second World War. The French again relied on product differentiation and on individualistic styling, based on entrepreneur-innovators who were often products of top-echelon educational institutes. So German technical efficiency did not always lead to process efficiency.

This was because the meticulous care in technical development, as taught in polytechnics and similar institutes, and by apprenticeships, did not vouchsafe high levels of workflow, and indeed often counted against them. Visiting Americans of the late nineteenth and early twentieth centuries were scornful of the 'over-engineering' of German (and Swiss) products and production methods. The so-called American 'invasion' of European markets, beginning in the final years of the nineteenth century, rested on more standardized products, sold through Yankee marketing flair. Only after the Second World War, with the help of British and American army experts, did the German motor car industry achieve a sustainable market niche though selling reliability and product quality. Process efficiency in terms of workflow continues to be its Achilles heel. This may seem surprising in view of the extensive role of engineers and technicians in the German manufacturing system, but can be explained by their focus on the technical aspects of engineering, rather than 'production engineering'.

Italy

The pattern described above for France to some extent began to give way in the interwar period in France itself,[37] and since the Second World War it is Italy that has come to be most identified with such processes. The networked SMFs found in the 'Third Italy' and elsewhere have been considered exemplars of 'flexible specialization', and even regarded as a major new divide in the history of industrial organization,[38] though others believe this view to be exaggerated. These SMFs have developed and diffused techniques for process efficiency. A good example is provided by Porter, of the introduction of roller kilns into SMFs in the Italian ceramic tile industry in the mid-1970s, which cut the cycle time for single-firing from 16–20 hours to 50–55 minutes.[39] These firms were very small, typically consisting of just three or four people. Thus time-saving in the form of rapid throughput was a major aspect of their survival.

The networking of these small firms in localized districts, however, helped to make this diffusion possible. The district as a whole has to become 'collectively entrepreneurial'.[40] At the heart of the 'Third Italy' in the province of Emilia-Romagna, the city of Modena acted as a regional hub for advanced engineering skills – Modena was the home of companies celebrated for high technical and design sophistication, such as Ferrari, Maserati and Lamborghini.[41] Overall purpose and direction comes from combining the decentralization of production capability in specialized SMFs (often family-based) with social integration, given by the sense of local community. In towns such as Modena, the latter was provided by local government (the Communist Party in this particular case) setting up local industrial parks through land expropriation and covenanted building programmes, installing practices of peer review and loan guarantees in place of formal banking practice for finance, and offering communal marketing and other services to share overheads. It was then up to the small family firms in the district to adopt individual designs via both competition and collaboration, and this was what was meant by being 'collectively entrepreneurial'.

Larger firms as well as local governments had an important role to play as 'hubs' in this networked system. Large firms like Benetton acted to diffuse knowledge concerning efficient production techniques on the supply side, and to diffuse information that permitted *rapid* redesign of fabrics and garments in the SMFs which supplied them on a sub-contract basis, in accordance with changes in broader demand patterns.[42] This in turn required such large firms to develop advanced IT systems, allowing them to gather and transmit information as rapidly as possible – obtained from their global network of franchised shops and quickly communicated to their sub-contracted suppliers. Similarly, in Baden-Württemberg in Germany, another region associated with 'flexible specialization', the regional government was again noteworthy, but so also were educational establishments, trade associations, banks, etc.[43]

USA

North America also borrowed British industrial products and technologies in the nineteenth century, but wasted little time before re-engineering them to suit American conditions. While the new technologies developed in the USA were rather modest contributions to the sum total of human technological knowledge before the twentieth century, it would also be inaccurate to describe those used in US industry as simple copies of the British. It was less a case of imitation than of re-invention, in the eyes of Marshall.[44] A major element in that re-invention procedure was speeding up British practices; examples include the ring spindle in place of the mule in the US cotton spinning industry,[45] and 'hard driving' in the US steel industry.[46] In other words, the Americans took the British heuristics even further than the British themselves, in contrast to many continental European countries which partly dethroned time-saving in favour of product quality or technical efficiency. Again, one can give reasons on both the demand side and the supply side for the accentuated time-saving.

The demand-side argument relates to the nature and composition of domestic US demand. The US population halfway through the nineteenth century was already somewhat wealthier than Britain's (real wages were around 20–40 per cent higher). More important still was the structure of that demand, dominated by large numbers of rural households owning modest amounts of land.[47] This had substantial effects not only on marketing but also on production. Whereas many British items were customized for wealthy purchasers, Americans concentrated on cheaper, more standardized items for the whole community – an example much referred to in the mid-nineteenth century was guns, where (military purposes aside) the British concentrated on sporting pieces for the aristocracy while the Americans produced rifles and later pistols in large quantities for the small farmers and cowboys. Thus American demand sought, or at least appeared satisfied with, homogeneous goods for undifferentiated and extensive markets (mass consumption), which made it relatively straightforward to move towards mass production. Standardization was the key to American industrialization, including the standardization of units of weights and measures.[48] Even items that might be expected to be individually tailored were vastly more standardized in the USA, such as boots and shoes.[49]

On the supply side, the composition of factor inputs differed substantially from that in the Old World. The US techno-economic system in the nineteenth century was dominated by the availability of abundant supplies of land, obtained with varying degrees of subterfuge from the native population. These huge tracts of land were settled by small to medium farmers under such provisions as the Homestead Act (1862), who gave rise to the demand patterns just mentioned. By contrast, the conventional factor inputs of labour and capital were scarce and inelastic in supply. Both deficiencies were partly met by massive influxes of labour (mass immigration) and capital (inward investment), especially from the middle of the nineteenth century; but even these were insufficient to redress the balance. This spurred on a quest to speed up the output of the scarcer inputs (labour and capital) through adopting the machinery paradigm, in US agriculture as well as in manufacturing. Cheap land inputs also went with cheap timber and water inputs, which in turn led to cheap energy; with effects on speeding up machinery converse to those operating in continental Europe where energy was expensive.[50]

American technology in this era is often described as labour-saving. Despite a voluminous literature, there is no agreement about the theoretical explanations for such a bias when capital as well as labour was restricted in supply. An alternative empirical perspective is that, while technological changes in the narrower sense may have been labour-saving, the organizational changes were capital-saving.[51] The former pattern is perhaps accounted for by complementarities between labour and raw materials in the production processes.[52] This can be subsumed into the more general argument that I would make, that these outcomes reflected 'technological opportunities' (and organizational opportunities). So far as the equipment was concerned, these promoted a bias towards labour-saving, because it was there that the mechanical opportunities were greater.[53]

What first attracted British attention to the fact that they had a major new industrial rival, however, was not American technologies or even products, but American processes of manufacture. The very idea of assembly of components was so alien to the British observers in the 1850s – who coined the phrase, the 'American system of manufactures' – that whenever it was mentioned in their reports it was placed in inverted commas thus: 'assemble'.[54]

What permitted such routine assembly in turn was the development of inter-changeable parts, dating back to inventors such as Eli Whitney and Simeon North at the beginning of the nineteenth century. In their turn, interchange-able parts required a high degree of standardization and precision manufac-ture of the components. Interchangeable parts saved the time variously of the designers (only one design needed to be established), the producers (through dispensing with expensive and time-consuming handicraft labour), and the consumers (being able to replace any defective part with another equally useable). Throughput speeds were increased, as the above-mentioned British observers expressly noted, and there were knock-on dynamic effects of fur-ther developing the specialized machines and tools, effectively creating the machine tool industry.

Ultimately, interchangeable parts would lead towards the assembly line and continuous processing, as introduced in automobiles (though with more primitive antecedents in other industries) by Ford in Detroit after 1909.[55] On such huge, dedicated production lines, the components flowed successively to each worker, who stayed in the same place, thus minimizing the static loss which Adam Smith had described from workers having to move between jobs, and maximizing throughput and 'scale'. Ford evaluated the success of the moving assembly line by the reduction of labour-time per chassis, and so on. Labour-saving occurred *as a result*.[56]

While Fordism was seen as solving the problems of 'capital process', there was a large area of operations left undisturbed by the assembly line. The equivalent to Fordism when one turned to 'labour process' became known as 'Taylorism', after the publication of F.W. Taylor's short but influential work, *The Principles of Scientific Management* (1911). Taylor argued that the needs of employers and employees could be reconciled through combining high wages with low labour costs, and the way to do this was to get employees to work at the fastest possible pace consistent with productive efficiency.[57] While Ford wanted maximum throughput from machines, Taylor wanted it from workers, typically in bureaucratic organizations.[58] A task such as shov-elling or bricklaying could be reduced to a 'science' to determine the maxi-mum speed for the task (determined by 'speed' and 'feed') and the optimum speed for the worker.[59] Taylor thus espoused such principles as tight supervi-sion, effort-related payment systems (differential piece rates, etc.), bureau-cratic task allocation, and work-planning methods, such as the notorious 'time and motion' studies. In practice, Taylorism became embodied in spe-cialized equipment and embedded in hierarchical organizations, and was thus subverted into capital process and Fordism.

USSR

One of the issues in the great industrialization debate of the 1920s in the Soviet Union, less emphasized in later discussion but just as important, was that over the organization of industry. The choice was seen as coming down clearly between a German pattern, based as above on skills, moderate throughput and SMFs, and an American pattern, as just described, replacing skills, building large plants and achieving high throughput from advanced process technologies and Fordist–Taylorist working practices. The west European model was accepted to be more appropriate to the existing industrial situation, and the problems associated with the rigidity of the American mass production model were equally accepted.[60] Nevertheless, the Soviets plumped unhesitatingly for the latter, partly because of fears that the USSR lacked a skilled labour force, and partly on the positive grounds that this was seen as the route to fast catch-up. Lenin was extremely impressed by the potentialities of Taylorism, and argued: 'We must organize in Russia the study and teaching of the Taylor system and systematically try it out and adapt it to our ends.'[61] This emphasis on new construction and giant plants long continued: thus heavy chemical plants in the 1970s were typically 60–70 per cent larger than their US counterparts.[62]

It was assumed that scale economies would be maximized by building plants as big as total output (regional or national) required.[63] Whether giant plants really did achieve static, much less dynamic, cost reductions when set against counteracting forces such as managerial diseconomies of scale is more dubious. Such giant enterprises were often denounced as 'gigantomania'. In practice, there was no real effort to imitate the core of the 'American system of manufactures', which was the provision of interchangeable parts and sub-assemblies. This was owing partly to the lack of a large enough market, but also to the lack of development of complementary inputs – leapfrogs like this needed to be grounded in much greater accumulation of knowledge.[64] The Soviets instead believed Henry Ford: that workers could be trained rapidly on the job. Peasant youths and untrained women were preferred as employees to recruiting artisans from SMFs.[65] Continuous-flow production ebbed away as a result of such deficiencies.[66]

While the problems of product innovation had to do mainly with the lack of economic incentives from the demand side, for process innovation the main problems were organizational.[67] In a context of exacting production targets, process technologies were required to meet the objectives of reduced downtime, fast throughput, machine co-ordination and systemic co-ordination discussed above. Early attempts to augment throughput focused on labour process, best known via the 'Stakhanovite' movement in 1935, whereby employment was reorganized to attain very high output per shift. This was

interpreted by Soviet scholars as a Marxian reduction of the socially necessary labour-time, and can be regarded as time-saving in our sense, in that
output increased per unit of time from an undiminished labour force – though
later there did arise some concern over technological unemployment.[68] The
second phase of Stakhanovism in 1939 instead concentrated on machine
productivity, i.e. 'capital process', again time-saving but in relation to equipment.[69] Despite their high propaganda value, neither phase took hold in a
permanent way. Only to a limited extent were they directed at innovation, as
distinct from speeding up existing technology.[70] Engineering solutions were
developed to solve problems of capital process, such as 'group technology',[71]
but their diffusion was disappointing.

There were frequently voiced complaints about lags in delivery times for
new equipment orders – the annual planning process meant that each stage in
turn usually had to be planned for the following year without any cross-
consultation, so delivery might take several years longer than necessary simply because of the bureaucratic delays arising out of planning. Downtimes
were high because of low labour skills, poor-quality components and lack of
supplies at vital times. The problem of distancing between innovation producer and user raised the added complication that often the equipment supplied was incompatible with what was already in place – thus systemic
co-ordination was weak. If fast throughput was attained, it was regarded as
being achieved by sacrificing product quality, all too often to an unacceptable
degree.

'Economies of speed' in the systemic sense were seriously deficient in the
face of such problems. Lilja *et al.* (1989) compared two paper mills in the
perestroika period (late 1980s), one in Finland and one just over the border in
the USSR, with virtually identical plant and equipment. They found that
machine output per minute in the Finnish mill was twice that in the Soviet
mill, expected shutdowns in the Soviet mill were three to five times those in
the Finnish mill, and yet first-quality paper represented 97 per cent of the
Finnish output as compared with 65 per cent of the Soviet. Thus the key
heuristic of time-saving was ignored in the Soviet Union in favour of large
production units and central control.

Japan

The Japanese also placed primary emphasis on process development rather
than products, but with vastly greater success. Japanese companies based
themselves on the doctrine of continuous improvement (*kaizen*). The main
achievement of the 'Japanese system of manufactures' has been learning to
learn about process innovation. Products could be imitated, but in processes
the Japanese were evolving something hitherto unique.[72] Mansfield (1988)

found that about two-thirds of Japanese R&D was *process*-oriented, whereas two-thirds of American company R&D was *product*-oriented.

The time-saving arrangements in the organization of production have been orientated towards creating 'lean production systems',[73] and it is these that western companies have struggled hardest to copy. Such lean production systems present the most immediately recognizable form of Japanese industrial superiority, not least from the results in terms of high physical productivity per unit of time to which they give rise; for example, the much lower number of man-hours required to produce an average motor car than in the USA.[74]

One of the most celebrated constituents of the lean production system is the adoption of 'just-in-time' (JIT) production scheduling. Components required for assembling a particular line of products are thus ordered to arrive at the moment they are needed for incorporation into the work in progress. This is in obvious contrast to the traditional western 'just-in-case' scheduling, where large stocks of each possible component are kept at hand, in case they turn out to be needed when the product line is altered. Indeed, in the west, JIT is often simply regarded as a better method of inventory (stock) control, cheapening the cost to the firm of holding inventories of such components. However, as Schonberger (1982) argues, the more significant impacts of JIT appear to be dynamic rather than static gains, especially in raising worker commitment and motivation as each is responsible for the ordering, etc.; equally, each had only himself or herself to blame if mistakes were made. Changes were also required within the factory in capital process, including 'downsizing' of special-purpose machinery to reduce the minimum efficient size of plant, and reduction of changeover times including methods for rapid tool change ('single-minute exchange of dies').[75]

The other well-known constituent of lean production is the adoption of 'total quality control' (TQC). Paradoxically, notions of TQC came from ideas advanced by US advisers to Japanese industry in its period of reconstruction after the Second World War, especially Deming in 1950 and Juran in 1954. In Japan the implementation of higher product quality began with *ex post* statistical sampling of product runs to detect any defective items, as also occurred in progressive western companies. From this, however, it steadily moved towards *ex ante* reduction – and, if possible, elimination – of defects before the production process began, i.e. at source. Thus, for instance, wastage arising out of half-building a car before the problem from a faulty component became recognized could be overcome – this was the policy of 'zero defects' as fully worked out. 'Quality circles' have been increasingly directed at identifying potential *future* problems. Quality control remained the responsibility of the shopfloor, in contrast with the USA, where it was seen as a tool of management.[76]

The main dynamic gains came from the combination of these two concepts, given their overlapping nature. JIT production plus the scrapping of *ex post* quality control not only reduced buffer inventories and induced fast feedback on defects, but in dynamic terms led to heightened awareness of problems and their causes, and thus on to their solutions.[77] For the firm as a whole, it not only led to static cost gains from lower material and labour inputs, having the effects of saving working capital and saving time, but also to faster market response, better forecasting and leaner administration.[78] In industries like automobiles, the Japanese found that there did not have to be a trade-off between throughput and quality – on the contrary, guaranteed component quality permitted an acceleration of throughput. JIT and TQC in combination fitted best into the Japanese style of management, based as they were on consensual approaches (as in the 'quality circles') plus bottom-up decision-making for routine operations (individual worker responsibility for orders, etc.). Because of this, they were often much less statically and dynamically efficient when introduced as management techniques in western companies.

Just-in-time relationships require close integration of the manufacturing (assembling) firms with the suppliers of components. Otherwise, all that happens when the assembly company reduces its inventories is that it pushes the burden of carrying such inventories upwards to the components suppliers, and in western companies which attempted to introduce JIT this occurred all too frequently. For JIT to benefit the production process at large, 'arm's length' supplier–user relationships are not good enough: suppliers need to remain continuously well-informed about the prospective needs of their manufacturing customers.[79] Japanese manufacturers are thus painstaking in the attention they devote to a careful choice of suppliers, to guarantee both zero defects in the supplied components and forethought to future needs. The main issue in the connection is a basis in commitment to *quality and reliability* – price is much less significant than for suppliers based on market-only linkages, as in the usual western circumstances.

One possible solution is to integrate vertically, which was typically what happened in US industries where control of input quality was crucial. Much the same occurred in early Japanese industry, in the *zaibatsu* ('money-cliques'). Their postwar structure came more to resemble that of other industrial groups – the *keiretsu* – which became established around emerging large firms (the *kaisha*). Sub-contracting was the typical basis of these relationships – instead of formal vertical integration, this has been described as 'quasi integration'.[80]

The 'Flying Geese'

While the first efforts in the Meiji era were aimed at indiscriminate copying of foreign techniques, there were sustained efforts thereafter to indigenize the technology, in order to limit the external dependence. Japanese technology borrowing in the twentieth century, up to the present day, has often limited the import component to the first plant only of each generation of the technology, requiring domestic industry to construct subsequent plants. Thus 'reverse engineering' and similar strategies have loomed large. About one-third of Japanese R&D in the modern era is considered as being spent on 'processing' foreign technologies.[81]

Similar policies have been pursued by other East Asian countries, following Japan. Both Taiwan and South Korea have copied foreign products, with production often undertaken on the type of relationship known as 'OEM' (original equipment manufacturer), i.e. fabrication and assembly to the designs of American, European or Japanese corporations, which then 'badged' the product and sold it under their own brand names. The primary emphasis was instead placed on processes and on rapid indigenization. Only later, when domestic manufacturing capabilities were reasonably advanced, was very extensive use made of foreign licensing (FL) as a means of acquiring new technologies. Amsden (1977) thus claims that the Taiwan machine tool industry used FL generally when sufficiently strong to be able to judge which foreign designs had the greatest growth potential in a Taiwanese setting.

Development of indigenous technological capabilities (ITCs) was the cornerstone of industrial advance in East Asia, with the aims of minimizing foreign control as quickly as possible and generating export competitiveness, including that among SMFs. Operation of the early petrochemical plants was expected to be grasped within one year in Korea.[82] Beyond the operation stage, 'imitator' strategies based on reverse engineering, using very close copying, were more common in the earliest years; but later there was a shift to 'apprenticeship' strategies, with adaptations carried out as the imports were duplicated.[83] 'Turnkey' projects, i.e. importing the whole plant in a state ready to be switched on, were restricted as much as possible to the scale-intensive process industries like petrochemicals, and even there they were progressively indigenized in later plants. Foreign engineers had been completely supplanted by Koreans in the first petrochemical plant (Hanyang) within four years.[84] Production capability and investment capability were achieved at practically the same time, and innovation capability followed within a handful of years – twenty years after the giant Korean steel firm, POSCO, was founded, it was exporting its technology to the USA.[85] Formal R&D expenditures were not very large, as the main emphasis lay on importing and indigenizing foreign technologies.[86]

Low wages constituted one early basis for cost efficiency in processes, but wages rose very rapidly, especially for production workers: 'workers were paid relatively high wages not because of a shortage of particular skills but in order to induce them to exercise their intelligence and make imported technology work'.[87] This reflected the emphasis on *process* change, which required especially adaptable workers. In many such industries, the modes of learning were uncodified, which placed even more responsibility on the employees; this contrasted with 'supplier-dominated' industries like textiles, where the changes were to a large extent embodied in capital goods.[88] Following Japan, a major objective was to seek technological changes that saved time, especially through reducing downtime.[89] A second significant objective was to upgrade quality, for example through introducing quality circles.

High adaptability of workers has been seen as an objective of accelerating programmes for education – the claim has been made that the East Asian Tigers were 'building education ahead of demand'. This is suggested by the unduly high expenditures on education relative to average per capita incomes over time.[90] However, the claim is strongly disputed by Amsden, who argues that the *quality* of education, especially in the vocational field, was by no means high enough to initiate growth.[91] Mass education was instituted mainly for 'social control',[92] a proposition that also probably held in the nineteenth-century USA. However, the provision of a *generalized* (non-vocational) primary and secondary educational system represents a key contribution to development, in providing 'training for training'.[93] At the same time, one can hardly disagree with Porter that there have to be complementary investments by firms and industries in specialized training and education.[94]

In the end, the key factor endowment indeed proved to be human capital (knowledge): the East Asian countries accumulated it and successfully underwent structural change, while other countries trying to catch up as newly industrializing countries, e.g. in Latin America, have to date been far less successful in both respects. In a dynamic sense, the issue was shown to be not one of choosing 'appropriate' technologies to fit the existing factor endowments, but how quickly the endowments themselves could be augmented in the interests of long-run industrial advantage.

WHAT IS THE OPTIMAL STRATEGY FOR TECHNOLOGICAL ADVANCE?

This is a crucial reason for not necessarily taking the advice often proffered by western economists, of aiming to grow through *exploiting* existing comparative advantages and factor endowments, as, for instance, is suggested in Wall and Yin (Chapter 9 in this volume). I am not in a position to know whether Wall and Yin are correct in their assessment of the current situation in China, that the optimal strategy is to develop high-technology industries using low-technology (labour-intensive) methods. This work is based on much research and extended observation of the Chinese situation. However, there are two aspects of this general line of argument which trouble me. The first is the implicit belief that it is sufficient to continue depending on more traditional processes, and limiting high-tech to the change of product structure. In terms of the second panel of Figure 11.1, this may move the country horizontally across the chart, but the tenor of my argument has been that the gains have been more substantial in most countries through moving downwards, i.e. through advancing process quality by means of faster overall rates of workflow. I shall return to this point in the context of China in the conclusion below.

The second reservation is the one just stated: that static (existing) comparative advantages and factor endowments are not appropriate to assessing the opportunities for rapid growth – we need to assess the *dynamic* comparative advantages and *enhancements* of factor supplies. The experience of Japan provides conclusive evidence in regard to this argument. The Ministry of International Trade and Industry (MITI), as reconstituted after 1949, rejected the advice tendered by worthies from the American Occupation and financial sources within Japan, to aim at growth through exploiting the existing factor endowment of labour intensity and existing comparative advantage of light industry. MITI instead went for a strategy of rapid growth through developing capital-intensive industry in the 1950s and '60s, and knowledge-intensive industries after 1971. MITI made several mistakes, and was often unsuccessful in getting industry to do what it wanted. But few, I believe, could now dissent from the view that Japan grew *much* faster under this allegedly inappropriate strategy than it would have done through pursuing labour-intensive processes and light industrial products. MITI argued in favour of replacing comparative advantage with 'competitive advantage' – i.e. what I have called dynamic comparative advantage – with the competitive strength gained from a number of high-tech companies (*kaisha*) in high-tech industries.

The adoption of time-saving changes of the kind stressed in this chapter retains the benefit that there is no need to dispense with labour and generate unemployment in an economy that has a relative surplus of labour. True, the generation of employment in the manufacturing sector may not be as great in the short term as a more committed labour-intensive strategy would achieve. However, there have been examples of developing countries choosing labour-intensive intermediate technologies which failed to become competitive at any stage, much less grow rapidly – as for instance Sen (1960) showed for the case of *ambar charka* in textile production in India. More generally, it seems highly likely that the greater growth of output generated by time-saving (output-augmenting) technical changes will absorb a greater amount of employment in the long term than the labour-intensive alternatives. Finally, it should be emphasized that time-saving methods permit a fair range of modification to economic contexts that may favour labour-saving in some countries and labour-intensity in others – we can contrast how Ford saved labour as a result of saving time in the US situation with the use of large temporary labour forces to build tower blocks rapidly in present-day Beijing.

Part of the competitive advantage also derives from organizational changes, as in the Japanese *kaisha* and the creation of a dynamic managerial and administrative structure in the most progressive firms. To explore this point, let us return to Figure 11.1 and the question of scale and scope. The figure shows that rapid growth has come variously from large firms or small firms, from diversified firms or specialized firms. The *levels* of these parameters are thus of secondary importance; what is of consequence is their respective strengths in pursuing dynamism, as reflected in the lower panel of Figure 11.1 upon which this chapter has concentrated. Thus a giant-sized firm may possess advantages in rates of sheer throughput on given product lines, but this does not necessarily give it an advantage in regard to product flexibility, where dynamic SMFs may have the edge in terms of product redesign and the like, which may emerge through differences in downtime (or through differences in market success). Historically, smaller firms have been especially successful in exploiting *technological* synergies at upstream stages (e.g. in machine tools, by producing similar tools for a diversity of industrial users), and in exploiting *product* synergies downstream (e.g. in higher-quality textiles). But to obtain some efficiency in the processes which link their technologies to their products, they may need to be closely aligned with larger-scale operations. The latter may be single large firms, like the Japanese *kaisha* or Italian hub producers, or may be local trade associations, or may come from regional government or similar support and guidance. Some kind of umbrella organization is required to channel information to where it is needed most. A networked system has many advantages overall in combining the capacity of the smaller unit (or decentralized corporation) for knowledge accumulation with that of the larger unit for information acquisition.

THE CHOICE FOR CHINA

China's development since the Second World War has involved a quite high degree of decentralization, certainly by comparison with the USSR. Its industrial structure has grown up under the legacy of 'walking on two legs' to the point of a considerable degree of dualism in the size/scope pattern of firms. The impression which comes out strongly from the Chinese chapters in this volume, notably that of Jiang (Chapter 7), and from our own factory visits, is that this dualistic structure remains somewhat divided – rather along the lines of prewar Japan or postwar South Korea. At the same time, there have been especially strong rates of growth in certain regions of the country, notably the provinces of Huanan noted by Zheng (Chapter 10). These considerations lead to the suggestion that the pattern of development that might prove most suitable for China is one along the lines of the recent experiences of Italy or southern Germany. The latter have conventionally been called examples of 'flexible specialization', but the term needs to be interpreted carefully. I have argued that success involves due consideration of process flexibility as well as product flexibility, and this in turn may necessitate bringing the smaller firms under the umbrella of larger organizations (be they firms, trade associations, local governments, or whatever). In this way dualism is preserved, but it is dualism of a more integrated and responsive kind than has been the case hitherto.

Ideally this pattern may lead to something like the Japanese *keiretsu*, with strong bonds between suppliers and customers. In this way, Japan has been able to outstrip the usual limitations of trading off greater product quality against greater process quality (see the second panel of Figure 11.1). The evidence, however, suggests that these industrial groups take much time and effort to develop, and that at present China (like South Korea) does not make use of close user–producer relationships, instead relying mainly on market-mediated linkages. The more that can be done in this respect, the better the situation is likely to become, but the cost and time involved may prove to be rather high.

In practice, therefore, China may realistically aim to move towards the 45° frontier implied in Figure 11.1. The question then becomes where China can best be located on this frontier. This chapter has pointed out that the historical experience has awarded greatest growth rates to downward movements in the diagram, i.e. to increasing the overall workflow. Both productivity and market potential have contributed in this way. However, in export markets – and eventually in domestic markets as well – there are long-term advantages to be sought in improving product as well as process quality. Japan came to dominate export markets in its chosen fields from the 1960s by producing medium- to high-quality products at medium to low costs. Only by a commitment to process improvement can these two desiderata be successfully combined.

The point was also made by a lead article in *China Daily*, published during our stay in Beijing, and quoting the official Chinese-language *Economic Information Daily*:

> The economy has arrived at a crossroads after 16 years of reforms and opening to the outside. The economic scale has expanded immensely in quantitative terms, so

it is high time to highlight the qualitative side of economic growth. When China blindly sought rapid growth in output, products invariably failed to improve in performance and quality. ... Outstanding production ability is indeed important. All enterprises and governments at all levels should be aware that the economic growth rate does not truly represent a country's economic strength.[95]

There are older examples that China can consider for indigenizing in order to achieve such flexibility and qualitative change; not only drawn from among the leaders in the 'flying geese' formation in East Asia but also from regions of western Europe and even North America. The policy implication of this chapter is that responsiveness to product markets involves process change. Time-saving changes allow efficient production of higher-quality products a well as of larger-quantity products, and can do so without necessarily threatening other social achievements such as high rates of employment. My impression is that attention in China has been focused rather too much on 'scale and scope', and especially on the size of firms – there are dangers here of repeating the USSR's 'gigantomania' – and not enough as yet on the question of production processes.

NOTES

1. Krugman (1979, p. 259).
2. Pacey (1990, ch. 5).
3. Katz (1985, 1987); Westphal *et al.* (1985).
4. von Tunzelmann (1995b).
5. E.g. Chandler (1990).
6. Caves and Porter (1977).
7. Scazzieri (1993).
8. E.g. Porter (1985).
9. See also Pavitt (1986).
10. It is true that the patterns across countries are very diverse, and there may be periods (such as the present, perhaps) when the trend towards income equality is reversed.
11. von Tunzelmann (1995b).
12. Ibid., ch. 2.
13. Smith (1776/1976, pp. 13ff).
14. E.g. Mill (1848/1909, pp. 125–8).
15. Smith (1776/1976, p. 17).
16. Ibid., pp. 31–2.
17. E.g. Marx (1859/1971, p. 37).
18. Marx (1887/1965, pp. 409–17); von Tunzelmann (1978, pp. 216–18).
19. Marx (1858/1973, p. 705, etc).
20. Marx (1857/1973, pp. 688–9); (1909/1977, pp. 261–2).
21. Marx (1858/1973, p. 539); (1919/1967, p. 320); (1909/1977, pp. 244–5).
22. White (1962, p. 62); Cipolla (1976/1993, p. 139).
23. von Tunzelmann (1995a).
24. Harris (1988, p. 40).
25. Marshall (1919, p. 60).
26. von Tunzelmann (1993, p. 267).

27. Pollard (1965, p. 33).
28. Speed-up also characterized the garments industry from the 1860s, based on the sewing machine, but by way of 'sweated industry', usually in the worker's own home; cf. Lazonick (1990, p. 48).
29. Rostow (1960/1971, ch. 4).
30. Steuart (1767/1966, pp. 249–50); Marshall (1919, p. 111).
31. Palmade (1972, p. 23).
32. Marshall (1919, p. 116).
33. Ibid., p. 120.
34. Milward and Saul (1973, pp. 176–7, 319).
35. Ibid.
36. von Tunzelmann (1978, ch. 11).
37. Lévy-Leboyer (1980).
38. Piore and Sabel (1984).
39. Porter (1990, p. 217).
40. Best (1990, p. 234).
41. Porter (1990, p. 212).
42. Belussi (1987).
43. Herrigel, in Kogut (1993).
44. Marshall (1919, p. 774).
45. Sandberg (1974, chs 2–3).
46. Temin (1964, ch. 7).
47. Rosenberg (1972, p. 48).
48. Veblen (1904, ch. 2); Marshall (1919, passim).
49. Ibid., p. 233.
50. von Tunzelmann (1978, ch. 11).
51. Field (1987, 1992).
52. Ames and Rosenberg (1967); David (1975, ch. 1).
53. Cf. Habakkuk (1962, p. 163).
54. Rosenberg (1969; 1972, p. 94).
55. Ford (1922, ch. 5); Hounshell (1984, ch. 6).
56. Ford (1922, pp. 82–90).
57. Taylor (1911, ch. 1).
58. Littler (1982); Hounshell (1984, pp. 251–3).
59. Taylor (1911, ch. 2).
60. Granick (1967, pp. 24–5).
61. Braverman (1974, p. 12).
62. Amann and Cooper (1982, p. 128).
63. Rosenberg (1992).
64. Granick (1967, pp. 44–7).
65. Ibid., pp. 92–3.
66. Ibid., pp. 112–15.
67. Amann and Cooper (1982, pp. 18, 249).
68. Berliner (1976, pp. 158–69).
69. Granick (1954, p. 86).
70. Ibid., pp. 247–8.
71. Amann and Cooper (1982, ch. 3).
72. Rosenberg (1994, ch. 7).
73. Best (1990, p. 14); Womack *et al.* (1990, passim).
74. Cf. ibid., ch. 4.
75. Abegglen and Stalk (1985, ch. 5); Best (1990, pp. 150–3).
76. Lazonick (1990, p. 292).
77. Schonberger (1982, Figure 2-3).
78. Ibid.
79. Best (1990, p. 15).
80. Aoki (1988, ch. 6).

81. Mansfield (1988).
82. Enos and Park (1988, p. 69).
83. Amsden (1989, ch. 9).
84. Enos and Park (1988, pp. 103–9).
85. Amsden (1989, ch. 12); Wade (1990, p. 319).
86. Enos and Park (1988, pp. 43–7).
87. Amsden (1989, p. 190).
88. Ibid., p. 265.
89. Ibid., ch. 7; see also p. 253 for textiles; p. 272 for shipbuilding; p. 305 for steel; cf. Porter (1990, p. 465).
90. Kim (1993, p. 359).
91. Amsden (1989, ch. 9).
92. Ibid., p. 219.
93. Kim (1993); von Tunzelmann (1995b).
94. Porter (1990, ch. 12).
95. *China Daily* (1995).

REFERENCES

Abegglen, J.C. and Stalk, G. Jr (1985), *Kaisha: The Japanese Corporation*, New York: Basic Books.
Amann, R. and Cooper, J. (eds) (1982), *Industrial Innovation in the Soviet Union*, New Haven, Conn., and London: Yale University Press.
Ames, E. and Rosenberg, N. (1968), 'The Enfield Arsenal in theory and history', *Economic Journal*, 78, 827–42.
Amsden, A.H. (1977), 'The division of labor is limited by the type of market: the Taiwanese machine tool industry', *World Development*, 5, 217–33.
—— (1989), *Asia's Next Giant: South Korea and Late Industrialization*, New York and Oxford: Oxford University Press.
Aoki, M. (1988): *Information, Incentives, and Bargaining in the Japanese Economy*, Cambridge: Cambridge University Press.
Belussi, F. (1987), 'Benetton: the innovation potential of traditional sectors', Science Policy Research Unit Occasional Paper, no. 25.
Berliner, J.S. (1976), *The Innovation Decision in Soviet Industry*, Cambridge, Mass., and London: MIT Press.
Best, M.H. (1990), *The New Competition: Institutions of Industrial Restructuring*, Cambridge: Polity Press.
Braverman, H. (1974), *Labor and Monopoly Capital*, New York: Monthly Review Press.
Caves, R.E. and Porter, M.E. (1977), 'From entry barriers to mobility barriers: conjectural decisions and continued deterrence to new competition', *Quarterly Journal of Economics*, 91, 241–61.
Chandler, A.D. Jr (1990), *Scale and Scope: The Dynamics of Industrial Capitalism*, Cambridge, Mass., and London: Belknap Press.
China Daily (1995), 'Percentages mislead, quality really counts', 8 April.
Cipolla, C.M. (1976), *Before the Industrial Revolution: European Society and Economy, 1000–1700,* London: Methuen; quoted from 3rd edn, London: Routledge, 1993.
David, P.A. (1966), 'The mechanization of reaping in the ante-bellum Midwest', in H. Rosovsky (ed.), *Industrialization in Two Systems: Essays in Honor of Alexander Gerschenkron*, New York: John Wiley, 3–39.

——— (1975), *Technical Choice, Innovation and Economic Growth: Essays on American and British Experience in the Nineteenth Century*, London and New York: Cambridge University Press.

Enos, J. (1997), 'The adoption of innovations and the assimilation of improvements', Chapter 6 in this volume.

——— and Park, W.-H. (1988), *The Adoption and Diffusion of Imported Technology: The Case of Korea*, London: Croom Helm.

Feinstein, C. (1997), 'Technical progress and technology transfer in a centrally-planned economy: the experience of the USSR, 1917–1987', Chapter 3 in this volume.

Field, A.J. (1987), 'Modern business enterprise as a capital-saving innovation', *Journal of Economic History*, 47, 473–85.

——— (1992), 'The magnetic telegraph, price and quantity data, and the new management of capital', *Journal of Economic History*, 52, 401–14.

Ford, H. (1922), *My Life and Work*, with S. Crowther, London: Heinemann; quoted from 1924 edn.

Granick, D. (1954), *Management of the Industrial Firm in the USSR: A Study in Soviet Economic Planning*, New York: Columbia University Press.

——— (1967), *Soviet Metal-fabricating and Economic Development: Practice versus Policy*, Madison, London: University of Wisconsin Press.

Habakkuk, H.J. (1962), *American and British Technology in the Nineteenth Century: The Search for Labour-saving Inventions*, Cambridge: Cambridge University Press.

Harris, J.R. (1988), *The British Iron Industry, 1750–1850*, Basingstoke, Hants.: Macmillan.

Hounshell, D.A. (1984), *From the American System to Mass Production, 1800–1932: The Development of Manufacturing Technology in the United States*, Baltimore, Md, and London: Johns Hopkins University Press.

Jiang Xiaojuan (1997), 'On the Chinese government policy towards science and technology and its influence on the technical development of industrial enterprises', Chapter 7 in this volume.

Katz, J. (1985), 'Domestic technological innovations and dynamic comparative advantages: further reflections on a comparative case-study programme', in Rosenberg and Frischtak (1985, 127–66).

——— (ed.) (1987), *Technology Generation in Latin American Manufacturing Industries*, London: Macmillan.

Kim, L. (1993), 'National system of innovation: dynamics of capability building in Korea', in R.R. Nelson (ed.), *National Innovation Systems: A Comparative Analysis*, New York and Oxford: Oxford University Press, 357–83.

Kogut, B. (ed.) (1993), *Country Competitiveness: Technology and the Organizing of Work*, New York and Oxford: Oxford University Press.

Krugman, P. (1979), 'A model of innovation, technology transfer, and the world distribution of income', *Journal of Political Economy*, 87, 253–66.

Lazonick, W. (1990), *Competitive Advantage on the Shop Floor*, Cambridge, Mass., and London: Harvard University Press.

Lévy-Leboyer, M. (1980), 'The large corporation in modern France', in A.D. Chandler Jr and H. Daems (eds), *Managerial Hierarchies: Comparative Perspectives on the Rise of the Modern Industrial Enterprise*, Cambridge, Mass., and London: Harvard University Press, 117–60.

Lilja, K. *et al.* (1989), 'Adjusting to perestroika: the case of Svetogorsk mills', working paper, Helsinki School of Economics.

Littler, C. (1982), *The Development of the Labour Process in Capitalist Societies*, London: Heinemann.

Mansfield, E. (1988), 'Industrial R&D in Japan and the United States: a comparative study', *American Economic Review, Papers & Proceedings*, 78, 223–8.

Marshall, A. (1919), *Industry and Trade: A Study of Industrial Technique and Business Organization...* London: Macmillan.

Marx, K. (1857–8), *Grundrisse: Foundations of the Critique of Political Economy*, English edn, ed. N.I. Stone:, Chicago, 1904; paperback edn, trans. M. Nicolaus, Harmondsworth, Middx: Penguin Books, 1973.

—— (1859), *A Contribution to the Critique of Political Economy*, German edn, 1859; English edn, trans. S.W. Ryazanskaya, ed. M. Dobb, Moscow: Progress Publisher; London: Lawrence & Wishart, 1971.

—— (1887), *Capital: A Critical Analysis of Capitalist Production*, vol. I: *Capitalist Production*, German edn, Hamburg: O. Meissner; New York: L.W. Schmid, New York: Hamburg: O. Meissner; New York: L.W. Schmidt, 1867; English edn, trans. S. Moore and E. Aveling from 3rd German edn, 1883); quoted from 1965 edn, Moscow: Progress Publishers London: Lawrence & Wishart.

—— (1919), *Capital: A Critique of Political Economy*, vol. II: *The Process of Circulation of Capital*, German edn, ed. F. Engels, O. Meissner: Hamburg, 1885; English edn, ed. Charles H. Kerr, Chicago, 1919; quoted from 1967 edn, Moscow: Progress Publishers.

—— (1909), *Capital: A Critique of Political Economy*, vol. III: *The Process of Capitalist Production as a Whole*, German edn, ed. F. Engels, O. Meissner, Hamburg, 1894; English edn, ed Charles H. Kerr, Chicago, 1909; quoted from 1977 edn, Moscow: Progress Publishers; London: Lawrence & Wishart.

Mill, J.S. (1848), *Principles of Political Economy, with Some of Their Applications to Social Philosophy* ; ed. W. J. Ashley, London: Longmans, Green, 1909.

Milward, A.S. and Saul, S.B. (1973), *The Economic Development of Continental Europe, 1780–1870*, London: Allen & Unwin.

Pacey, A.J. (1990), *Technology in World Civilization*, Oxford: Blackwell.

Palmade, G.P. (1972), *French Capitalism in the Nineteenth Century*, trans. G.M. Holmes, Newton Abbot, Devon: David & Charles; French edn, Paris: Librairie Armand Colin, 1961.

Pavitt, K. (1986), 'Technology, innovation and strategic management', in J. McGee and H. Thomas (eds), *Strategic Management Research*, London: John Wiley, 171–90.

Piore, M.J. and Sabel, C.F. (1984), *The Second Industrial Divide: Possibilities for Prosperity*, New York: Basic Books.

Pollard, S. (1965), *The Genesis of Modern Management: A Study of the Industrial Revolution in Great Britain*, London: Edward Arnold.

Porter, M.E. (1985), *Competitive Advantage: Creating and Sustaining Superior Performance*, New York: Free Press.

—— (1990), *The Competitive Advantage of Nations*, New York: Free Press

Rosenberg, N. (1963), 'Technological change in the machine tool industry, 1840–1910', *Journal of Economic History*, 23, 414–46.

—— (ed.) (1969), *The American System of Manufactures*, Edinburgh: Edinburgh University Press.

—— (1972), *Technology and American Economic Growth*, New York: Harper & Row.

—— (1992), 'Economic experiments', *Industrial and Corporate Change*, 1, 181–203.

—— (1994), *Exploring the Black Box: Technology, Economics, and History*, Cambridge: Cambridge University Press.

—— and Frischtak, C. (eds) (1985), *International Technology Transfer: Concepts, Measures, and Comparisons*, New York: Praeger.

Rostow, W.W. (1960), *The Stages of Economic Growth: a Non-Communist Manifesto*, Cambridge: Cambridge University Press, 2nd enlarged edn, 1971.

Sandberg, L.G. (1974), *Lancashire in Decline*, Columbus: Ohio State University Press.

Scazzieri, R. (1993), *A Theory of Production: Tasks, Processes, and Technical Practices*, Oxford: Clarendon Press.

Schonberger, R.J. (1982), *Japanese Manufacturing Techniques: Nine Hidden Lessons in Simplicity*, New York: Free Press.

Sen, A.K. (1960), *Choice of Techniques: An Aspect of the Theory of Planned Economic Development*, Oxford: Blackwell.

Smith, A. (1776), *An Inquiry into the Nature and Causes of the Wealth of Nations*, London: W. Strahan and T. Cadell; bicentennial edn, ed. R.H. Campbell, A.S. Skinner and W.B. Todd, Oxford: Clarendon Press, 1976.

Steuart, J. (1767), *An Inquiry into the Principles of Political Oeconomy ...* , London: A. Millar & T. Cadell; ed. and abridged A.S. Skinner, Edinburgh and London: Oliver & Boyd, 1966.

Taylor, F.W. (1911), *The Principles of Scientific Management*, New York: Harper.

Temin, P. (1964), *Iron and Steel in Nineteenth-century America: An Economic Inquiry*, Cambridge, Mass.: MIT Press.

Veblen, T. (1904), *The Theory of Business Enterprise*, repr. New York: Augustus M. Kelley, 1965.

von Tunzelmann, G.N. (1978), *Steam Power and British Industrialization to 1860*, Oxford: Clarendon Press.

—— (1993), 'Technological and organizational change in industry during the Industrial Revolution', in P.K. O'Brien and R. Quinault (eds), *The Industrial Revolution and British Society*, Cambridge: Cambridge University Press, 254–82.

—— (1995a), 'Time-saving technical change: the cotton industry in the English Industrial Revolution', *Explorations in Economic History*, 32, 1–27.

—— (1995b), *Technology and Industrial Progress: The Foundations of Economic Growth*, Aldershot, Hants.: Edward Elgar.

Wade, R. (1990), *Governing the Market: Economic Theory and the Role of Government in East Asian Industrialization*, Princeton, N.J.: Princeton University Press.

Wall, D. and Yin Xiangshuo (1997), 'Technology development and export performance: is China a frog or a goose?', Chapter 9 in this volume.

Westphal, L.E., Kim, L. and Dahlman, C.J. (1985), 'Reflections on the Republic of Korea's acquisition of technological capability', in Rosenberg and Frischtak (1985, 167–221).

White, L. Jr (1962), *Medieval Technology and Social Change*, Oxford: Oxford University Press; quoted from Oxford Paperbacks edn, 1964.

Womack, J.P., Jones, D.T. and Roos, D. (1990), *The Machine the Changed the World: Based on the MIT Study of the Future of the Automobile*, New York: Rawson.

Zheng Youjing (1997), 'Economic growth and technical transfer in China', Chapter 10 in this volume.

Index